Praise, Praise, Praise for Roses For Dummies!

"As an all-organic gardener, I've always dreamed of having a rose expert/enthusiast come to my gardens for tea and spend the afternoon sharing and teaching me all about roses. Roses For Dummies is written as a friend, answering all my puzzling questions and providing easy solutions that are budget friendly."

> — Jan Weverka, Editor of *The Rose Garden,* a monthly organic newsletter

"This book is fun to read and loaded with information — just what I'd expect from Lance Walheim, who really knows gardening from the ground up. It takes the mystery but not the magic out of growing roses. Beginners as well as advanced rose growers will find advice that's abundant and extremely helpful."

> — Bill Marken, Editor-in-Chief of eHow.com and former Editor-in-Chief of *Rebecca's Garden*

Praise, Praise, Praise for Gardening For Dummies!

". . . this is an outstanding reference for beginners and first-time homeowners . . . clearly explains how to retrieve garden information online."

> — Carol Stocker, *Boston Globe,* Boston, Massachusetts

". . . a thorough, readable beginners' guide. . . . Readers will enjoy the straightforward, yet light-hearted tone."

> — Cheryl Dorschner, *Burlington Free Press,* Burlington, Vermont

"This book has much to recommend it . . . a simple, well-laid-out introduction to basic gardening . . ."

> — *Library Journal*

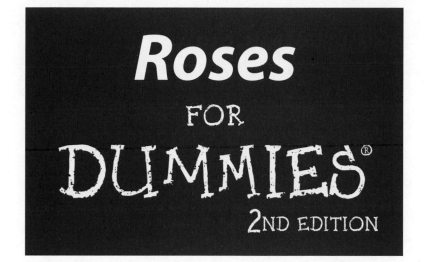

Roses

FOR

DUMMIES®

2ND EDITION

Roses
FOR
DUMMIES®
2ND EDITION

by Lance Walheim and the Editors at the
National Gardening Association

Wiley Publishing, Inc.

Roses For Dummies®, 2nd Edition

Published by
Wiley Publishing, Inc.
909 Third Avenue
New York, NY 10022
www.wiley.com

Copyright © 2000 by Wiley Publishing, Inc., Indianapolis, Indiana

For general information on our other products and services or to obtain technical support, please contact our Customer Care Department within the U.S. at 800-762-2974, outside the U.S. at 317-572-3993, or fax 317-572-4002.

Wiley also publishes its books in a variety of electronic formats. Some content that appears in print may not be available in electronic books.

Library of Congress Cataloging-in-Publication Data:

Library of Congress Control Number: 99-67174

ISBN: 0-7645-5202-3

Manufactured in the United States of America

10 9 8 7

About the Authors

Lance Walheim has been gardening most of his life. He got his start when his father forced him to turn the soil and plant tomatoes in the family vegetable garden as punishment for a deed he can't recall. Funny thing was, he found that he enjoyed working in the soil and has been doing it ever since. In 1975, he graduated from the University of California, Berkeley, with a degree in botany. Shortly after, he started writing and researching books on gardening and since has authored or contributed to over 40 titles on subjects ranging from citrus to rhododendrons. He has contributed to, or written, three books on roses, not including this one. He has also served as a writer for *Sunset* and *National Gardening* magazines and is part-owner of California Citrus Specialties, marketers of specialty citrus fruit. But his true loves are family and gardening, the "composts" that enrich his heart and soul.

The National Gardening Association is the largest member-based, nonprofit organization of home gardeners in the U.S. Founded in 1972 (as "Gardens for All") to spearhead the community garden movement, today's NGA is best known for its bimonthly publication, *National Gardening* magazine. Reporting on all aspects of home gardening, each issue is read by some half-million gardeners worldwide.

For more information about the National Gardening Association or its magazine, write to 180 Flynn Ave., Burlington, VT 05401, USA. Send e-mail to nga@garden.org, or visit the Web site at www.garden.org.

Dedication

We dedicate this book to anyone who can't walk by a rose without sticking his or her nose into it.

Authors' Acknowledgments

We have relied on information from many chapters, members, and publications of the American Rose Society. Without their help and expertise, this book would not have been possible. To them, we say many thanks. We would also like to thank Weeks Roses, Upland, California; Jackson & Perkins, Medford, Oregon; Sequoia Nursery, Visalia, California; Garden Valley Ranch Nursery, Petaluma, California; and the Pasadena Tournament of Roses, Pasadena, California.

There are many individuals to thank. Ann Hooper, a special consultant, made so many contributions to this book that listing them all is impossible. Tom Carruth of Weeks Roses, F. Harmon Saville of Nor'East Miniature Roses, David P. Kidger of Primary Products, and American Rose Society Consulting Rosarians Martha Chapin, Dr. Thomas Cairns, Robert Ardini, Malcolm Lowe, Louise Coleman, Frank Benardella, Jackie Clark, and Rich Baer were all extremely helpful. And to Bob Martin, the technical reviewer, humble accolades for double-checking everything in here and alerting us to errors and omissions.

Certainly and effusively we thank the team at Hungry Minds, Inc., which includes in Chicago: Kathy Welton, Holly McGuire, and Jill Alexander. All were essential to this project. In Indianapolis, Kathy Cox (project editor) and Kathleen Dobie (copy editor) worked with us in the trenches and contributed enormously to this book — many thank-yous to you both. We also continue to acknowledge the contributions of Pam Mourouzis and Tammy Castleman, project editor and copy editor respectively of the first edition, which set the high standard for this book.

Publisher's Acknowledgments

We're proud of this book; please send us your comments through our Dummies online registration form located at www.dummies.com/register/.

Some of the people who helped bring this book to market include the following:

Acquisitions, Editorial, and Media Development

Project Editor: Kathleen M. Cox

Acquisitions Editor: Holly McGuire

Copy Editor: Kathleen Dobie

Technical Reviewer: Bob Martin, Consulting Rosarian, American Rose Association

Acquisitions Coordinator: Jill Alexander

Cover Coordinator: Jonathan Malysiak

Editorial Manager: Pamela Mourouzis

Editorial Assistant: Carol Strickland

Cover Photograph: Tony Stone, © Daniel Bosler

Production

Project Coordinator: Maridee Ennis

Layout and Graphics: Karl Brandt, Angela F. Hunckler, Clint Lahnen, Tracy Oliver, Jill Piscitelli, Anna Rohrer, Brent Savage, Brian Torwelle, Maggie Ubertini, Dan Whetstine

Special Art: DD Dowden

Proofreaders: Laura Albert, Corey Bowen, Nancy L. Reinhardt, Marianne Santy

Indexer: Sharon Hilgenberg

Special Help
Corey Dalton, Patricia Yuu Pan, Janet Withers

Publishing and Editorial for Consumer Dummies

Diane Graves Steele, Vice President and Publisher, Consumer Dummies

Joyce Pepple, Acquisitions Director, Consumer Dummies

Kristin A. Cocks, Product Development Director, Consumer Dummies

Michael Spring, Vice President and Publisher, Travel

Brice Gosnell, Associate Publisher, Travel

Suzanne Jannetta, Editorial Director, Travel

Publishing for Technology Dummies

Andy Cummings, Vice President and Publisher, Dummies Technology/General User

Composition Services

Gerry Fahey, Vice President of Production Services

Debbie Stailey, Director of Composition Services

Contents at a Glance

Cartoons at a Glance

By Rich Tennant

"Well that's just _amazing_! Look at the size of those Grandifloras, and with the heat we've had!"

page 313

"Would you ask the men with the pink 'Simplicity' boutonnieres not to group around the 'Butterscotch' rose bush? It plays havoc with the entire color scheme of my garden."

page 97

"Plenty of sunshine, organic matter, and the right soil will keep them bright and colorful. And what that won't do, a box of fluorescent felt tip markers will take care of."

page 65

What I like about this routine, Stacey, is the way Marcos maintains the health of the rose by drooling a liquid rooting hormone from his mouth onto the flower's cut end.

page 203

"Well that's just STUPID! You breed a special rose in my honor, and it looks just like any other dumb rose! Except for those stupid giant thorns sticking out all over! What's that about?!"

page 9

"Well, that's a lovely hybrid rose, Muriel. But why do you call it 'Whack-on-the-head'?"

page 295

Fax: 978-546-7747
E-mail: richtennant@the5thwave.com
World Wide Web: www.the5thwave.com

Table of Contents

Introduction

*I*t's hard to believe it has been three years since we published the first edition of *Roses For Dummies*. Things change so quickly in the gardening world, especially when it comes to roses. Nearly 100 varieties are described in this edition that weren't included in the first. Many of them are new, but some of them are pretty old, usually added because readers told us about their dependable favorites. In fact, letters and comments made by readers of the first edition have contributed significantly to this new and improved edition. For that, we say thank you very much.

Controlling insects and diseases that attack roses has also changed since the first edition of this book. Many of the new varieties we've added have exceptional disease resistance and are easy to grow without spraying. But if trouble does arise, in Chapter 21 you'll find out about safe new products and techniques for controlling pesky problems like black spot and powdery mildew, as well as insects like aphids and Japanese beetles.

No matter how much has changed, some things stay the same. And many of the words we wrote in the first edition still ring true.

If you asked ten people to name their favorite flower, probably nine would name the rose. Why? Well, that question is pretty easy to answer. What other flower offers so much? There's the wonderful, almost sensuous way a rose opens — the petals slowly unfurling, so softly, so gently. And the colors are so intense, so vivid, and sometimes just so wild. And what about the fragrance? Even though rose fragrance seems to surround us in perfumes, air fresheners, and what have you, there's still nothing more refreshing or revitalizing than sticking your nose in a rose and taking a deep breath. Oh, the fragrance!

But our meager attempt at describing the beauty of roses as perfect flowers can never stand up to those of poets, painters, artists, and writers, who for centuries have tried to capture that beauty in words and pictures. Even though roses have been loved for so long and are so popular today, their use and appreciation as flowering shrubs — hardworking plants that can form the backbone of a landscape as hedges, ground covers, and sources of season-long color — may be only in its infancy.

Even rose experts are often bewildered by how huge and versatile this group of plants is. Roses are wonderful landscape plants that are unmatched for the length of the season in which they bloom and the amount of color they produce. But who really thinks of them as utilitarian plants? Not enough people, that's for sure.

And no matter what you've heard, roses are not hard to grow. In fact, many roses are tough plants that fit perfectly into the low-maintenance gardens of the modern world. Sure, they need a little care, but the pleasure they give in return is well worth it.

About This Book

This book aims to change the way you think about roses. They are not finicky plants that need constant attention and a social security pension to keep them healthy. Roses are plants for the 21st century — blooming unselfishly, pleasing the eye and nose, and asking only for your appreciation in return.

The first thing we want you to realize is that a rose is not just a rose. Even if you already grow roses, maybe have for years, you can still find plenty of new information to excite you.

Before you get your hands dirty, get to know roses — how the plants grow, how the flowers form, and what makes them smell so good. You can find it all in this book, and in easy-to-understand language. And realize that where you live influences how roses perform and how you need to care for them.

Even though the rose family is huge, the goal of this book is to make roses easy to understand. We tell you not only how to distinguish one type of rose from another, but also how to best use each type and color, whether you want one plant for a bouquet or 100 plants for a hedge. This book can help you make roses work for you.

And you don't have to read this book cover to cover to understand the wide world of roses. You'll find a great deal of interesting and useful information, but we've put it together in a way that is easy to access. If you have a question, you can answer it quickly and then put the book down until you need it again.

Conventions Used in This Book

Rose gardeners, or any gardeners for that matter, have their own jargon. Although most words are straightforward and down to earth (most of you won't have any trouble figuring out watering, fertilizing, or pruning, for example), one area is a bit trickier: the names of specific plants. To ensure that we all know which plant we're talking about, gardeners have a system of plant naming based on Latin and Greek.

So following conventional garden nomenclature, we list the common names of plants in normal type, usually lowercase (dog rose, for example). From there, naming gets a bit more complex. Every plant is a member of a larger horticultural family, sharing general horticultural characteristics with other members. For roses, that family is *Rosaceae*. All roses share the same family, but, interestingly enough, other common garden plants are also members of the rose family, including pyracanthas, apples, and hawthorns.

Plant families are divided into groups of closer relatives, indicated by a group or genus name. This genus name is always written in italics with the first letter capitalized. Thus, the genus name for rose is *Rosa*.

The next name is the species name. Like the genus, this name is written in italics, but the first letter is lowercase. Only some of the oldest roses, such as *Rosa multiflora,* are described by species. Most modern roses are grouped by class instead of species: hybrid teas, floribundas, grandifloras, climbers, and so on. You'll find out more about those in Chapter 1. Within each group are the varieties. We won't bore you with all the reasons why, but these are usually enclosed in single quotation marks. These names, like 'Mister Lincoln' and 'Double Delight', are types of names that you will become most familiar with. On a rare occasion, a botanical rose variety, meaning that the rose was found flourishing in the wild rather than having been created by a rose breeder, is listed as the third part of the botanical name, in italics with the first letter in lowercase. But you need not lose sleep over that.

Modern Roses 10, published by the American Rose Society in 1993, is our reference for rose names.

Foolish Assumptions

In writing this book, we're assuming a few things about you and your experience with roses:

- ✔ You've been one of the lucky ones to receive a bouquet of roses from a florist, or you've envied those friends, relatives, or coworkers who were.
- ✔ You enjoy gardening or want to give it a try.
- ✔ You're interested in growing your own roses, or you already grow them and want to find greater success and at the same time enjoy these wonderful flowers more.
- ✔ You've stuck your nose in a rose and enjoyed its exquisite fragrance.
- ✔ You think that roses are very colorful and want to bring some of that color into your own garden or home.

How This Book Is Organized

This book is organized into parts, each of which contains several chapters.

Part I: Roses 101

Roses are a diverse group of plants. Having a basic understanding of the different classes of roses, from the beautifully formed hybrid teas to the floriferous shrub roses to the sprawling climbers, and how they grow and bloom, helps you appreciate their versatility. Part I tells all about rose plants, rose flowers, and rose fragrance. It also explains why where you live influences which roses you can grow and how you grow them.

Chapter 1 gives you a basic introduction to rose types and the lingo used to describe them, and tells how you can use roses in the landscape.

Chapter 2 introduces you to rose flowers: how they form, which colors they come in, and what distinguishes their character.

Chapter 3 is about rose fragrance and how to enjoy it fully. It tells you which varieties smell best and why.

Chapter 4 gives you everything you need to know about rose climates. It includes lists of varieties that are proven performers in your geographic area and gives you tips on how to recognize the best place to plant them in your yard.

Part II: Using Roses in Your Garden

Here's where we put roses to work in the garden.

Chapter 5 tells you how to use roses in the landscape as hedges, screens, edgings, ground covers, and everywhere else you'd never think to plant them.

Chapter 6 is about combining roses with other plants, such as flowering perennials and herbs.

Chapter 7 tells you the basics on growing roses in containers, from which type of pot and soil to use to choosing the best varieties to caring for them.

Part III: All the Roses You Need to Know

You can choose from literally thousands of rose varieties. In this part, we help you make the best choices.

From Chapter 8 to Chapter 14, we list the most widely available and popular roses. We start with hybrid teas and move on through grandifloras, floribundas and polyanthas, miniatures, climbers, shrubs, and old garden and species roses. Hundreds of varieties are described, organized by flower color.

Color Pictures

In about the center of this book, you'll find more than one hundred color pictures of roses. Just as all the roses described in the text are arranged by type and by color, here the roses are arranged by type and by color, with some fragrance favorites thrown in, along with pictures to help you identify common rose pests and other problems. Whether you choose by type, by color, or by fragrance, you'll see some of our favorites in blooming color.

Part IV: Growing Healthy Roses

This part gives you the nuts and bolts on everything you need to know about growing roses, from picking them out at the nursery to keeping them free from pests and diseases.

Chapter 15 describes the different ways roses are sold and which may be the best for you.

Chapter 16 takes you through the proper techniques for planting roses.

Chapter 17 covers the basics on watering and mulching. Don't worry; we tell you how much water to apply and how often to apply it.

Chapter 18 is about the nutrients you can apply to keep your roses healthy and blooming on and on.

Chapter 19 makes pruning roses simple. It's all here — the tools you need, when to prune, and no-nonsense talk on the exact technique.

Chapter 20 helps you get your roses through chilly winters.

Chapter 21 is about insects and diseases and what to do to prevent them while still keeping your garden a healthy and happy place.

Chapter 22 shows you how to increase your rose collection and, if you're so inclined, even create your own unique varieties.

Chapter 23 is about drying rose flowers and using them to make wonderfully fragrant potpourris.

Part V: The Part of Tens

This part contains all the rest of the fun stuff that doesn't fit neatly anywhere else.

Chapter 24 answers the most commonly asked questions about roses — no nonsense, quick, and to the point.

Chapter 25 tells you about roses you should be shy about planting, unless you really want them for a specific reason. With so many terrific varieties available, why make more work for yourself?

Chapter 26 focuses on one of the best ways to use roses: as cut flowers.

Chapter 27 is a lighthearted look at roses and rose gardens that have made history.

Part VI: Appendixes

One thing about growing roses — they grow on you, and fast. You always want more information about where to find them, tricks for growing them right in your neighborhood, even how you can show them off when everything goes right and you grow the perfect flower.

Rose societies are everywhere — the flowers are that popular. Join one and you have a wealth of information and expertise at your fingertips. You can also enter your flowers in rose shows. In Appendix A, we tell you what rose societies offer and how to sign up.

Public rose gardens are not only beautiful; they're informative, too. Visit one nearby and you'll see what a rose should look like when it's grown in your area. In Appendix B, we provide a list of public rose gardens throughout the world.

Mail-order catalogs sell everything you need, from the most obscure rose varieties to the latest irrigation technology. And you don't have to leave home to shop. Appendix C lists our favorite mail-order rose catalogs, as well as some other catalogs that specialize in gardening equipment we think you may want to have. These catalogs are beautiful, informative, and fun to read.

Icons Used in This Book

We use the following icons throughout the book to point out particularly important information:

Helps you avoid common pitfalls or dangerous situations.

Demystifies gardening lingo. (Although we've made this book as jargon-free as possible, you need to know some terms.)

Gives addresses and/or phone numbers for ordering special gardening equipment, supplies, or specific plants. (You can also find sources in Appendix C.) Information next to this icon may help you find useful tidbits for your rose growing.

Flags inside information that even some experienced gardeners may not know.

Marks varieties that are pictured in the color section of this book. Some of these are also easy growers.

If you're still a little intimidated by some of the thornier rose-growing issues, try roses marked with this arrow. They're widely recognized as easy growers that pack beautiful blooms for minimal effort. Of course, most of the roses in this book, such as the floribundas, are easy to grow. We just mark these to help get you started.

Where to Go from Here

If you're just beginning and want to find out why the rose is one of the most beloved flowers, go to Part I. If you want to know how to use roses in the landscape or grow them in containers, go to Part II. Head to Part III if you're trying to decide which rose to buy. Go to Part IV if you want to learn all there is about growing roses, from buying them in nurseries to planting, watering, and fertilizing to controlling common pests. If you're just looking for some fun facts about roses, go to Part V.

Part I
Roses 101

The 5th Wave   By Rich Tennant

"Well that's just STUPID! You breed a special rose in my honor, and it looks just like any other dumb rose! Except for those stupid giant thorns sticking out all over! What's that about?!"

In this part . . .

The rose is America's National Flower. It's been called the Queen of Flowers, and people have revered it for as long as people have been in existence. Cro-Magnon man probably brought a bouquet of roses back to the cave for his mate. And she was undoubtedly as thrilled to receive them as people are today.

Rose hobbyists, otherwise known as rosarians, would have the world believe that roses require more fertilizer, more water, more love, more attention, more time, and more money than any other flowering plant — probably because rosarians usually enter their blossoms in rose shows and are in a never-ending search for the perfect rose. Although we admit that rosarians grow some pretty spectacular roses, we also want to assure you that everyday gardeners can get great results with very little effort.

This part familiarizes you with the unique language and culture that have developed around roses and helps you find out how roses are classified, how the plants grow, how the flowers form, what colors they come in, and which varieties are fragrant and why. We also have to do some geo-positioning. Most roses grow and bloom anywhere they get proper care. But one of the tricks of growing great roses with a minimum of hassles is to choose varieties that are well adapted to your climate. And that means knowing a little about your climate — whether the summers are hot and dry, hot and humid, or cool and humid, and whether the winters are cold and icy or warm and mild. Once you become weather-wise, you can choose the right varieties — for example, ones that are hardy enough to survive your cold winters, that resist disease where it's hot and humid, or that bloom beautifully despite cool summers. To give you suggestions, this part also provides lists of recommended roses for different types of climates.

Chapter 1

Everything You Need to Know about Roses

In This Chapter

▶ Why roses are easy to grow
▶ Where roses come from
▶ Why you need to know the definition of budding
▶ Which roses to grow
▶ How roses are grouped
▶ Where new rose varieties come from

*W*hether you just want to mix a couple of roses in with your other perennials or you get so hooked that you want to make roses your hobby, you can find no plant more beautiful and satisfying. Roses are fun and easy to grow, particularly if you know a little about them before you start.

Of course, no book can include everything about roses, but we think that this one comes close to having all you need to know in order to buy, plant, grow, and care for just about any rose.

If you want to go out and dig a hole this very minute, stop. Read this chapter first. But if you've already dug yourself into a hole by jumping in without knowing what you were doing, remember the old adage:

If at first you don't succeed, read the directions and try again.

Are Roses as Hard to Grow as Everyone Says?

If you get one thing from this book, we want it to be the easy answer for anyone who tells you that roses are hard to grow. Plain and simple, that's a myth. But, like many stereotypes, it contains a grain of truth.

We may be stretching the point, but we're using an analogy with cars anyway (any automobile enthusiast can relate): Some cars are expensive, and some aren't. Some look great, and some don't. Some are easy to maintain, and some aren't. Yet they're all cars. If you're wary of working on cars, you wouldn't buy an antique Jaguar or Triumph. You probably wouldn't buy a new Lamborgini, either. If you want basic, care-free transportation, you buy a basic, easy-to-maintain vehicle.

It's like that with roses. If you don't want to fuss over your roses after you plant them, don't choose the fanciest, most beautiful, most fragrant long-stemmed hybrid tea. Look for something a bit more . . . well, practical. And please don't assume that an "easy" rose doesn't look so good. 'Iceberg' is one of the easiest roses to grow, and it's also one of the world's most beautiful white roses (see Chapter 10). We mark many of these easy-to-grow varieties with a "Can't Miss" icon. These are sure-fire roses — easy-to-grow and color-ful performers. Some groups of roses, like the shrubs and floribundas, are almost all easy to grow. What we're saying is that out of the thousands of roses available, some are the easiest, most trouble-free plants you'll ever meet, and some thrive on the indulgent fussing that some gardeners love to provide.

Which Rose Should I Grow?

Which rose should you grow? Good question — and exactly the subject of a good portion of this book. Unfortunately, no one can answer this question for you. You have to become familiar with what's available, develop some prefer-ences (for a color or fragrance, for example), and give some thought to the type of rose likely to thrive in your garden (and to how much care you're will-ing to provide).

We think that color is one good place to start, and that's why we include some pages of color pictures in this book that include roses selected by color. You can find a rose color you like and then refer to the chapters that describe the specific roses, which are also described according to color. You also find lists of roses throughout this book: roses that look good, smell good, grow well, are cold hardy, and what have you. Chapter 4 includes sev-eral lists of roses for various climates. And, of course, many people are entranced by types — some love hybrid teas while others want a grandiflora garden. There's a rose for every passion.

Finally, again and again in this book, we recommend that you consult with a local rose expert (a *rosarian*) and visit public gardens that offer substantial displays of roses (we list some in Appendix B). If you do either of these, you'll know for a fact whether a particular rose grows well or really struggles in your area.

Where Do Roses Come From?

Botanists believe that roses in some form flourished long before humans inhabited the earth, and it's thought that people have been cultivating roses for more than 5,000 years. Many of these early rose varieties, called *old garden roses* or *species roses* (you can read about them in Chapter 14), are still around. But humans have been applying their genius to rose culture (growing) and rose breeding (hybridizing) for a long time. Now gardeners can have the best of both worlds — species and old garden roses as well as modern hybrids.

Most of the rose plants you can buy today are grown by commercial rose growers in huge rose fields in fairly temperate climates. In the United States, nearly all rose plants are grown commercially in California's San Joaquin Valley, in Arizona, and in Texas. These plants are grown in fields for two years before they're harvested while *dormant* (during their normal winter rest period). The rose plants are stored *bareroot* (a descriptive term meaning that they have no soil on their roots) in huge, moist, refrigerated facilities to keep them from growing before being shipped to gardeners, nurseries, and garden centers nationwide in winter or early spring. You can find out more about shopping for roses in Chapter 15.

You may wonder whether roses are ever grown from seed. Most of the roses you buy are not. A rose grown from seed is usually not what you expect in terms of flower color and form. However, many of the varieties available may originate as seedlings. These are *hybrids* from crosses of two other roses. The seed from the original cross-breeding experiment grew into a beautiful rose and so the hybrid was grown and offered to other rose growers. You can find out more about all this seed stuff in Chapter 22.

What's in a rose?

For all their perceived mystery, roses are pretty simple plants, as Figure 1-1 shows. They consist of *roots* that take up water and nutrients from the soil, and *canes* (or stems) that grow from the *crown* of the plant (where the canes end and the roots begin). The canes usually have thorns (ouch) but some varieties have fewer than others, and a few (see the roses with "smooth" in their name in Chapter 8) are completely thornless. The leaves and branching canes grow from *bud eyes,* small buds that sprout at intervals along the cane. The leaves are usually produced in five-leaf *leaflets.* As a plant thrives, new canes sprout both from the crown of the plant and from the junction of the cane and the leaflets.

The flowers of the rose plant are called *roses, flowers, blooms,* or *blossoms.* A rose flower stays on the plant and looks like a rose for a certain length of time, depending on the variety. When the flower fades, falls apart, or otherwise dies, it is called a *spent bloom* and should be cut off the plant to encourage repeat flowering. Cutting off dead flowers is called *deadheading,* which we discuss in Chapter 19. The rate at which a rose plant can form a new flower is called *repeat.*

Most modern roses — those that have been bred since the late 19th century — are *ever-blooming or free blooming* which means that they are repeat bloomers and flower almost continuously throughout the growing season. Many old roses, like the damask variety 'Marie Louise' bloom only once a season. To find out more about rose flowers, see Chapter 2.

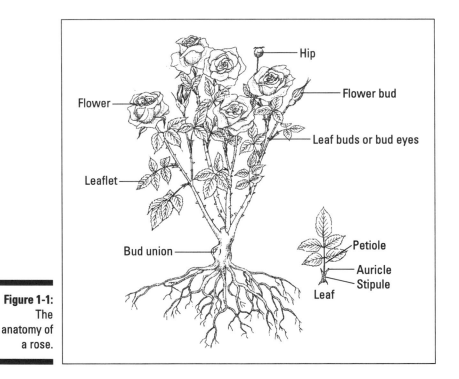

Figure 1-1:
The anatomy of a rose.

How does budding make a rose?

Many types of roses are grafted, or, more correctly, *budded,* onto a rootstock (you can find out more about rootstocks in Chapter 15), as opposed to growing on their own roots as most perennials do. The reasons for this are: Many commercial growers believe that certain varieties of roses perform better on vigorous rootstocks; with a good rootstock, new plants take less time to establish their root systems; and growers get a larger percentage of roses to thrive on rootstock than they do with roses on their own roots.

The keeper of all the world's rose knowledge

The history of roses is obviously a rich one, and keeping track of new varieties and of new developments in the rose world is important. This responsibility falls, in part, upon the American Rose Society — the United States' largest specialized plant society. Not only does the American Rose Society maintain a large membership of rose hobbyists, but it publishes a monthly magazine on roses, holds local and national rose shows, and certifies a large number of Consulting Rosarians, who make house calls to help people with their rose questions. The American Rose Society also administers the International Registration Authority – Roses (IRAR). The IRAR registers new varieties of roses to ensure that accurate records are kept regarding rose names, descriptions, ownership, and trademark and patent information.

For more information about the American Rose Society, and similar groups in other parts of the world, see Appendix A.

Commercial growers take canes from the rose varieties they want to propagate. They cut off the *bud eye* (a dormant bud that will eventually grow into a cane) at the junction of the cane and a leaflet, and insert it under the bark on the cane of a rootstock plant. When the canes and foliage above the bud are cut off the rootstock plant, all the plant's energy goes toward making the newly budded eye grow. The bud eye from the desired variety has all the genetic material needed to create a new plant that's identical to the original.

The point at which the bud is inserted into the bark of the rootstock plant is called the *bud union.* On mature plants, the bud union looks like a knob. As the plant grows in your garden, new, large canes grow from above the bud union.

In cold climates, the bud union is the part of the plant that's most important to protect in winter. Plant the bud union several inches below the ground in cold-winter climates, and protect it by covering it with a mound of soil during the winter months. (For more about growing roses in cold regions, see Chapter 20.)

How Are Roses Grouped?

Rosaceae is the third largest plant family. This family includes many ornamental landscape plants, fruits, and berries, including apples, cherries, raspberries, and pyracantha, characterized by the shape of the *hip* (the part of the flower where the seeds develop) and by petals in groups of five. Roses are members of the plant genus *Rosa.* Within that genus, roses are grouped into classifications based on the characteristics that each particular plant displays.

Your choice of rose depends on how you plan to use it and on your personal preferences. Some rose gardeners grow only one or two types of roses, and others grow many types. Our advice is to try growing one or two in each class and see which rose types you prefer. The following list tells you about the basic differences between the various types of roses:

> ✔ **Hybrid teas** (see Figure 1-2) bear large flowers that commonly grow one to a long stem, and bloom continually throughout the growing season. The bush can grow quite tall, with an upright *habit* (a term rosarians to describe the shape or look of a plant). Hybrid tea roses are usually budded onto a vigorous rootstock, and are a great choice if you like large flowers with a pleasant rose form (you find out more about this in Chapter 2) and if you like to make rose arrangements or have cut flowers in the house. Chapter 8 describes hybrid teas.

Figure 1-2:
A hybrid tea rose plant.

> ✔ **Grandifloras** (see Figure 1-3) are upright plants with hybrid tea-type flowers. The flowers often grow in clusters, but the stems on each flower within a cluster are long enough for cutting. Grandifloras are almost always budded and are a good choice if you like lots of blooms for color in the garden and stems for cutting, all on the same plant.

Grandifloras normally grow to between 3 and 6 feet tall. We talk about grandifloras in Chapter 9.

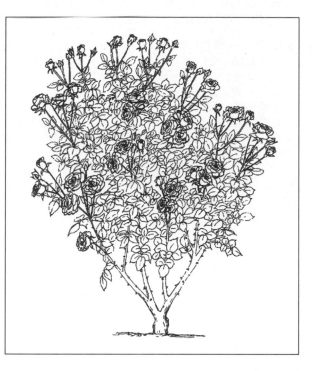

Figure 1-3:
A grandiflora rose plant.

✔ **Polyanthas** are the forerunners of modern floribundas. The plant itself can be quite large, covered with small flowers. Their usual habit is compact, hardy, and generous-blooming. The variety you see most often is 'The Fairy' — a wonderful variety, covered with small pink flowers on a plant that can spread to several feet in height and width. Because they are so similar, we group the polyanthas with the floribundas in Chapter 10.

✔ **Floribundas** (see Figure 1-4) have flowers that are smaller than hybrid teas and which grow in clusters on short stems. The bush is usually quite compact and blooms continually throughout the growing season. Most floribundas are budded, but commercial growers are beginning to grow them on their own roots. Choose floribundas if you need fairly low-growing plants that produce great numbers of colorful flowers. Floribundas are described in Chapter 10.

Figure 1-4:
A floribunda
rose plant.

✔ **Miniatures** (see Figure 1-5) are extremely popular small plants, usually
between 6 and 36 inches in height, with their leaves and flowers in perfect
proportion. They customarily grow on their own roots, and are not
budded, which makes them hardier in cold climates. Most mini varieties
bloom profusely throughout the growing season and are a great choice for
lots of color in a small space. You also can grow miniatures indoors in
pots on a sunny windowsill or under a fluorescent light. Recently, the
American Rose Society classified roses thought to be too large to be
miniatures and too small to be floribundas as "mini-floras." This name has
not yet been completely accepted by nursery workers so we continue to
group these varieties as miniatures. Miniature roses are covered in
Chapter 11.

✔ **Climbers** (see Figure 1-6) don't really climb like clematis or other true
vines that wrap around or attach themselves to supports. They do, however, produce really long canes that need to be anchored to a fence, trellis, or other support. Otherwise, the plants sprawl on the ground.
Flowers bloom along the whole length of the cane, especially if the cane
is tied horizontally, such as along a fence. Some climbers bloom only
once in the spring, but many modern climbers produce flowers throughout the growing season. Climbing roses are described in Chapter 12.

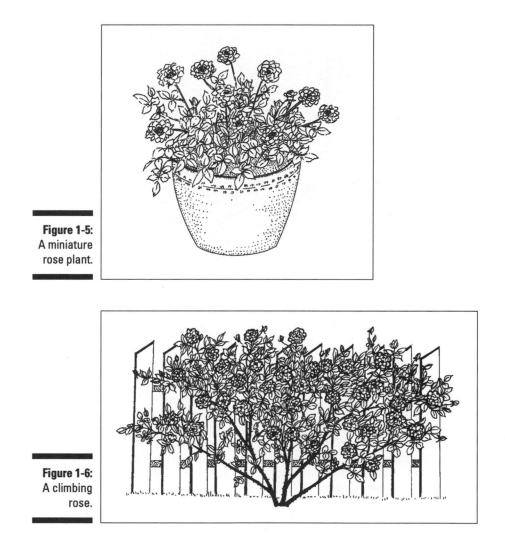

Figure 1-5:
A miniature
rose plant.

Figure 1-6:
A climbing
rose.

↙ **Shrubs** (see Figure 1-7) have become very popular in recent years because most are quite hardy and easy to grow, and great for landscaping. They are generally large plants, and most, particularly the modern shrubs, bloom profusely throughout the season. If you want to fill a large space with color, the shrub category offers a great many choices. For more information, see Chapter 13.

Figure 1-7:
A shrub
rose.

✔ **Old garden roses** are those discovered or hybridized before 1867. The classification "old garden roses" is made up of many subclasses of roses, including alba, bourbon, China, hybrid perpetual, damask, and the species roses. They are often referred to as Antique roses. Many old garden roses bloom only once during the growing season. Old garden rose aficionados enjoy the history and study of these lovely and often fragrant plants. We describe them in Chapter 14.

✔ **Tree roses, or standards,** aren't included among the basic categories because nearly any rose that is grafted (or budded) onto a tall trunk is a tree rose. Most often, hybrid teas, floribundas, and miniatures are used as tree roses. These plants really aren't even trees. Most just have that lollipop tree look, as shown in Figure 1-8, but are only 2 to 6 feet high. They are wonderful either in the ground or in containers but are very susceptible to winter damage, and in cold climates you must either bury the entire plant in the ground or bring it into a cool garage.

When you go to a garden center to choose your rosebushes, knowing which classification of rose you want is important. The classification gives you hints about you can use it in your garden. The variety you choose (see the following section) depends on your personal preference as to color, hardiness, and so on. You don't want to plant a once-blooming old garden rose in a spot where having season-long color is important.

Figure 1-8:
A tree rose trained to grow as a tree.

A marketing ploy by any other name . . .

Everything we tell you in this chapter is proof that the rose world is one neat and tidy bundle of orderly delight, right? Not quite. Selling roses is big business. Think about it — over 50 million roses are sold each year in the United States alone — times, say, 10 bucks apiece. Holy cow! Talk about a cash cow!

Selling roses is also a competitive business, so it's only natural that companies look for a marketing edge. One way they do it, and it has become a lot more prevalent since the first edition of this book, is to give their own names to the proprietary classes or groups of new rose varieties they introduce. Sometimes a new

group of roses falls into one of the standard groups of roses (for example, the David Austin roses are grouped as shrubs. But more often it's hard to tell where they fit). New groups of roses like Romanticas, Generosas, and the Sunblaze varieties, don't always fit neatly where you think they should. Worse, the breeders don't always tell you where they belong.

So anyway, we point out where we think these roses belong in the appropriate chapters of this book. Just realize that the future looks more confusing and you may not be able to tell what a rose is really like. Reading rose descriptions carefully has never been more important.

Where Do Rose Varieties Fit In?

Within each classification of roses are varieties. If you're talking to a bona fide rose snob, however, be sure to say *cultivar* (a combination of cultivated and variety), not variety, even though the two terms mean the same thing. Either word indicates a particular plant within a classification (which is much less complicated than it sounds). Each variety is a distinct individual and every plant so named is identical.

For example, the variety 'Olympiad' is classified as a hybrid tea rose. So if you're looking for a lovely red rose with a classic rose form which grows on long stems, suitable for cutting, you may want to consider the hybrid tea 'Olympiad'. If instead you want a fragrant, orange- yellow hybrid tea, you may want to go with 'Sutter's Gold'. Varieties of all types or classifications of roses are described in Part III of this book.

How does a rose get its name?

The American Rose Society oversees international rose registration to ensure that names and descriptions of rose varieties are original and correct. But who thinks up some of these wild names? Most of the time, it's just the people who bred the rose.

We asked Tom Carruth, horticulturist for Weeks Roses, one of the largest commercial growers of roses in the United States, what they look for when they name a new rose. "What you name a rose is very important. Naturally, we look for something that will help sell the rose and gives someone an idea of what it's like. A mediocre name can ruin a great rose just as a good name can sell a mediocre rose. Some of the names I

really think work include 'St. Patrick', which you just know is a green rose; 'Scentimental', which tells you right off that this rose is fragrant; and 'Gourmet Popcorn', which gives you an immediate image of the flower."

Sometimes roses are named after a favorite person, relative, or celebrity, such as 'Princesse de Monaco'. Of course, in such cases you have to get permission from the owner of the name. Many old roses have French names. You can probably thank Empress Josephine, wife of Napoleon I. Her collection of roses from all over the world (see Chapter 27) really launched rose growing to new heights.

Where Do New Roses Come From?

Many new varieties of roses are introduced to the gardening public each year. Some of them are so fabulous that you can't resist buying them for the pleasure of seeing them grow in your own garden. But who invents new rose varieties? Well, rose breeders, more correctly called *rose hybridizers,* are unique people. Some are amateurs — usually *rosarians* (people who are very serious about growing roses) who take their hobby a step further and try their hand at hybridizing. Some are independent hybridizers, who develop new varieties and sell them to commercial rose growers. But the most successful (and financially secure) rose hybridizers are employed by commercial rose growers — companies that can afford to support large-scale hybridizing programs and the years of development needed to bring a new rose to the market.

Roses are cross-bred by pollen exchange. The hybridizer must be an expert in rose genetics in order to choose existing varieties whose desirable characteristics will be passed on to a new variety and whose undesirable characteristics will not.

After pollen is exchanged, the hybridizer leaves the rose hip to ripen. At harvest, the hip is cut off the plant and broken open, and the seeds are stored for a few weeks before they're planted in flats in a carefully controlled greenhouse. In one hybridizing season, hundreds of thousands, perhaps half a million, seeds are planted. From the seedlings, eventually only three or four are deemed worthy of selling to gardeners.

New seedlings are tested for several years to ensure that the new variety grows well in all climates, is not a haven for every pest and disease that comes along, and has pleasing flowers and a desirable growth habit. It's not unusual for a new rose variety to be tested for ten years or more before it comes to market.

Rose denominations

To further complicate the issue of rose names, here's a tidbit of information that won't affect you in any way unless you want to grow roses commercially, or want to be a contestant on *Jeopardy!*: Each variety of rose has a denomination, or code name. The denomination identifies the rose plant no matter what commercial name the plant is given. Sometimes, roses bred in Europe are introduced in the United States under another variety name (and vice versa). For example, the floribunda 'Livin' Easy' is called 'Warm Welcome' in Europe. But the denomination is the same in Europe and in the United States.

The variety denomination is usually a "code name" that consists of three capital letters that indicate the company that owns the rights to the rose, plus a bunch of usually meaningless (although sometimes they give you a clue about the parentage of a variety) lowercase letters that indicate the particular cultivar. The floribunda 'Livin' Easy' (or 'Warm Welcome' in Europe) is ultimately identifiable by its denomination, *HARwelcome. HAR* indicates that the rights to the plant are owned by Harkness & Company in England, and *welcome* tells you that the plant is the orange floribunda you know and love (see Chapter 10).

Rose breeders and commercial rose growers go through all this rigmarole so that the rose has one identifying name everywhere in the world and can therefore be protected with patents, trademarks, or the like. A plant patent lasts for 20 years, so the owner of the rights may collect a royalty on each plant that's sold for 20 years. Unfortunately for rose breeders, patents are not always honored worldwide, and, in fact, only a small portion of new varieties are actually patented.

Next time you buy a rosebush, notice the metal tag attached to it. The denomination is printed under the variety name, either in parentheses or after the abbreviation *cv* (for cultivar). For example:

- Timeless™
  (JACecond)

- Scentimental™
  cv. WEKplapep

JAC is the abbreviation for Jackson & Perkins, and WEK is the abbreviation for Weeks Roses. The small letters identify the parentage. For example *plapep* means the variety resulted from crossing 'Playboy' with 'Peppermint Twist'.

Chapter 2

It's All about Flowers

*F*lowers are the reason people grow roses. No matter what kind of roses you like, the flowers are endlessly fascinating. Rose flowers come in almost every color and many shapes. Some plants flower once, some all season long. To make sure that the rose you buy has the color, shape, size, and blooming schedule that suits your yard, your climate, and your expectations, you should know what to look for.

Rose flowers have enthralled human beings throughout the ages. In fact, the Empress Josephine — you know, Napoleon's main squeeze — made rose gardening the "in thing" for generations of gardeners, right up to today. Starting in 1798, she attempted to collect every known variety of rose for her garden at Malmaison, near Paris. By the time she died in 1814, she had collected 250 different varieties.

Today, you can find thousands of rose varieties, all, in one way or another, descended from the early roses.

What endears roses to people is the color, the shape, the substance, the fragrance, the size, and the overall appeal of the flowers. We heard one rose grower say, "I started growing roses because the flowers were so perfect. God really screwed up when he made people, but didn't he do a great job when he designed roses?" Nothing makes the heart sing the way a perfect rose does. And roses never dump you for someone else.

And, like preferences for blond or brunette, blue eyes or brown, tall or petite, what's perfection to you may not be perfection to someone else. Visiting a few gardens at the height of their spring bloom is a good way to try to determine your idea of rose perfection. (You can find a list of public rose gardens in Appendix B.) If you love them all, that's okay, too.

Anatomy of a Rose

Speaking of love — like most plants, the flowers of a rose plant are sexual beings. The petals surround the sexual parts of the plant, which include both male and female organs. Yep, roses have both male and female parts, all in one lovely flower, making them able to self-pollinate. Maybe the flowers are so pretty that they fall in love with themselves!

Figure 2-1 shows a cross section of a rose flower. The *stamens,* so lovely in many varieties of roses, are the male parts of the rose. The *anthers,* at the top of the stamens, produce the pollen that fertilizes the *ovules,* or eggs, located at the bottom of the *pistil,* the female part of the flower, inside the hip of the flower. Rose flowers can self-pollinate, but the resulting plant is rarely as good as the original. You can find out more about the sex life of roses in Chapter 22.

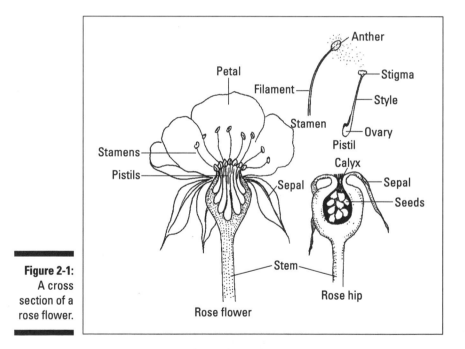

Figure 2-1:
A cross section of a rose flower.

The *sepals* are leaf-like structures that cover the rose buds before they open, protecting them. Sepals slowly separate to reveal the color of the developing flower and finally pull away entirely, allowing the petals of the bud to unfurl. The sepals are often a very attractive part of the flower, particularly if their feathery ends extend above the top of the bud. When they drop, allowing the petals to open, they are often a very decorative underpinning to a beautiful flower.

How many petals does it take to make a rose?

You can find much beauty in all the parts of a rose flower, but what most people consider perfection in a rose bloom is the petals — their color, their substance (See "But does it have substance" in this chapter for more), their arrangement, and their fragrance.

A rose may have no petals at all, like the famous green rose, *Rosa chinensis viridiflora*. What appear to be the petals of the flower are actually lots of sepals. Many people consider the green rose uglier than several miles of bad road, but others find a strange beauty in its greenness. The green rose is of the China family of old garden roses roses, and, as with all Chinas, this plant is tender in cold winter climates and must be brought inside during the chilliest months. Unlike most other old garden roses, however, the Chinas, including the green rose, bloom all season long. (See Chapter 14 for more about old garden roses.)

A rose can also have so many petals that it won't open in anything but the hottest weather. Sometimes these many-petaled roses are so fabulous that they're worth growing, even if you see only a few blooms a year during a heat wave. The most notorious rose for having so many petals that many of the flowers end up as squishy rotten balls at the top of a strong cane is the hybrid tea 'Uncle Joe'. The plant is a large one, often reaching 6 or 7 feet tall, with wonderful, deep green foliage. In hot weather, when the flowers do open, they are among the most beautiful of the red hybrid teas.

The most common petal formations fall into three categories:

- ✔ **Single:** Many beautiful roses have only a single row of petals (usually 5), as shown in Figure 2-2. Like the wonderful 'Dainty Bess', a single hybrid tea with five large, pale pink petals surrounding bright red stamens, single-petaled roses can be very lovely. 'Eyepaint' is another beautiful single rose. Both are pictured in the color section.

- ✔ **Semi-double:** Roses considered semi-double may have only two or three rows of 12 to 16 petals, as shown in Figure 2-3. The pink floribunda 'Simplicity', which Jackson & Perkins sells as a hedge rose, has semi-double flowers.

- ✔ **Double or fully double:** These roses have lots of petals, as Figure 2-4 shows. A rose is considered double if it has more than 17 petals. Sometimes roses with 26 to 40 petals are called fully double and those with over 40 petals are called very double. Double roses are generally larger and showier than singles or semi-doubles. The red hybrid tea 'Mister Lincoln' has double flowers and is shown among the "Fragrant Favorites" in the special color section.

Figure 2-2:
A single rose has a single row of petals.

Figure 2-3:
A semi-double rose has two or three rows of petals.

In the descriptions in Part III of this book we try to include the number of petals for each variety to help you visualize the flower. Unfortunately, the petal counters must have run out of steam at the end of the day because exact petal counts couldn't be found for some varieties. So go out and try counting them yourself, if it matters to you. In any case, whether you choose roses with single, semi-double, or double flowers makes no difference. If you like them, they're perfect.

Figure 2-4:
A double rose has many petals.

What puts a rose in top form?

The way a flower's petals unfurl is called *form*. Whether a rose is considered to have good form depends on the kind of rose you're looking at, as well as your own idea of what's attractive. Many people think that the *quartered form* (in which the center petals are folded into quarters) often found in old garden roses is very attractive. Other people prefer the complete lack of form found in other old garden roses, with floppy petals that jut out in every direction. Many old garden roses with little or no form are very charming.

But really, when you talk about rose form, you're talking about modern roses. Modern roses, including hybrid teas, floribundas, grandifloras, and miniatures, can have two types of form:

✔ **Exhibition or formal:** Many-petaled rose flowers with great (or formal) form are often called *exhibition roses*. The flowers are gracefully shaped, with the petals symmetrically arranged in an attractive circular outline coming to rest in a high, pointed center. The arrangement of the unfurling petals should be symmetrical and evenly spaced, with no evident gaps. The center of the bloom should be perfect — well-defined, high, and pointed. From the side view, you should notice a symmetry of structure as the petals unfurl uniformly from the high, pointed center. The outer row of petals should be as close as possible to a horizontal plane.

> Each variety has its own inherent characteristics. Exhibition roses are at their perfect phase of bloom when they are one-half to three-quarters open.
>
> ✔ **Garden decorative or informal:** Decorative (or informal) form is evident when a rose does not have a well-defined, high, pointed center. A decorative rose may be *ruffled* (wavy) or *cupped* (curved inward) and can have a low center. Decorative roses usually have fewer petals. These roses are often referred to as *garden roses,* as opposed to exhibition roses.

Climate conditions, culture, and weather can affect rose form. But if you want to grow roses with consistently good form, choose varieties genetically graced with it. As you get involved in the rose hobby, you may find that form becomes more important to you. If so, buy varieties known as exhibition varieties. Doing so isn't as difficult as it sounds. If a rose has exhibition form, the catalog description generally says so. Not quite as many roses with exhibition form are available as roses with decorative form, but you still have plenty to choose from.

Following is a list of hybrid teas that we think are top-notch in the exhibition form department:

- ❀ **'Crystalline':** White hybrid tea
- ❀ **'Keepsake':** Pink hybrid tea
- ❀ **'Moonstone':** White and pink hybrid tea
- ❀ **'Signature':** Deep pink hybrid tea
- ❀ **'St. Patrick':** Yellow hybrid tea

The following are pictured in the color section:

- ❀ **'Stainless Steel':** Silvery lavender hybrid tea
- ❀ **'Touch of Class':** Pink hybrid tea

Miniature rose form is judged like hybrid tea form. Here's our list of top exhibition minis:

- ❀ **'Figurine':** Light pink miniature
- ❀ **'Jean Kenneally':** Apricot miniature
- ❀ **'Kristin':** Red and white miniature
- ❀ **'Minnie Pearl':** Pink miniature
- ❀ **'Rainbow's End':** Yellow and red miniature
- ❀ **'Snow Bride':** White miniature

Unless you're planning to exhibit your roses at a rose show, however, form really doesn't matter much, as long as it's pleasing to you.

But does it have substance?

Substance is a quality in a rose that is extremely important to the stability and durability of its form and to its *keeping quality,* or vase life. *Substance* is the amount of moisture in the petals, and it is manifested in the texture, firmness, crispness, thickness, and toughness of the petals. You can determine the presence of substance in rose petals by feeling the thickness of the petals and seeing an opalescent sparkle and sheen in pastel-colored roses or a velvety appearance in red roses.

When you touch a rose's petals, you can't help but be impressed with the thick velvety feel of some varieties. They truly are a work of art. Some of the people we know should have as much substance as some roses do!

Should you care whether it's pink or mauve?

Colors of roses! So many exist that we hardly know where to begin. Well, we can start by talking about the elements that contribute to a rose's color:

- ✔ **Brightness:** This refers to the clarity and vividness of the color, and the absence of cloudiness or muddiness.
- ✔ **Hue:** This component gives visual impact to the eye and distinguishes one color from another.
- ✔ **Chroma:** The purity and intensity of the hue is called the chroma. Ideal chroma has virtually no gray or white in the hue.

So ideal hue is a combination of ideal brightness and ideal chroma.

The American Rose Society, keeper of the world's rose knowledge, divides rose colors into 18 color classes. Every rose fits into one of these categories, and when anyone registers a new rose with the International Registration Authority – Roses, they must specify one of these 18 color classes. Mail-order rose companies may describe colors of roses in terms that are more accurate or whimsical, such as "candy apple red" or "salmon orange," but the official color class is one of the 18 listed here:

- White (includes near-white and white blend)
- Light yellow
- Medium yellow
- Deep yellow
- Yellow blend
- Apricot (includes apricot blend)
- Orange (includes orange blend)
- Orange-pink
- Orange-red
- Light pink
- Medium pink
- Deep pink
- Pink blend
- Medium red
- Dark red
- Red blend
- Mauve (includes mauve blend)
- Russet

Oh, and for the record, a *blend* is a rose with different shades of one color, or two or more different colors on the same flower, and they're most often grouped by the most dominant color. If a rose is several shades of one color, we describe it in Part III under that color. If a rose has several colors, it's a "multicolored rose" in this book.

Although these 18 color categories are the official colors of roses, we simplified them in this book. In the color section of this book, we group roses into seven color groups: red, pink, orange, yellow, white, lavender, and multicolored or blends. In describing the varieties in Part III of this book, we stick to the same simplified groups and use adjectives that we hope help you imagine the rose accurately. And as Chapter 4 points out, rose color can change slightly when a rose is grown in different climates. That's why "official" color descriptions sometimes vary from the color in a photograph or the color of the rose in your own garden.

The search for a black or blue rose

When someone develops a blue rose or a black rose, the American Rose Society will have to add new categories. But you probably won't see those colors during your lifetime. Hybridizers have about given up on black because the dark tissue of the petals absorbs so much heat that the flower dies before it opens.

As for blue, well, a couple of research groups send out media releases every year or so saying that they almost have a blue rose. Then their funding gets a shot in the arm. It's pretty unlikely, though, that a blue rose will appear in the foreseeable future. The problem is that roses have no natural blue pigment. The pigment that makes mauve roses mauve is really a red pigment which is altered by the pH in the rose's cells. An interesting note: The red pigment in

mauve roses doesn't photograph well, showing up as pink on film. That's why the color of many mauve roses is not quite accurate in most catalog photos unless, of course, the photo is doctored, something we would never do.

Making a blue rose will require some big-time gene splicing, and because biologists haven't even identified most of a rose's genes, splicing 'em will be pretty hard. Also, the chemical response to the pH in the cell, once altered, would have to react favorably with the process of photosynthesis and with the plant's metabolism. A plant scientist could make this project his or her life's work. But if the scientist were successful, he or she would be rich beyond anyone's dreams!

Becoming Flower-Full

You know what makes a good rose a good rose — all that stuff about form and substance and colorful petals — but how do those naked-looking sticks you plant in the spring get to the flower stage? The process is nothing short of miraculous.

With the chemical element phosphorus working with elements in the soil that plants need to promote *photosynthesis* (you remember from high school science: light and carbon dioxide go in the leaf, water and oxygen come out), your rose plant develops new canes from two places:

- ✔ From the crown of the plant (the bud union on budded roses)
- ✔ From the bud eyes located at intervals along the canes

Rose flowers form at the top of a new cane. You can watch the tiny bud as it forms and grows.

Hybrid tea roses

Hybrid teas usually form flowers one to a stem in early spring, but subsequent blooming during the summer often produces two or more buds to the sides of the large main bud. The energy the plant must expend to make the side buds grow takes vitality away from the larger central bud, so all the flowers will be small.

If you want your hybrid tea flower to reach its full size and potential, you must disbud it when the tiny side buds are forming. You can *disbud* easily by snapping off the side buds when they are very small. Doing so allows the main bud to reach its maximum size. If you like more flowers per plant and don't care about their size, don't bother to disbud.

Floribunda roses

Floribundas usually form flowers in clusters, often called *sprays.* A cluster forms at the top of a cane, just like a single flower. But instead of only one bud, there are several.

As the buds grow, the center, or terminal, bud grows faster than the others in the cluster and opens several days sooner than the others. If you want all the flowers to open at the same time, you must nip out the center bud. From that point on, all the buds in the cluster mature at the same time. (See Figure 2-5 for an example of a floribunda cluster.)

Having all the flowers in a cluster open at the same time is important only if you're going to exhibit the spray in a rose show. In home flower arrangements it's not all that important.

Figure 2-5:
A cluster of
floribunda
roses.

So When Do They Bloom, Anyway?

Few flowering plants are truly *ever-blooming,* producing new flowers from spring to late fall. But roses do bloom on and off throughout the season (from mid spring to fall), making them among the most desirable garden plants. At least, most modern hybrid teas, floribundas, grandifloras, miniatures, and modern shrubs are called *ever-blooming, repeat blooming* or *free-flowering (remontant),* while many old garden roses flower either once a year) or once in the spring and again in the fall.

You can expect your roses to bloom for the first time about six to eight weeks after growth starts in the spring. The flower needs that long to form and mature. The first bloom in the spring, when all your roses are in full bloom, is always the most spectacular, making that time of year — whenever it may be in your area — a favorite time for everyone who loves roses. Modern roses continue to produce flowers throughout the season, and the process for repeat flower development takes the same six weeks or so. But the plants almost always have flowers at different stages of growth, making for a continuous display.

Roses That Bloom Once a Season

Roses that bloom once a season are called *once-flowering*. These are usually old garden roses or antique roses — those discovered or hybridized before 1867. Some antique roses, namely the hybrid musks, hybrid perpetuals, noisettes, Chinas, teas, and about 60 percent of the rugosas, are ever-blooming. But all the others — like albas, centifolias, damasks, and gallicas — bloom only once.

"So why grow 'em?" you may ask. The answer is: "For the display they put on when they do bloom." As if they're saving up all their energy for a whole year and then throwing it all away in an explosion of bloom, old garden roses that bloom only once can produce as many as 50 times more total flowers than ever-blooming roses.

These great roses bloom only once a year in spring. You can read more about them, and others like them in Chapter 14:

- **'Empress Josephine':** This old garden rose has rich pink, semi-double flowers, loosely shaped with large, wavy petals and well-branched growth.

- **'Harison's Yellow',** *Rosa harisonii:* This flower has cupped, soft yellow blooms with golden stamens.

- **'Ispahan':** This damask rose has bright pink flowers which are loosely double and very fragrant. Though it blooms only once, its bloom season is long.

- **'Königin von Dänemark':** The pale pink flowers of this alba rose have a darker center. Very full, medium-sized, fragrant blooms are produced by this vigorous grower.

- **'Mme. Hardy':** A damask rose whose flowers are pure white, occasionally tinged pale pink, with a green center. The plant grows vigorously, producing very fragrant, cupped, large blooms.

- **'Mme. Plantier':** The flowers of this hybrid alba rose are creamy white changing to pure white, with very fully double, flat blooms in clusters. The plant is fragrant, vigorous, and bushy.

To stop telling you about the flowers of rose plants is no easy task. After all, these flowers have inspired poets, artists, and lovers for generations. Perhaps it's enough to offer you this warning: Be careful when you start growing roses, or you, too, may fall in love with them.

Chapter 3

Rose Fragrance

● ●

In This Chapter

▶ Understanding what makes a rose fragrant

▶ Enjoying different scents

▶ Timing and techniques for making the most of rose scentsations

▶ Recognizing James Alexander Gamble Fragrance Medal winners

▶ Describing our favorite fragrant roses

● ●

*F*ragrance isn't the main reason most people grow roses, but it sure is a nice benefit. Many of the world's most beautiful modern roses have little or no fragrance, but they're wonderful to look at. (There was a time when scent wasn't as desirable an attribute as it is now, and roses were bred for other characteristics.) More and more people think that fragrance is an important characteristic in a rose, however, and are now, more than ever, seeking out only fragrant varieties.

An estimated 25 percent of all roses have no fragrance or only a small amount, 20 percent are intensely fragrant, and the remainder lie somewhere in the middle. So if you shop only for fragrant roses, you may miss out on some of the world's most beautiful varieties. But when a rose is both fragrant and beautiful, what more can you ask for?

Rosarians have been asking rose hybridizers to try to breed fragrance into new varieties, especially hybrid teas, which, as a group, have long been bred for flower form and are often scentless. And there's probably not one rose hybridizer in the world who doesn't try. But breeding for fragrance isn't as easy as it sounds. A single gene isn't responsible for fragrance — a series of genes is. And that series is elusive. You may think that if you cross one fragrant rose with another, you'll get a fragrant rose. Not so. In fact, when you cross two fragrant varieties, you're just about guaranteed to get no fragrance at all! So when a hybridizer does come up with a new fragrant rose, it's cause for great excitement throughout the rose world.

Nearly every part of a rose can emit fragrance — even the thorns. On moss roses (see Chapter 14 for more information about them), the fragrance is concentrated in the moss, or the hairs on the hip and sepals (Chapter 2 explains the anatomy of a rose flower). But most often, fragrance, or at least the highest concentration of it, is in the petals of a rose.

This chapter can help you pick out particularly fragrant varieties and make the most of their tantalizing fragrances. Just follow your nose!

What Makes the Fragrance

The fragrance of a rose is, like everything else in the living world, the product of a series of chemical reactions — both within the rose, and with the atmosphere around the rose. Several chemical groups are responsible for floral fragrance, including aromatic alcohols, aldehydes, carbonic acid, essential oils and resins, fatty acids, and phenols.

Certain other chemicals, such as citronellol and phenylethyl, have been identified as being responsible for certain scents, but this chemical stuff is complicated (and you probably don't care, anyway). Better to know how your nose interprets those chemicals in everyday terms.

What the nose knows

There are just about as many rose fragrances as there are noses. Certainly, everyone gets something different when they bury their nose in a rose. But several individual scents have been more or less definitively identified. It is thought that a connection exists between fragrance and other rose characteristics:

- ✔ Darker roses are generally more fragrant than lighter colored ones.
- ✔ Heavily petaled roses have a stronger or more intense scent than those with fewer petals.
- ✔ Red and pink varieties are more closely associated with the classic rose scent.
- ✔ The aromas of yellow and white roses are often compared with the fragrance of orrisroot, nasturtiums, and violets, along with other flowery and lemony scents.
- ✔ Orange roses are often associated with a fruity scent.

You can, however, count on exceptions to all these "rules."

The following list includes the most commonly identified scents, and at least one rose considered representative of that fragrance:

- ❀ **Apple:** 'New Dawn', 'Honorable Lady Lindsay'
- ❀ **Apple and clove:** 'Souvenir de la Malmaison'
- ❀ **Apple, clove, parsley, and lemon:** 'Eden Rose'
- ❀ **Apple, rose, and clove:** 'Zéphirine Drouhin'
- ❀ **Bay:** 'Radiance'
- ❀ **Classic rose:** 'Scentsational', 'Seattle Scentsation'
- ❀ **Clove:** 'Dainty Bess'
- ❀ **Fern and moss:** 'Queen Elizabeth'
- ❀ **Fruit:** 'Fragrant Plum'
- ❀ **Lemon:** 'Confidence'
- ❀ **Lily of the valley:** 'Madame Louis Lévêque'
- ❀ **Linseed oil:** 'Persian Yellow'
- ❀ **Nasturtium:** 'Buccaneer'
- ❀ **Orrisroot:** 'Golden Masterpiece'
- ❀ **Orrisroot and raspberry:** 'Kordes' Perfecta'
- ❀ **Orrisroot and violet:** 'Golden Dawn'
- ❀ **Quince:** 'Sutter's Gold'
- ❀ **Raspberry:** 'Angels Mateu'
- ❀ **Rose and clove:** 'Chrysler Imperial', 'Dolly Parton', 'Fragrant Cloud'
- ❀ **Rose and lemon:** 'La France', 'Mirandy', 'Tiffany'
- ❀ **Rose and nasturtium:** 'Sarah Van Fleet'
- ❀ **Rose and parsley:** 'American Beauty'
- ❀ **Spice:** 'Soleil d'Or', 'Scentimental', 'Ain't She Sweet', 'Secret'
- ❀ **Violet:** 'Margaret McGredy'
- ❀ **Wine:** 'Vandael'

Not all these roses are widely available, or even described in this book. But the next time you go to one of the public rose gardens listed in Appendix B (or to visit your rose-growing Uncle Floyd), try comparing the fragrances of different roses. Doing so is kind of fun, especially for kids.

Enhancing your sniffing pleasure

Although fragrance is a genetic characteristic present in some roses and not in others, other factors affect the strength of the fragrance within a fragrant variety. Excellent *culture,* including planting in good soil with correct pH, and watering and fertilizing, is vital to ensuring that a rose's fragrance reaches its full potential. Even more important is the amount of moisture in the soil. Rose fragrance is sweetest when plants have adequate water — another good reason to read Part IV, "Growing Healthy Roses."

 Temperature, humidity, wind conditions, and time of day also affect fragrance strength. Scent is more pronounced on warm, sunny days, is significantly reduced on cloudy days, and is hard to detect when the weather is overcast and cold. And roses emit more fragrance later in the day than they do in the morning.

Chapter 26 tells you how to get the most out of cut roses for bouquets. After a rose is cut, its fragrance stays with the petals, but the scent is strongest when the room is warm and the air is more humid than dry.

Choosing Fragrant Varieties

Because fragrance is a great selling point, mail-order rose catalog descriptions never keep fragrant varieties a secret. To further narrow your choices, you can always look for those that have been awarded the American Rose Society's James Alexander Gamble Rose Fragrance Award.

Not only must a nominee be fragrant, it must also possess a number of other attributes, including vigor, pest-and disease-resistance, form, substance, color, and extreme popularity for more than five years. (Chapter 2 talks about rose characteristics.) These qualities, of course, make any rose wonderful, which is why all the Gamble Award winners, even though they have a little age on 'em, should still be readily available at your local garden center.

The following list includes all the roses ever to have won the prestigious Gamble Fragrance Award:

- ✔ **1961:** 'Crimson Glory', red hybrid tea
- ✔ **1962:** 'Tiffany', pink and yellow blend hybrid tea
- ✔ **1965:** 'Chrysler Imperial', red hybrid tea (pictured under "Fragrant Favorites" in the color section)

- **1966:** 'Sutter's Gold', orange-yellow hybrid tea

- **1968:** 'Granada', red multicolored hybrid tea

- **1970:** 'Fragrant Cloud', orange-red hybrid tea (pictured under "Hybrid Tea" in the color section)

- **1974:** 'Papa Meilland', red hybrid tea

- **1979:** 'Sunsprite', yellow floribunda (pictured under "Fragrant Favorites" in the color section.)

- **1986:** 'Double Delight', red and white bicolored hybrid tea (pictured under "Hybrid Teas")

- **1997:** 'Fragrant Hour', orange-pink hybrid tea

You may have noticed that most of these roses are hybrid teas. As we said earlier, many hybrid teas don't have strong fragrance, which is true. But isn't it also interesting that some of the most fragrant roses are hybrid teas? What a wacky world.

Some of our favorite fragrant old garden roses are the following:

- **'Alfred de Dalmas':** Light pink moss

- **'Ispahan':** Medium pink damask

- **'Mme. Hardy':** White damask

- ***Rosa gallica officinalis:*** Light crimson gallica

- **'Sombreuil':** White tea

But don't for one moment believe that a whole bunch of newer roses aren't fragrant and great plants, too. The following varieties are readily available and wonderfully fragrant:

- **'Melody Parfumée':** Plum grandiflora

- **'Fragrant Plum':** Mauve grandiflora

- **'Scentimental':** Red-and-white-striped floribunda (pictured under "Fragrant Favorites" in the color section)

- **'Scentsational':** Pink and mauve miniature (pictured under "Miniatures")

- **'Secret':** Pink and white hybrid tea (pictures under "Hybrid Teas")

And don't forget the David Austins, Generosas (find more on both in Chapter 13) and Romanticas (check out Chapter 8 for more). Most have great fragrance.

That's all we "nose" about rose fragrance. Now go smell the roses!

Chapter 4

The Climates of the Rose

*T*here's virtually no place in the world where you can't grow nearly any type of rose you want. Of course, you may have to turn yourself inside out to keep the rose alive and thriving, but you can do so if you're masochistically inclined.

Finding roses naturally suited to the climate in which you live, however, is a much better idea (not to mention easier and more satisfying). The rose family is a diverse group of plants that thrive in a wide range of conditions. For nearly every climate, the list of roses you have to choose from is a long one.

Like all plants, each classification of rose, and even specific varieties within a classification, has its own tolerances to high or low temperatures, wind, and other climate factors that can affect its performance, if not its very survival. And equally important, your climate dictates how you care for your roses — how often you need to water, which diseases you should watch out for, when to fertilize — and when to do the other stuff that gardeners do.

Climate factors can also affect roses in more subtle ways. For example:

✔ The color of a rose variety can be surprisingly different when grown in two different climates, or even in the same climate in different seasons.

✔ The size of a plant's flowers can vary also, and certain varieties, especially ones with many petals, may have different climatic requirements in order to open properly.

Unless you want to spend your life trying to get your roses to thrive, you should be familiar with the climate you live in and understand how it affects the types of roses you want to grow and dictates the care you give them.

So that's what this chapter is all about — getting to know the climate you live in and its influence on the roses you choose and the way you care for them. We brief you on the climate basics, but often refer you to other parts of this book for more specifics on how climate can impact how you should care for your roses. Within each climate section, we give you a list of rose types recommended for specific climate regions.

How Roses React to Climate

The general climate of your region — that is, the city or county you live in — is determined by a complex mix of factors: how cold the winters are; how warm the summers are; how sunny or cloudy it is, how humid or dry it is; and a whole bunch of other circumstances you can probably guess at. And most of these factors affect how different types of roses grow or perform. The more you know about climate factors, the better rose gardener you can be.

Using zone maps

If you live in a cold-winter area, make sure that you choose roses that can survive the winter with a minimum of injury. But how do you know how cold it usually gets in your area? If you live in North America, the easiest way is to look at the USDA Plant Hardiness Zone Map. (The Quick Reference Card right inside the front cover of this book includes a USDA Zone and temperature conversion chart.) This system of plant hardiness zones divides North America into 11 regions, based on average winter minimum temperatures. The warmest, Zone 11, has an average winter minimum above 40°F (4°C). Each succeeding zone down to Zone 1 averages 10 degrees colder. Zones 1 through 10 are further divided into *a* and *b* regions in order to distinguish zones where minimum winter temperatures differ by 5 degrees.

Zone maps based on the average lowest temperature are available for most regions of the world. Unfortunately, because each region is mapped independently, there is no single map of plant climate zones for the world.

Choosing the right roses for your zone

When you know how climate affects the way roses grow and how to care for them in your particular climate, you can use that knowledge to decide which roses to plant. The world is rich with lists of recommended roses for specific areas, and you should be able to find a variety that can thrive where you live. Most of these lists are published by local rose societies. (For more information about rose societies, see Appendix A). But many retail nurseries and cooperative extension offices offer lists of recommendations as well. You can also visit a local public rose garden and see for yourself how specific roses do in your area. A list of such gardens is found in Appendix B.

But to get you started, we compiled lists of roses recommended for specific climates. We collected them from local rose societies and rose experts who have years of experience in growing great roses in those areas.

One thing to keep in mind about these lists is that they may not include some of the newest varieties. The newer varieties were introduced so recently that there hasn't been enough time to evaluate them completely. However, many of the newer varieties, especially the award winners, grow well in nearly all climates. Some of them look so great that you may want to throw caution to the wind and evaluate them for yourself. What a novel idea!

The following sections give you the scoop on how different climate factors affect roses.

Hardiness: How Cold Can You Grow?

Different types of roses have different tolerances to cold winter temperatures. The lowest temperature a rose can withstand without injury is called its *winter hardiness*.

Several factors influence whether a plant reaches its full hardiness, and consequently, a plant's hardiness is generally given in a range. For example:

- Most popular hybrid teas, floribundas, climbers, and grandifloras can survive 10° to 20°F (–12° to –6°C) temperatures without any winter protection.
- Miniatures, because they grow on their own roots and don't have that vulnerable bud union, are hardier.
- Many species and shrub roses are hardier still. For example, rugosa roses are said to be hardy to about –35°F (–37°C).

But, even within groups of roses, different varieties can be hardier than others. For example, the lovely white hybrid tea 'Pristine' doesn't seem to like temperatures much below 30°F (–1°C). Rosarians in cold-winter climates who can't live without 'Pristine' treat it like an annual and replant it each year.

Most rose books and some catalogs list hybrid tea roses as being hardy to between −10° to −20°F (−23° to −29°C), but that's with some type of winter protection, such as mounding soil over the base of the plant. Without protection, modern roses, like hybrid teas, floribundas, and most climbers, are often damaged by temperatures of 10°F (−12°C) and colder.

Messin' with your hardiness head

Rose hardiness isn't at all precise. In fact, sometimes it's downright confounding. Early cold snaps in fall, or late ones in spring, can damage plants that you normally think of as being hardy. And different types of cold damage exist. Sometimes, just the tips of the canes die; other times everything above the ground dies; and occasionally, the whole plant ends up deader than a doornail. To further complicate things, dry winter winds, bright sunshine, and even how you care for a rose prior to cold weather affect its capability to withstand winter weather. Luckily, most roses are relatively easy to protect from the ravages of winter. (For that information, go to Chapter 20.)

Growing roses in cold winter climates

If you live where temperatures regularly drop below 10°F (−12°C), use these strategies to give your roses a fighting chance:

- **Plant hardy roses.** Many roses have good cold hardiness. You may also want to check out some of the mail-order catalogs listed in Appendix C. Many single out the hardy varieties that they sell.

- **Grow own-root roses.** Hardier than budded roses because they grow on their own roots (like most miniatures and many old garden roses and shrubs) and don't have that vulnerable bud union that most modern roses have. If winter kills your own-root rose to the ground (but not below the ground), it is more likely than a budded plant to resprout true-to-type in the spring. For more on own-root roses, see Chapter 15.

- **Plant deep.** If you don't buy own-root roses, plant deeper than normal so that the bud union is well below the soil surface and protected by the layer of soil above it. For more information about bud unions and planting, see Chapter 16.

- **Use winter protection.** For various techniques, see Chapter 20.

Where winters are really brutal (−30°F or −34°C and colder — U.S. Zones 1 through 4), you're best off with the hardiest shrub roses, particularly any of the Morden and Explorer series from Canada and any of the rugosas.

A sampling of winter-hardy roses

Table 4-1 lists roses that not only survived winters in Minnesota without protection but also bloomed the following season even when canes that died in the winter were pruned almost to the ground in the spring. Testing was done at the University of Minnesota, where winter temperatures regularly drop below −35°F (−37°C).

Table 4-1	Really Hardy Roses for the North	
Name	*Type*	*Flower Color*
'Applejack'	Shrub	Pink spotted with crimson
'Carefree Beauty'	Shrub	Pink
'Champlain'	Shrub	Dark red
'Eutin'	Floribunda	Red
'Golden Wings'	Shrub	Yellow
'John Cabot'	Shrub	Red
'John Franklin'	Shrub	Red
'Morden Amorette'	Shrub	Pink
'Morden Centennial'	Shrub	Pink
'Prairie Dawn'	Shrub	Pink
'Prairie Princess'	Shrub	Pink

Some modern roses are hardier than others. We compiled the list of plants in Table 4-2 from recommended lists compiled in cold-winter regions of the United States. We don't list all the hardy roses recommended for each area — only those that showed up on two or more lists. Most shrub or landscape roses are very hardy, including the entire Meidiland series. But the ones in Table 4-2 come up again and again.

Table 4-2	Hardier-Than-Most Roses	
Name	*Type*	*Flower Color*
'All That Jazz'	Shrub	Salmon-orange
'Altissimo'	Climbing	Red

(continued)

Table 4-2 *(continued)*

Name	Type	Flower Color
'America'	Climbing	Pink
'American Spirit'	Hybrid tea	Red
'Betty Prior'	Floribunda	Pink
'Black Jade'	Miniature	Red
'Bonica'	Shrub	Pink
'Carefree Beauty'	Shrub	Pink
'Carefree Delight'	Shrub	Pink and white
'Carefree Wonder'	Shrub	Pink and white
'Chicago Peace'	Hybrid tea	Pink and yellow
'Child's Play'	Miniature	White and pink
'China Doll'	Polyantha	Pink
'Chrysler Imperial'	Hybrid tea	Red
'Class Act'	Floribunda	White
'Dainty Bess'	Hybrid tea	Pink
'Don Juan'	Climbing	Red
'Dortmund'	Climbing	Red and white
'Double Delight'	Hybrid tea	White and red
'Europeana'	Floribunda	Red
'Eyepaint'	Floribunda	Red and white
'Figurine'	Miniature	White and pink
'Fragrant Cloud'	Hybrid tea	Coral-orange
'Garden Party'	Hybrid tea	White
'Gene Boerner'	Floribunda	Pink
'Gold Medal'	Grandiflora	Yellow
'Golden Showers'	Climbing	Yellow
'Granada'	Hybrid tea	Pink and yellow

Name	Type	Flower Color
'Handel'	Climbing	Pink and white
'Iceberg'	Floribunda	White
'Impatient'	Floribunda	Orange-red
'Improved Blaze'	Climbing	Red
'Ivory Fashion'	Floribunda	White
'Jean Kenneally'	Miniature	Apricot
'Judy Fischer'	Miniature	Pink
'Little Darling'	Floribunda	Salmon-pink and yellow
'Love'	Grandiflora	Red
'Magic Carrousel'	Miniature	White and red
'Medallion'	Hybrid tea	Apricot-orange
'Midas Touch'	Hybrid tea	Yellow
'Minnie Pearl'	Miniature	Pink
'Mister Lincoln'	Hybrid tea	Red
'New Dawn'	Climbing	Pink
'Olympiad'	Hybrid tea	Red
'Party Girl'	Miniature	Yellow
'Pascali'	Hybrid tea	White
'Peace'	Hybrid tea	Yellow and pink
'Pink Parfait'	Grandiflora	Pink
'Pleasure'	Floribunda	Salmon-pink
'Queen Elizabeth'	Grandiflora	Pink
'Regensberg'	Floribunda	Red and white
'Rise 'n' Shine'	Miniature	Apricot-yellow and pink
'Secret'	Hybrid tea	White and pink
'Sexy Rexy'	Floribunda	Pink
'Sheer Bliss'	Hybrid tea	White and pink

(continued)

Table 4-2 *(continued)*

Name	Type	Flower Color
'Showbiz'	Floribunda	Red
'Simplicity'	Floribunda	Pink
'Singin' in the Rain'	Floribunda	Orange
'Snow Bride'	Miniature	White
'Starina'	Miniature	Red
'Summer Dream'	Hybrid tea	Apricot-pink
'Sunsprite'	Floribunda	Yellow
'Swarthmore'	Hybrid tea	Red
'The Fairy'	Polyantha	Pink
'Tiffany'	Hybrid tea	Pink
'Touch of Class'	Hybrid tea	Pink
'Tournament of Roses'	Grandiflora	Pink
'Tropicana'	Hybrid tea	Coral-orange
'White Lightnin'	Grandiflora	White

Let the Sun Shine . . . or Block It Out

The sun shines in most places, but the duration and intensity varies a whole lot from one place to another and from one season to the next. In some coastal areas, summer fog is common, and roses lap up every minute of sunshine. But at the other extreme, in desert areas, the sun is so hot that it stresses plants and even bleaches out the color of some roses.

Dealing with too much or too little sunlight is really a matter of choosing appropriate varieties for your climate and choosing an appropriate planting site around your home. Figure 4-1 shows the perfect planting place.

In areas where temperatures rarely drop below 32°F (0°C), such as in the deep southern areas of the United States and parts of southern California, roses grow and bloom almost year-round. But don't think that you're getting off easier than those people who have to protect their roses from winter.

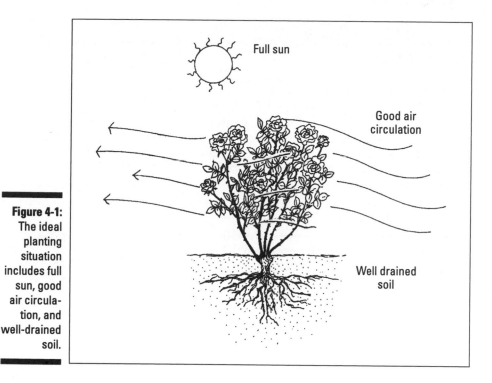

Full sun

Good air circulation

Well drained soil

✔ First, because your roses grow and bloom for a longer period, you need to water, deadhead, and fertilize more often.

✔ And, just as people need a rest once in a while, so do roses. In temperate areas, you almost have to force them into dormancy with winter pruning and even a little leaf pulling.

For details about pruning, see Chapter 19. Make sure to check out Chapter 18, which covers fertilizing, too.

Heat tolerance: When your roses are red hot

Hot weather during the day and at night has some surprising effects on how roses perform and how you care for them. Probably most interesting is how temperature affects the color and character of roses.

More petals, more heat

Red roses with many petals (more than 45 to 50), like 'Chrysler Imperial', need heat, especially at night, to open properly. In cooler areas, such as near the coast in the western United States, the flower petals tend to stay in a ball and don't unfurl completely. Consequently, in cooler climates, roses with fewer petals are often preferable.

Warmth fuses color

Bicolored roses, like the miniature 'Rainbow's End' and the hybrid tea 'Double Delight', also can look remarkably different in different temperatures. When summers are warm, their colors meld together in beautiful fusion, and it's hard to tell where one shade starts and the other ends. When it gets cooler, the distinctions between colors are more pronounced, with the colored edges on the petals becoming more distinct.

Heat slows growth

Growth really slows down when the temperature climbs over 90°F (32°C). Flowers are smaller than they are in the cooler temperatures of early spring or late fall, and flower production, or repeat, takes longer. Also, the petals on some varieties, like the wonderful 'Scentimental', a striped floribunda, may scorch or wilt in super-hot sun. Varieties like this are definitely worth the extra effort, but they benefit from being planted where they get partial shade during the hottest hours of the afternoon.

More heat means more water

The hotter it is, the more often you have to water. The soil in which roses are planted should never dry out, but especially in hot weather, roses really take a beating if they don't have plenty of water. If the heat combines with summer rainfall or high humidity . . . well, that's a horse of a different color.

A sampling of roses for hot, dry climates

The rose societies of both Tucson and Phoenix, Arizona, provided the recommendations in Table 4-3.

Table 4-3	Roses That Stand Up to Heat	
Name	**Type**	**Flower Color**
'Altissimo'	Climbing	Red
'America'	Climbing	Coral pink
'Angel Face'	Floribunda	Lavender
'Apricot Nectar'	Floribunda	Apricot
'Arizona'	Grandiflora	Orange, yellow, and pink
'Beauty Secret'	Miniature	Red
'Black Jade'	Miniature	Red

Name	*Type*	*Flower Color*
'Brandy'	Hybrid tea	Orange
'Brass Band'	Floribunda	Apricot
'Celebrity'	Hybrid tea	Yellow
'Centerpiece'	Miniature	Red
'Cherish'	Floribunda	Pink
'China Doll'	Polyantha	Pink
'Chrysler Imperial'	Hybrid tea	Red
'Cl. First Prize'	Climbing	Pink
'Cl. Iceberg'	Climbing	White
'Class Act'	Floribunda	White
'Cl. Queen Elizabeth'	Climbing	Pink
'Cupcake'	Miniature	Pink
'Don Juan'	Climbing	Red
'Double Delight'	Hybrid tea	White and red
'Dream Weaver'	Climbing	Pink
'Dreamglo'	Miniature	Red and white
'Dublin Bay'	Climbing	Red
'Europeana'	Floribunda	Red
'Figurine'	Miniature	White and pink
'First Prize'	Hybrid tea	Pink
'Fragrant Plum'	Grandiflora	Lavender
'French Lace'	Floribunda	White
'Gene Boerner'	Floribunda	Pink
'Gingersnap'	Floribunda	Orange and yellow
'Gold Medal'	Grandiflora	Yellow
'Handel'	Climbing	White and pink
'Holy Toledo'	Miniature	Apricot and yellow
'Honor'	Hybrid tea	White

(continued)

Table 4-3 *(continued)*

Name	Type	Flower color
'Iceberg'	Floribunda	White
'Impatient'	Floribunda	Orange-red
'Intrigue'	Floribunda	Lavender
'Ivory Fashion'	Floribunda	White
'Joseph's Coat'	Climbing	Yellow and red
'Judy Fischer'	Miniature	Pink
'Just Joey'	Hybrid tea	Apricot
'Kristin'	Miniature	Red and white
'Lace Cascade'	Climbing	White
'Lavender Jewel'	Miniature	Lavender
'Little Artist'	Miniature	Red and white
'Love Potion'	Floribunda	Purple
'Loving Touch'	Miniature	Apricot
'Magic Carrousel'	Miniature	White and red
'Marina'	Floribunda	Orange
'Mary Marshall'	Miniature	Orange
'Medallion'	Hybrid tea	Apricot
'Minnie Pearl'	Miniature	Pink
'Miss All-American Beauty'	Hybrid tea	Pink
'Mister Lincoln'	Hybrid tea	Red
'Montezuma'	Grandiflora	Salmon-pink
'Moonstone'	Hybrid tea	White and pink
'New Day'	Hybrid tea	Yellow
'Old Glory'	Miniature	Red
'Olé'	Grandiflora	Red-orange
'Olympiad'	Hybrid tea	Red
'Oregold'	Hybrid tea	Yellow
'Over the Rainbow'	Miniature	Red and yellow

Name	Type	Flower Color
'Pacesetter'	Miniature	White
'Paradise'	Hybrid tea	Lavender
'Party Girl'	Miniature	Apricot-yellow and pink
'Peace'	Hybrid tea	Yellow and pink
'Peaches 'n' Cream'	Miniature	Orange
'Perfect Moment'	Hybrid tea	Yellow and red
'Piñata'	Climbing	Red, yellow, and orange
'Playboy'	Floribunda	Orange and red
'Pristine'	Hybrid tea	White and pink
'Puppy Love'	Miniature	Orange, pink, and yellow
'Purple Tiger'	Floribunda	Purple, white, and pink
'Queen Elizabeth'	Grandiflora	Pink
'Rainbow's End'	Miniature	Yellow and red
'Redgold'	Floribunda	Yellow-red
'Rio Samba'	Hybrid tea	Yellow and orange
'Rise 'n' Shine'	Miniature	Yellow
'Royal Highness'	Hybrid tea	Pink
'Sarabande'	Floribunda	Scarlet-orange
'Scentimental'	Floribunda	Red and white
'Sequoia Gold'	Miniature	Golden yellow
'Sheer Bliss'	Hybrid tea	White
'Sheri Anne'	Miniature	Orange-red
'Showbiz'	Floribunda	Red
'Shreveport'	Grandiflora	Orange and yellow
'Signature'	Hybrid tea	Pink
'Simplex'	Miniature	White
'Singin' In The Rain'	Floribunda	Apricot
'Snow Bride'	Miniature	White

(continued)

Table 4-3 *(continued)*

Name	Type	Flower Color
'Sonia'	Grandiflora	Pink and yellow
'St. Patrick'	Hybrid tea	Yellowish green
'Starina'	Miniature	Red-orange
'Summer Sunshine'	Hybrid tea	Yellow
'Sun Flare'	Floribunda	Yellow
'Sundowner'	Grandiflora	Pink
'Sunsprite'	Floribunda	Yellow
'Tempo'	Climbing	Red
'The Fairy'	Polyantha	Pink
'Timeless'	Hybrid tea	Pink
'Touch of Class'	Hybrid tea	Pink and orange
'Tournament of Roses'	Grandiflora	Pink
'Trumpeter'	Floribunda	Orange-red
'White Lightnin'	Grandiflora	White
'Winsome'	Miniature	Lavender
'Yellow Doll'	Miniature	Yellow

Sultry summers and sweaty roses

We can't say it often enough, and it's certainly worth pounding into your head: The drier or hotter it is, the more often you have to water your roses.

But what if there's too much rain? Roses drown, that's what.

Many parts of the southeastern United States get so much rain, and soil drainage is so poor, that the only way to grow roses is in raised beds or containers. You can find out how in Chapter 7.

Humidity attracts pests and disease

That said about water, the level of atmospheric humidity in summer, which is often related to the amount of rainfall or fog (or just plain mugginess), has an important impact on the diseases, and sometimes the insects, that attack roses.

For example:

- ✔ Where it's hot, humid, and rainy in summer, or where days are hot and nights are cool, *black spot,* a fungus that makes round black spots on rose leaves and causes them to fall off, can be a problem.

- ✔ Where nights are humid and cool, *powdery mildew,* a fungus that distorts new growth and causes silvery fuzz on rose leaves, may show up.

- ✔ Where days are warm and nights cool and humid, *rust,* another fungus that looks like orange spots on leaves and stems, can cause plants to defoliate. And, if you don't take preventive measures, *spider mites,* microscopic spiders that suck the life out of rose leaves, appear.

So, you need to be familiar with the pests and diseases likely to show up in your area. When you're in the know, you can choose rose varieties resistant to those problems, or at least know when to expect to have to do battle. For more information on that battle, see Chapter 21.

A sampling of roses for areas with warm, humid summers

The list of roses in Table 4-4 was compiled from rose societies in the deep south of the United States.

Table 4-4	Roses That Don't Wilt in Humidity	
Name	*Type*	*Flower Color*
'All That Jazz'	Shrub	Orange
'Altissimo'	Climbing	Red
'America'	Climbing	Pink
'Angel Face'	Floribunda	Lavender
'Apricot Nectar'	Floribunda	Apricot-orange
'Betty Prior'	Floribunda	Pink
'Black Jade'	Miniature	Red
'Carefree Wonder'	Shrub	Pink and white
'Cherish'	Floribunda	Pink
'Chicago Peace'	Hybrid tea	Pink and yellow
'Child's Play'	Miniature	White and pink
'China Doll'	Polyantha	Pink

(continued)

Table 4-4 *(continued)*

Name	Type	Flower Color
'Class Act'	Floribunda	White
'Dainty Bess'	Hybrid tea	Pink
'Don Juan'	Climbing	Red
'Dortmund'	Climbing	Red and white
'Double Delight'	Hybrid tea	White and red
'Europeana'	Floribunda	Red
'Figurine'	Miniature	White and pink
'First Prize'	Hybrid tea	Pink
'Fragrant Cloud'	Hybrid tea	Coral-orange
'Friendship'	Hybrid tea	Pink
'Gene Boerner'	Floribunda	Pink
'Gold Medal'	Grandiflora	Yellow
'Granada'	Hybrid tea	Red and orange
'Honor'	Hybrid tea	White
'Iceberg'	Floribunda	White
'Impatient'	Floribunda	Orange-red
'Ivory Fashion'	Floribunda	White
'Ivory Tower'	Hybrid tea	White
'Lady X'	Hybrid tea	Lavender
'Love'	Grandiflora	Red
'Loving Touch'	Miniature	Apricot
'Mikado'	Hybrid tea	Red
'Miss All-American Beauty'	Hybrid tea	Pink
'Mister Lincoln'	Hybrid tea	Red
'Montezuma'	Grandiflora	Salmon-pink
'Old Glory'	Miniature	Red

Name	Type	Flower Color
'Olympiad'	Hybrid tea	Red
'Paradise'	Hybrid tea	Lavender
'Pascali'	Hybrid tea	White
'Peace'	Hybrid tea	Yellow and pink
'Perfect Moment'	Hybrid tea	Red and yellow
'Perfume Delight'	Hybrid tea	Pink
'Pristine'	Hybrid tea	White
'Queen Elizabeth'	Grandiflora	Pink
'Redgold'	Floribunda	Yellow-red
'Rio Samba'	Hybrid tea	Yellow and orange
'Rise 'n' Shine'	Miniature	Yellow
'Rose Parade'	Floribunda	Pink
'Royal Highness'	Hybrid tea	Pink
'Shining Hour'	Grandiflora	Yellow
'Sonia'	Grandiflora	Pink and yellow
'Sun Flare'	Floribunda	Yellow
'Sunsprite'	Floribunda	Yellow
'Tiffany'	Hybrid tea	Pink
'Touch of Class'	Hybrid tea	Orange-pink
'Tournament of Roses'	Grandiflora	Pink
'Unforgettable'	Hybrid tea	Pink
'White Masterpiece'	Hybrid tea	White
'Winsome'	Miniature	Lavender

Roses for Areas with Cool Summers

The roses in Table 4-5 are recommended by the International Rose Test Garden in Portland, Oregon, and the San Francisco Rose Society. Varieties marked with an asterisk (*) have exceptional disease resistance — particularly to powdery mildew and rust, which are common where summers are cool and foggy.

Table 4-5	Roses for Cool-Summer Climates	
Name	**Type**	**Flower Color**
'All That Jazz'	Shrub	Orange
'Altissimo'	Climbing	Red
'Amber Queen'	Floribunda	Apricot-gold
'America'	Climbing	Coral-pink
'Beauty Secret'	Miniature	Red
'Betty Prior'	Floribunda	Pink
'Bonica'	Shrub	Pink
'Carefree Wonder'	Shrub	Pink and white
'Caribbean'	Grandiflora	Orange
'Cinderella'	Miniature	White
'Class Act'*	Floribunda	White
'Color Magic'	Hybrid tea	Pink
'Dainty Bess'	Hybrid tea	Pink
'Dortmund'*	Climbing	Red and white
'Double Delight'	Hybrid tea	Red and white
'Dublin Bay'*	Climbing	Red
'Europeana'*	Floribunda	Red
'Eyepaint'*	Floribunda	Red and white
'Folklore'	Hybrid tea	Orange
'Fragrant Cloud'*	Hybrid tea	Coral-orange
'French Lace'*	Floribunda	White
'Gold Medal'	Grandiflora	Yellow

Name	Type	Flower Color
'Golden Showers'	Climbing	Yellow
'Golden Wings'	Shrub	Yellow
'Graham Thomas'	Shrub	Yellow
'Handel'*	Climbing	Pink and white
'Holy Toledo'*	Miniature	Orange and yellow
'Honor'	Hybrid tea	White
'Iceberg'*	Floribunda	White
'Joseph's Coat'	Climbing	Yellow and red
'Just Joey'*	Hybrid tea	Orange
'Las Vegas'	Hybrid tea	Orange, red, and yellow
'Little Artist'*	Miniature	Red and white
'Little Darling'	Floribunda	Yellow
'Little Jackie'	Miniature	Orange
'Love'*	Grandiflora	Red
'Magic Carrousel'	Miniature	White and red
'Marina'	Floribunda	Orange
'Medallion'	Hybrid tea	Apricot-pink
'Minnie Pearl'	Miniature	Pink
'New Beginning'	Miniature	Orange and yellow
'New Day'	Hybrid tea	Yellow
'Olympiad'*	Hybrid tea	Red
'Paradise'	Hybrid tea	Lavender
'Party Girl'	Miniature	Yellow and pink
'Pascali'*	Hybrid tea	White
'Peace'*	Hybrid tea	Yellow and pink
'Playboy'*	Floribunda	Red-orange
'Playgirl'*	Floribunda	Magenta-pink
'Precious Platinum'	Hybrid tea	Red

(continued)

Table 4-5 *(continued)*

Name	Type	Flower Color
'Prima Donna'	Grandiflora	Pink
'Pristine'	Hybrid tea	White
'Prominent'	Grandiflora	Orange
'Queen Elizabeth'*	Grandiflora	Pink
'Rainbow's End'	Miniature	Yellow and red
'Redgold'	Floribunda	Yellow-red
'Regensberg'	Floribunda	Pink and white
'Rise 'n' Shine'	Miniature	Yellow
'Sally Holmes'	Shrub	White
'Sarabande'*	Floribunda	Orange-red
'Sexy Rexy'	Floribunda	Pink
'Sheer Elegance'	Hybrid tea	Pink
'Showbiz'*	Floribunda	Red
'Simplex'*	Miniature	White
'Simplicity'	Floribunda	Pink
'Sonia'	Grandiflora	Pink
'Starina'*	Miniature	Red-orange
'Sun Flare'	Floribunda	Yellow
'Sunsprite'	Floribunda	Yellow
'Tiffany'	Hybrid tea	Pink
'Touch of Class'	Hybrid tea	Pink
'Tournament of Roses'	Grandiflora	Pink
'Trumpeter'*	Floribunda	Orange-red
'Voodoo'*	Hybrid tea	Orange, yellow, and red

Tiny Climates Are Not Just for Tiny Roses

This chapter gives you a pretty good idea of how climate factors such as winter low temperatures, summer heat and humidity, and the amount of sunshine can affect the roses you want to grow. But take things a step further. You know that big block of wood, nails, bricks, and concrete that sits in the middle of your property and that you call home? Well, its overwhelming size affects small areas of your garden and makes their climate just a little different from the overall climate of your neighborhood. These little areas are called microclimates. *Microclimates* are localized climates that, because of their proximity to large buildings or trees, or because of the way the land slopes, differ from the overall climate of an area.

If you walk around your home in the morning and again in the afternoon on a summer day, you can probably see the following microclimates, illustrated in Figure 4-2:

- ✔ The south side is mostly sunny and warm all day.

- ✔ The west side is shady and cool in the morning and hot and sunny in the afternoon.

- ✔ The east side is nice and sunny in the morning and cool and shady in the afternoon.

- ✔ The north side is shady almost all day. It's probably not a good place for roses.

As you walk, you may also notice that other large objects, especially trees, create microclimates that change from morning to afternoon. Even a south-facing slope is warmer than other parts of the garden, simply because it bathes in sun almost all day.

After you identify the microclimates around your home, you can choose just the right spot for planting roses. In general, roses want sun all day. But, as in the hot desert of the American southwest, for example, too much sun can harm roses. In that case, you may want to plant on the east side of the house so that the roses get a little shade during the hottest part of the day.

On the other hand, if you live in an area with cool summers, the extra heat caused by a west-facing wall may be just what you need to open those heat-loving red roses.

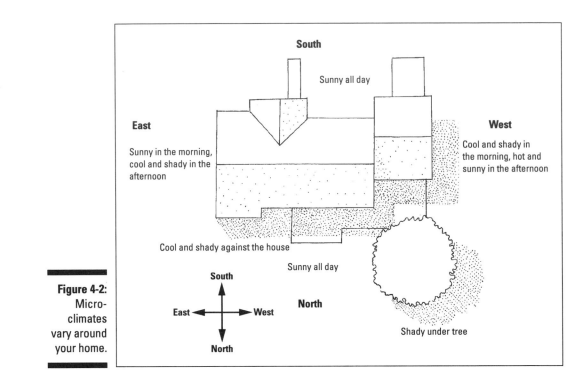

South

Sunny all day

East

Sunny in the morning, cool and shady in the afternoon

West

Cool and shady in the morning, hot and sunny in the afternoon

Cool and shady against the house

Sunny all day

South

East ← → West

North

North

Shady under tree

Figure 4-2: Micro-climates vary around your home.

Part II
Using Roses in Your Garden

The 5th Wave   By Rich Tennant

"Plenty of sunshine, organic matter, and the right soil will keep them bright and colorful. And what that won't do, a box of fluorescent felt tip markers will take care of."

In this part . . .

This is probably the most useful part of this book. Many people overlook the fact that roses not only are hard-working garden plants but also are one of the most colorful flowering shrubs.

Next time you do some landscaping, think of roses instead of, say, junipers or cotoneaster. When you want summer color, use roses along with your marigolds and petunias. When you want some color on your front porch, put roses in a container. Roses work in fantastically colorful ways.

Chapter 5

Landscaping with Roses

● ●

In This Chapter

▶ Landscaping with versatile rose shrubs

▶ Using color in the garden

▶ Mixing and matching plant textures

▶ Putting roses to work as hedges, edgings, and ground covers

▶ Growing roses on fences, walls, trellises, and arbors

● ●

*H*ave you ever walked into a garden and thought, "Wow, this is beautiful — every plant in its place, just the right mix of colors and textures, and everything so well organized. Someone planned this garden perfectly!"

Good landscaping does take planning and organization. You can find some basic landscape techniques, such as drawing plans and laying paths and patios, described in *Gardening For Dummies,* 2nd Edition, by Michael MacCaskey, Bill Marken, and The National Gardening Association (IDG Books Worldwide, Inc.).

When dealing with roses, we hope that you really take one piece of advice to heart: Before you plant any rose, think carefully about where you want to plant it and the impact it will have on your garden or landscape.

Of course, you have to provide the plant with the requirements for healthy growth in terms of sunshine, soil, and the like, and we cover all that in Part IV of this book. But you also need to think about how roses can work for you, how they can fill basic landscape roles as hedges, screens, ground covers, barriers, and more. Even more importantly, how will their colors blend with the plants in the rest of your garden? What will the emotional effect be? Will they add excitement or serenity to your garden?

You may think that we've gone over the edge with these questions, but don't be so sure. Roses can fill traditional landscape roles that you may not have considered. And the colors they bring to a garden are bright and dramatic — they have an impact on the look of your yard. Unless you give those colors a little thought, your garden may end up looking like a box of crayons left out in the sun on a hot summer day.

This chapter can help you avoid melted-crayon syndrome and show you, not only how to use colors and plant texture wisely, but also how to make roses work hard as hedges, screens, ground covers, and more.

Painting the Landscape with Colorful Roses

Taste in colors is a personal thing. If your favorite color is red and you want a red rose, who can argue with that? Go for it! But if you want to create a harmonious display of color throughout your garden, think carefully about the colors you choose and how they blend with other plants, and even with the exterior of your home.

Different colors affect people's emotions differently. Red and orange are warm colors that can actually make a garden feel hotter, especially if you use them together. They can overpower a garden if they're used too much. Lavender, white, and pink have the opposite effect: They feel cool and soothing, especially when they're combined with a lot of green foliage. Yellow can go either way, depending on the colors you accent it with.

If you live in a hot-summer area, you may want to use cooler colors, such as white or pink. In cool climates, you can warm things up with red roses. If you want to attract attention to a certain area of the garden, use bright, deep colors in that spot — they're sure to attract the eye.

Choosing a color scheme for your entire garden and sticking to it is the best way to avoid turning your yard into an eye-burning kaleidoscope of mismatched colors.

Basically, colors combine in two ways:

- **Harmonious colors** blend together smoothly and have a soothing effect. They are usually different shades of one of the primary colors — red, yellow, and blue. Pink and red are harmonious colors, as are yellow and orange, and blue and green.

- **Contrasting colors** highlight each other, making each color appear brighter and stronger than it would by itself. You create the strongest color contrasts by putting one primary color next to another, such as blue salvia next to red 'Mister Lincoln' or yellow 'Sunsprite' next to blue petunias. In a garden, contrasting colors tend to attract the eye and stand out. They also make things appear closer when viewed from a distance. But, if you use them too much, they can overpower and dominate your garden. Your eyes need some place to rest.

If you feel a little uneasy about picking colors, keep your choices simple. Fewer colors often work better than more. Some of the most stunning gardens use just one flower color, such as white, yellow, or pink. Particularly where you have a good background of green foliage, this kind of simplicity offers a rare beauty. You might even go to a hardware store and pick up some paint chips and use them to experiment with different color combinations. After you find a combination you like, you can go to Part III and find roses to match.

Often you can get clues about good colors to use from the color of your house, from existing plants, or from landscape features. For example, using roses that combine well with the trim or siding color of your house can tie your whole landscape together into one harmonious picture.

You can also find potential color combinations in flowers themselves. For example, suppose that your favorite rose is the pink-and-white hybrid tea 'Secret'. If you combine that rose with other flowers in shades of white and pink, such as petunias or hardy geraniums, you have a guaranteed winner.

Mixing Plant Texture and Form

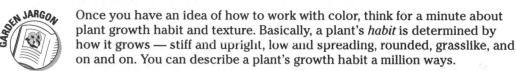

Once you have an idea of how to work with color, think for a minute about plant growth habit and texture. Basically, a plant's *habit* is determined by how it grows — stiff and upright, low and spreading, rounded, grasslike, and on and on. You can describe a plant's growth habit a million ways.

A plant's *texture* is most often related to the size and density of the foliage, and is usually described in terms of fine or bold, soft or coarse, or somewhere in between. Plants with many small or finely divided leaves, such as ferns, have fine, or soft, texture. Plants with larger or stiff leaves, such as camellias, are said to have bold, or coarse, texture. Bold plants tend to stand out and appear closer to the viewer. Soft-textured plants tend to recede and look like they're farther away.

The flowers also vary in texture. Most larger roses have to be considered bold flowers, especially when compared with smaller blooms like those of the annual lobelia or the perennial salvia. But some roses with smaller flowers are more finely textured.

Don't worry about exactly what texture or growth habit a plant has. Just realize that plants look different. What a news flash! When you're mixing roses with other plants, which is the topic of Chapter 6, you can create more natural and interesting situations by blending plants with different habits and textures, or even by combining roses that have different textures. For example, the soft foliage of miniature roses would get lost among other fine-textured plants. But when mixed with bolder plants, miniatures stand out and show their real character.

Many roses, especially the crinkly-leafed rugosas and the ferny moss roses (see Chapter 14), have foliage or stems with unique texture. They look good even when they're not in bloom.

Creating a Style All Your Own

On a very basic level, garden styles can be described as formal or informal. *Formal gardens* have a lot of straight lines and geometric shapes and seem very well organized. *Informal gardens* are less rigid and more natural, with plants growing the way they want, without severe pruning or shaping.

Even though distinguishing between formal and informal gardens is difficult (and who cares, anyway?), you should know that you can use roses to create either style. If you think that your garden needs a little more formality or organization, surround your cutting garden of hybrid teas with a low-growing, neatly clipped boxwood hedge. Voilà! — the formality of English kings. Planting long rows of floribundas, shrub roses, or miniature roses as hedges also creates formality, especially if you put a clipped hedge behind them.

If informality is more your style, plant some old or climbing roses way in the back of your yard and just let them have their way. They create a mounding, rolling background with a wonderfully wild look. Mixing shrub and floribunda roses in perennial borders or combining them with other blooming plants (the subject of Chapter 6) also results in a more informal style.

Here are some other tips to remember when landscaping with roses:

- ✔ **Keep short in the front, tall in the back.** Seems obvious, but people always forget. Keep shorter plants in front, adding gradually taller plants, with the very tallest ones in the back. That way, nothing is obscured.

- ✔ **Stick to odd-numbered groupings.** Roses, or any plants, for that matter, look more natural when grouped in odd numbers. Don't ask why this technique works; it just does.

- ✔ **Use soft colors in small spaces.** Lighter colors tend to recede and make a small garden look bigger. Darker or contrasting colors can make a small garden appear even more cramped.

- ✔ **Use repetition to provide continuity.** Even though mixing plants of different texture or form adds interest to a garden, repeating certain plants or groups of plants throughout a garden adds structure and order. So try to do a little bit of both.

Putting Roses to Work

Using roses in traditional landscape situations (that is, a landscape with hedges, ground covers, edgings, and so on) is becoming increasingly popular. And it's easy to see why. Roses offer one of the longest seasons of bloom of any flowering shrub, and newer varieties have been almost custom designed for landscape uses such as hedges, ground covers, edgings, and borders. What's the difference between a hedge and an edge? We define these as we proceed through this chapter.

In the following sections, we list our favorite roses to use in traditional landscape situations. We include the type of rose and its color so that you can easily find that plant in the appropriate section of Part III of this book.

Hedging your beds

You can plant some roses, mostly shrubs and floribundas, close together to create a continuous hedge. You won't get a formal hedge with neatly clipped edges; instead, the hedge has an informal style — less pruning enables the plants to bloom more. (For more information about pruning, see Chapter 19.)

Most of the roses in this section can also be used for continuous borders or for backgrounds to other plantings. A border differs slightly from a hedge in that a *border* can be viewed from only one side — for example, a row of roses planted at the base of a fence or wall. A *hedge* usually separates two areas and is attractive from both sides. To create either a hedge or border, plant the roses about 2 to 3 feet apart.

These plants create hedges that vary in height according to the variety you use and how often you prune the plant. But most range from 3 to 6 feet, depending on the climate you live in.

Some of our favorite hedge roses are pictured in the color section:

- ❀ **'Amber Queen':** Yellow floribunda
- ❀ **'Betty Boop':** Red and white floribunda
- ❀ **'Betty Prior':** Pink floribunda
- ❀ **'Bonica':** Pink shrub
- ❀ **'Brass Band':** Yellow, orange, and pink floribunda
- ❀ **'Europeana':** Red floribunda
- ❀ **'Iceberg':** White floribunda
- ❀ **'Kaleidoscope':** Lavender shrub

- 🌸 **'Knock Out':** Red shrub
- 🌸 **'Livin' Easy':** Orange floribunda
- 🌸 **'Sarabande':** Orange floribunda
- 🌸 **'Sexy Rexy':** Pink floribunda
- 🌸 **'Showbiz':** Red floribunda
- 🌸 **'Simplicity':** Pink floribunda
- 🌸 **'Sunsprite':** Yellow floribunda

Here are some more of our favorites:

- 🌸 **'Carefree Delight':** Pink and white shrub
- 🌸 **'Carefree Wonder':** Pink and white shrub
- 🌸 **'Cathedral':** Apricot floribunda
- 🌸 **'Cherish':** Pink floribunda
- 🌸 **'Class Act':** White floribunda
- 🌸 **'Easy Going':** Orange floribunda
- 🌸 **'First Edition':** Orange floribunda
- 🌸 **'Gene Boerner':** Pink floribunda
- 🌸 **'Golden Wings':** Yellow shrub
- 🌸 **'Mix 'n' Match':** Pink shrub
- 🌸 **'Playboy':** Orange-scarlet floribunda
- 🌸 **'Pleasure':** Pink floribunda
- 🌸 *Rosa rugosa:* Red, pink, purple, or white old garden rose (see Chapter 14 for more on this species rose and its excellent hybrids)
- 🌸 **'Sparrieshoop':** Pink shrub
- 🌸 **'Sweet Inspiration':** Pink floribunda
- 🌸 **'Trumpeter':** Orange-scarlet floribunda

Edging around

An *edging* is a continuous planting of low-growing plants at the base of taller plants, or along a walkway, patio, or other garden surface. To create a continuous edging, plant about 1 to 2 feet apart, depending on the height of the variety.

Edgings are one of the best ways to use miniature roses, which have a strong presence in the following list:

- 🌹 **'Angelica Renae':** Pink miniature
- 🌹 **'Beauty Secret':** Red miniature
- 🌹 **'Center Gold':** Yellow miniature
- 🌹 **'Child's Play':** White and pink miniature
- 🌹 **'China Doll':** Pink polyantha
- 🌹 **'Cherry Hi':** Red miniature
- 🌹 **'Cupcake':** Pink miniature
- 🌹 **'Debut':** Red miniature
- 🌹 **'Figurine':** Pinkish white miniature
- 🌹 **'Gourmet Popcorn':** White miniature
- 🌹 **'Jacquie Williams':** White and red miniature
- 🌹 **'Judy Fischer':** Pink miniature
- 🌹 **'Little Eskimo':** White miniature
- 🌹 **'New Beginning':** Orange miniature
- 🌹 **'Pride 'n' Joy':** Orange and yellow miniature
- 🌹 **'Renny':** Pink miniature
- 🌹 **'Rise 'n' Shine':** Yellow miniature
- 🌹 **'Starglo':** White miniature
- 🌹 **'Starina':** Orange miniature
- 🌹 **'Winsome':** Lavender miniature
- 🌹 **'Yellow Doll':** Yellow miniature

Covering ground

For the most part, rose varieties that make good ground covers are vigorous, spreading plants. However, many shrubby roses, such as low-growing floribundas, shrubs, and miniatures, can be spaced 2 to 3 feet apart and planted to cover a large area.

Also, vigorous old garden roses, like the bourbons and hybrid perpetuals (see Chapter 14 for more information), can be effective ground covers if you secure the ends of their long canes to the ground with wire pegs. This process, called *pegging,* is usually done during winter when the plants are dormant, but you generally have to repeat it throughout the growing season. The long, arching canes bloom along their entire length and stay close to the ground.

You can make your own pegs by cutting up wire coat hangers into 12-inch pieces and shaping each one into a U shape. Just put a peg over the end of each cane and push it into the ground.

The following are some of the best spreading roses for use as ground covers. Most should be planted 3 to 5 feet apart, depending on the vigor of the variety. Leave the most space between the most vigorous roses.

- **'Alba Meidiland':** White shrub
- **'Baby Blanket':** Pink shrub
- **'Dortmund':** Red and white climber
- **Flower Carpet roses:** Pink, white and red shrubs
- **'Jeeper's Creeper':** White shrub
- **'New Dawn':** Pink climber
- **'Pearl Meidiland':** White shrub
- **'Ralph's Creeper':** Red and orange shrub
- **'Red Cascade':** Red miniature
- **'Red Meidiland':** Red shrub
- **'Red Ribbons':** Red shrub
- *Rosa banksiae lutea:* Yellow old garden rose
- *Rosa bracteata* **'Mermaid':** Yellow species rose
- **'Scarlet Meidiland':** Red shrub
- **'Sea Foam':** White shrub
- **'The Fairy':** Pink polyantha
- **'White Meidiland':** White shrub

Climbing the walls

Training a climbing rose to sprawl on a fence, wall, or trellis is one of the most beautiful ways to work roses into the landscape and bring their flowers right up to eye level. (See Chapter 12 for more information about climbers.) However, you must realize that *training* is the key word here. Climbing roses are not true vines. They don't naturally cling to or wrap around a nearby vertical object like vines do. You must plant them near a support structure — such as a fence, post, arbor, wall, or trellis — and regularly tie their canes to that structure to make them stay put.

Following are several types of support structures for climbing roses. In all cases, the structure must be sturdy. A mature climber can be quite heavy and may break support not strong enough to handle the weight.

✔ **Arbors and pergolas:** Arbors and pergolas differ from trellises in that they have a horizontal top and are usually free-standing, supported by posts or trellis-like sides. (See Figure 5-1.) You train a rose up the support and then over the top. Like trellises, you can make arbors and pergolas from a variety of materials, from wood to plastic to metal. They also range in size from small enough to frame the entry to a yard or garden to large enough to cover a patio or entire walkway. Also like trellises, many arbors and pergolas are quite ornate or whimsical and can serve as the focal point of a garden.

Figure 5-1:
Create a stunning focal point for your garden by training a rose to climb over an arbor.

You can find many styles of prefabricated arbors in the mail-order rose catalogs listed in Appendix C. Or, if you're handy, you can build your own. You may want to consult a carpenter or builder for advice, though, especially if you plan to build a large arbor. One other tip: Use pressure-treated lumber, or rot-resistant wood like cedar or redwood, in any part of the structure that comes in contact with the soil. Remember to check out safety tips before using pressure-treated lumber.

- **Fences:** Split rail, chain-link, even barbwire — you can turn any sturdy fence into a colorful picture when you use it to support a climbing rose. If you have solid fences with few places to tie to, use a trellis or stretch wire between eye screws as described in the "Walls" bullet item.

- **Pillars:** A pillar is a sturdy, rot-resistant wood or metal post set in the ground. The size and shape of the pillar can vary as long as the pillar itself is firmly embedded. You then plant a climber at the base and tie it to the pillar as it grows.

- **Trellises:** A handsome trellis covered with a climbing rose can be a piece of art, turning a blank wall into a garden focal point. Trellises come in many shapes and sizes and are constructed from a variety of materials, including wood, metal, and plastic. They can be free-standing or attached to walls and fences. A trip to a local lumberyard or garden center or a browse through the rose catalogs listed in Appendix C of this book can give you a good idea of the variety available. Or, if you're handy, you can get a good idea of what you can make yourself.

  Lattice, one of the most common types of trellis, is designed for mounting on walls or fences. You can also attach it to fence posts for an inexpensive screen. When securing lattice directly to a solid surface, extend the connecting supports several inches beyond the surface so that the trellis doesn't lie directly on the surface. This space improves air circulation around the rose, which helps to reduce pest and disease problems.

  To make house painting or other maintenance easier, fasten the latticework to hinges at the bottom so that you can lay back the trellis for easy access to the wall. Use metal hooks and eyes to attach the trellis to the wall at the top.

- **Walls:** You usually have to attach some type of support to a wall. One way is to thread 14- or 16-gauge galvanized wire through eye bolts attached to the wall. If you have masonry walls, you have to use bolts with expanding anchors. But your local hardware store can help you make the right choice. Arrange the wires vertically, horizontally, or in a fan shape — whatever your fancy dictates. You can even attach the rose directly to the bolts and skip the wire altogether.

Creating thorny barriers

The thorny nature of most roses makes them formidable barriers for keeping people and animals from going where you don't want them to. Planting roses near windows to deter intruders from approaching your home is a great example. Although any thorny rose works, some types are nastier than others. 'Mermaid' is a classic "barrier" rose (see Chapter 25 for more advice on roses *not* to plant). Other good barriers include many of the David Austin English roses, species and old garden roses, shrubs, and climbers.

Chapter 6

Roses and Their Partners in the Garden

In This Chapter

▶ Combining plants with beautiful results

▶ Putting other plants in front of roses

▶ Mixing roses with herbs

▶ Highlighting your roses with attractive foliage

▶ Creating a white garden

▶ Using roses in ten classic combinations using roses

C ertain plants just seem to belong together. Maybe their shapes are a perfect contrast. Or maybe their flower colors blend together just right. Or possibly the plants share a common history. Whatever the reason, many plants (including other roses) combine well with roses, resulting in classic beauty.

That's what this chapter is all about: specific plants that form classic combinations with roses — plant combinations that give your garden an artist's touch. We list many plants here, but you need more information about heights, habits, and bloom times to combine them effectively. This kind of data is almost always included in garden catalog descriptions (or should be), or you can find it in books about types of plants. *Perennials For Dummies* by Marcia Tatroe and the National Gardening Association (also from IDG Books Worldwide, Inc.) includes many good ideas about using roses in perennial gardens and with perennial plants.

The Basics of Combining Plants

A lot of what this chapter covers conforms to the basic principles of combining colors and plant textures outlined in Chapter 5. The following list quickly repeats some of those principles and throws in some new suggestions as well:

✔ **Match cultural requirements.** Roses like full sun, regular water, and soil that's close to a neutral pH. The plants you combine with them should like those things, too. Otherwise, one or the other will be unhappy. And so will you. Many serious rosarians will tell you that roses should not be grown with other plants because roses don't like the root competition or being crowded. In truth, you shouldn't plant right next to a rose. You can damage roots, and crowding may encourage diseases like rust or black spot. That's why we recommend you use spreading plants in the upcoming section "Plants That Cover the Bases." Most of these can be planted a distance from the rose and they will still spread cover the base of the rose. It's also why we recommend you plant only disease-resistant rose varieties. Most of them are not only less likely to get disease, they are vigorous plants that can stand a little competition. Besides, a diverse planting attracts beneficial insects that reduce insect pests (see Chapter 21). If you're still not sold, skip this chapter, (fercryinoutloud). Go ahead and plant your roses in boring rows.

✔ **Consider bloom times carefully.** Most roses have a long bloom season, so make sure that the other plantings you use also look good over a long season. Combine plants with a staggered bloom season so that you have color in spring, summer, and fall. For example, plant early-blooming cool-season annuals like pansies and violets to complement your rose's spring bloom. When it gets hot, yank the cool weather flowers and replace them with heat-lovers like annual salvia or zinnias to highlight your roses all summer long. Use flowering perennials, shrubs, and annuals.

✔ **Give the roses room to grow.** Don't crowd the roses. Plant at least 18 inches to 2 feet away, depending on the size of the companion plant. Tall, spreading plants, such as ornamental grasses, need to be planted even further away (at least 3 feet).

✔ **Vary the heights of plants.** In general, use lower plants in front and taller ones in back. However, you don't have to follow this rule religiously. Mixing things up a bit can be interesting.

✔ **Mix and match plant textures.** Blend bold textures, like most shrubby roses, with soft textures such as ornamental grasses, vertical shapes with horizontal ones, and round plants with arching plants. Mix plants the way nature does.

✔ **Choose colors wisely.** Select the colors you want to work with — taking clues from the color of your house, garden structures, other plants, or whatever else in you have in your yard — and stick with them.

✔ **Don't forget the foliage.** One way to make sure that your garden always looks good is to combine roses with plants that have attractive foliage. We give you some ideas a little later in this chapter.

✔ **Use bright colors to direct the eye.** If you want to create a focal point in your garden, surround the area with bright or contrasting colors. Even one bright red rose draws the eye to a garden feature such as a small fountain or bird bath.

✔ **Unite the overall impression.** Repeat some plant combinations to add unity to the garden.

✔ **Keep it simple.** Always the best advice. Don't get carried away with too many colors or too many different kinds of plants. Simplify, and you won't go wrong.

Okay, now that you're an expert, you're ready to get to the good part: choosing your plants.

Plants That Cover the Bases

Many roses, especially hybrid teas and some tall floribundas, tend to get a bit open and sparsely foliaged at the base of the plant. To alleviate this problem, you can plant low-growing or spreading plants right in front of them. The easiest thing to do is to plant the companions at the same time you plant the roses, but you can do it anytime.

An obvious first choice is to use some of the compact miniature roses listed for use as edgings in Chapter 5. But many other options are available; the following sections list some favorite perennial and annual plants that you can use. See Figure 6-1 for an example of how perennial and annual plants can fill in around the base of roses.

Figure 6-1:
A rose with low-spreading plants growing around its base.

Perennials are plants that survive from year to year in your garden, usually at least three years but sometimes much longer. In other words, they don't have to be replanted every year. *Annuals* are plants that complete their entire life cycle from seed to seed in one growing season. They give your garden quick and glorious color but must be replanted each year.

Perennials

These low-growing (most stay under 1 foot high) perennials live on in your garden from year to year and combine well with roses in both flower and foliage:

- **Silver yarrow** *(Achillea clavennae):* Silver leaves and white flowers.

- **Sea pink** *(Armeria maritima):* Grassy leaves and pink flowers.

- **Basket-of-gold** *(Aurinia saxatilis):* Silver foliage and yellow flowers.

- **Swan River daisy** *(Brachycome):* Blue flowers, airy foliage.

- **Bellflower** *(Campanula):* Several low-growing species are available in many colors. The Serbian bellflower, *(C. poscharskyana)* has blue flowers on a hairy-leafed plant.

- **Grand morning glory** *(Convolvulus sabatius):* Lavender flowers, spreading silvery green foliage.

- **Sweet William** *(Dianthus):* Usually comes in reds, whites, and pinks; you can choose from one of many varieties.

- **Gazanias:** A creeping plant with bright, daisy-like flowers in a variety of shades.

- **Cranesbill** *(Geranium):* One of our favorites for its variety of color and attractive foliage.

- **Coral bells** *(Heuchera):* Great, heart-shaped foliage and delicate white, pink, or red flower spikes.

- **Candytuft** *(Iberis sempervirens):* The whitest of white flowers, deep green leaves.

- **Sea lavender** *(Limonium perezii):* Big, bold, dark green leaves and airy white and blue blooms.

- **Moss pink** *(Phlox subulata):* A compact plant with pink or blue flowers.

- **Lamb's ears** *(Stachys byzantina):* Soft, silvery leaves and small purple flowers on tall spikes.

- **Verbena:** *(Verbena)* Some species are used as annuals. The best rose companions are the blue and pink shades, either annual or perennial.

Annuals

Choosing different plants to compliment your roses each year can add interest and excitement to your garden. Some of our favorite rose-friendly annuals are:

- **Flossflower** *(Ageratum houstonianum):* Great blues.
- **Sapphire flower** *(Browallia speciosa):* Blue and white blooms.
- **Vinca** *(Catharanthus roseus):* Bright shades of white, pink, red, and purple.
- **Cosmos** *(Cosmos species):* A wide range of colors on upright, airy plants. New dwarf varieties stay under 18 inches high.
- **Lobelia** *(Lobelia erinus):* Beautiful blue, pink, or white flowers.
- **Sweet alyssum** *(Lobularia maritima):* Covered with pink, purple, or white flowers.
- **Petunias** *(Petunia hybrida):* Wonderful range of bright colors.
- **Johnny-jump-up** *(Viola tricolor):* A smaller version of a pansy, which comes in many colors.
- **Pansies** *(Viola wittrockiana):* Many colors to choose from.
- **Zinnias** *(Zinnia elegans):* Many colors — use the compact varieties like the Peter Pan series.

Roses and Herbs

Roses share many characteristics with aromatic herb plants — their fragrant flowers are used to make potpourri (see Chapter 23 for information about making potpourri), their hips can be used to make aromatic tea, and the fragrance of the flower can be extracted for perfumes. Hey, maybe roses are herbs!

In fact, roses and herbs are closely linked and have been planted together for centuries. Many of the very fragrant old garden roses, like the 'Old Blush' China rose and the autumn damask rose, share a long bond with herbs. But using any fragrant rose variety makes sense.

The family of plants called *herbs* is huge and includes many attractive species, so you have much to choose from. These are all beautiful plants and valuable ornamentals, but if you plan to harvest the edible ones, don't grow them with roses that have to be sprayed with pesticides. Keep those herbs in your vegetable garden. Here are some of our favorites:

- **Southernwood** *(Artemisia abrotanum):* Beautiful silvery foliage looks great with red and white roses.

- **Chamomile** *(Chamaemelum nobile):* Low-growing plant with yellow flowers.

- **Fennel** *(Foeniculum vulgare):* The variety with bronze foliage goes especially well with white, red or pink roses.

- **Lavender** *(Lavandula):* Blue flowers and aromatic foliage.

- **Scented geraniums** *(Pelargonium):* Many varieties to choose from with wonderfully fragrant, good-looking leaves and pretty flowers.

- **Parsley** *(Petroselinum crispum):* Bright green, ferny foliage goes great with yellow roses.

- **Rosemary** *(Rosmarinus):* Many shrubby types with blue flowers. Perfect with white, pink or blue roses.

- **Sage** *(Salvia officinalis):* The yellow-, purple-, or tricolor-foliaged varieties look great in front of any rose.

- **Santolina** *(Santolina):* Silvery leaves and yellow flowers.

- **Thyme** *(Thymus):* Many varieties to choose from — we especially like yellow-foliaged creeping thyme and pearly silver thyme.

Going for Leaves

Plants with attractive foliage can carry a garden through down times when little is in bloom. And, when roses are in bloom, the foliage of surrounding plants can really show off your roses and light up their colors.

By the light of the silvery leaves

To start, consider any plant with gray or silver foliage. These colors tie everything together and combine especially well with white, pink, red, and lavender flowers. Try one of the following plants:

- **Yarrow** *(Achillea):* Silver foliage and colorful flowers.

- **Artemisia 'Powis Castle':** Great texture and color.

- **Dusty Miller** *(Centaurea cineraria* or *Senecio cineraria):* Great annuals with purple or yellow flowers.

- **Snow-in-summer** *(Cerastium tomentosum):* A beauty with white flowers.

- **Crete dittany** *(Origanum dictamnus):* Soft leaves and purple flowers.

- **Sage** *(Salvia chamaedryoides):* Silver leaves and bright blue flowers.

- **Lavender cotton** *(Santolina):* The silver/lavender color of its foliage gives this variety its name, not its yellow flowers.

- **Lamb's ears** *(Stachys byzantina):* Wonderfully soft texture, small purple flowers.

- **Bush germander** *(Teucrium fruticans):* An airy shrub.

- **Silver thyme** *(Thymus vulgaris)* especially 'Argenteus': Low and aromatic.

Not-always-greener grassy leaves

These rose companions are interesting mostly for their grass or grasslike leaves. In addition, some of these plants produce flowers in late summer and fall — just when roses are putting on their last show of the season.

- **Lily-of-the-Nile** *(Agapanthus):* Strap-like leaves and bright blue summer flower balls.

- **Blue fescue** *(Festuca glauca):* Silver-blue leaves on a low, mounding grass.

- **Daylily** *(Hemerocallis hybrids):* Grassy leaves and mostly orange and yellow trumpet-shaped summer flowers.

- **Iris** *(Iris species):* Strap-like leaves and classic spring flowers in many shades.

- **Lily** *(Lilium):* Upright plants and colorful trumpet-shaped summer blooms.

- **Purple fountain grass** *(Pennisetum setaceum* 'Rubrum'*):* Purplish bronze leaves and soft reddish plumes in fall.

- **Feather grass** *(Stipa):* Graceful grasses and soft-textured plumes in fall.

These are just a few of the plants that we know work well as companions for roses, but hundreds of others exist. Keep your eyes peeled for good color combinations in other gardens. If something you try doesn't work, give the companion plants the old heave-ho and try something else. Besides, to paraphrase Duke Ellington's dictum about music that sounds good being good: If a plant combination looks good, it probably is.

White for When the Night Is Bright

Remember that whole thing about there being beauty in simplicity? Well, how about a garden with nothing but white flowers? Such a garden is stunning during the day (especially if you have a lot of green background), and has an unearthly beauty at night during a full moon. With good outdoor lighting, the garden comes alive every night.

Naturally, many white roses are available. The best are described in Part III, and a number are pictured in the color section of this book. But do you want the real truth?

Our favorite white rose is 'Iceberg', a floribunda. It gives more bloom for your buck than almost any other white rose.

Following are other white-flowering plants that you can use with roses in a moonlit garden. Some come in colors other than white, so make sure to choose the white-flowering varieties. Throw in as many silvery or gray foliaged plants as you want, too. They also reflect light. (For suggestions, see the "By the light of the silvery leaves" section earlier in this chapter.)

✔ **Snapdragon** *(Antirrhinum majus):* Tall spikes of flowers.

✔ **Jupiter's beard** *(Centranthus ruber):* Tall flower spikes.

✔ **Mums** *(Chrysanthemum):* Beautiful fall flowers.

✔ **Cosmos** *(Cosmos bipinnatus):* Airy foliage and daisy-like flowers.

✔ **Daisies:** Many different species with bright white flowers.

✔ **Dianthus** *(Dianthus):* Many varieties to choose from, some fragrant.

✔ **Candytuft** *(Iberis sempervirens):* Whitest of white on a compact plant.

✔ **Sweet alyssum** *(Lobularia maritima):* Ground-hugging carpet of white.

✔ **Geraniums** *(Pelargonium):* Great balls of white.

✔ **Petunias** *(Petunia hybrida):* Low-growing plant with trumpet-like flowers.

When combining any plants, don't forget to consider their height, habit, and growing requirements, as mentioned earlier in this chapter.

Ten of our favorite combinations

Some combinations just work — who cares why. These do.

✔ The blue blossoms of Lily-of-the-Nile combine wonderfully with the yellow 'Sunsprite' floribunda, and complement red climbers, like 'Dortmund' and 'Altissimo' also.

✔ Any red or pink rose stands out against a white fence or arbor

✔ 'Simplicity' pink floribunda, fronted by blue flowering salvia *(Salvia patens)* and silvery lamb's ears *(Stachys byzantina)* is a colorful treat.

✔ 'Iceberg' white floribunda with purple flowering Mexican sage *(Salvia leucantha)* and purple fountain grass *(Pennisetum setaceum 'Rubrum')* is a crisp, cool combination.

✔ Any pink floribunda or miniature rose planted around a red brick patio looks charming.

✔ Pink and red roses with pink and red geraniums *(Pelargonium)* fronted by light blue lobelia *(Lobelia erinus)* makes a cheery arrangement.

✔ 'Betty Prior' pink floribunda, set against gray-foliaged Artemisia 'Powis Castle', and blue flowering salvia *(chamaedryoides),* with candytuft *(Iberis sempervirens)* in front gives a variety of definite hues.

✔ Reddish purple hardy geraniums (Geranium species) with pink 'Carefree Wonder' shrub rose and white 'Iceberg' floribunda is an effective and attractive mix of color and texture.

Combining different types of plants with beautiful, or even just interesting, results is what gives a garden its personality. The plants you choose are what make the garden uniquely yours. Experiment! This is where gardening gets fun and rewarding.

Chapter 7

Growing Roses in Containers

- -

In This Chapter

▶ Which roses are best in pots?

▶ What are the different types of containers?

▶ How big should pots be?

▶ What's the truth about potting soil?

▶ How do you plant and care for container roses?

- -

Roses are great plants for growing in containers. Choose the right pot, and you turn any rose into a garden feature. Not only that, but growing roses in containers also makes the plants mobile — you can move them out front when they're in bloom, put them out of the way when they're not, and cart them off to a protected location in areas where winters get cold.

Growing roses in containers can also solve problems. If you have bad soil in your garden area, for example, you can fill a pot with a perfect soil mix purchased from a nursery and plant your rose in that. And you always have room for a pot or two even if you have a very small garden — especially if your "garden" is just a patio, porch, or balcony.

So gardening in containers really adds a wonderful new dimension to growing roses. But this kind of gardening is not quite the same as growing roses in open ground. You need to choose the right rose, the right pot, and the right soil. And after you plant the rose in a container, you need to care for it properly, which includes using some techniques that are a little different than the ones you use for in-ground plants. That's what this chapter's about: turning you into an expert container gardener.

Picking the Right Rose for the Pot

If you really set your mind to it, you can grow any rose in a pot, but after a while, some of the large types get very hard to care for and keep in bounds. Smaller, compact roses are really best for growing in containers. These include miniatures, polyanthas, floribundas, and some shrub roses. You also can grow any hybrid tea in a container, but to look their best, hybrid teas usually need to be combined with other low-growing plants. (For suggestions, see Chapter 5 for a list of plants that are useful for covering plant bases.)

Still, some floribundas, polyanthas, and shrub roses just fit in a pot better than others. The following are some of our favorites. Add to the list any miniature rose you like.

You can see these in the color section:

- ❦ **'Betty Boop':** Red and white floribunda
- ❦ **'Betty Prior':** Pink floribunda
- ❦ **'Bonica':** Pink shrub
- ❦ **'Brass Band':** Apricot-yellow floribunda
- ❦ **'China Doll':** Pink polyantha
- ❦ **'Europeana':** Red floribunda
- ❦ **'Iceberg':** White floribunda
- ❦ **'Knock Out':** Red shrub
- ❦ **'Sun Flare':** Yellow floribunda

Here are some more of our favorites:

- ❦ **'Baby Love':** Yellow shrub
- ❦ **'Carefree Delight':** Pink shrub
- ❦ **'Carefree Wonder':** Pink and white shrub
- ❦ **'Easy Going':** Golden yellow floribunda
- ❦ **'Flower Carpet':** Pink, white, or red shrubs
- ❦ **'Margaret Merrill':** White floribunda
- ❦ **'Margo Koster':** Coral polyantha
- ❦ **'Mix 'n' Match':** Pink floribunda
- ❦ **'Nearly Wild':** Pink floribunda
- ❦ **'Pillow Fight':** White shrub
- ❦ **'Regensberg':** White and pink floribunda
- ❦ **'Sarabande':** Orange-red floribunda
- ❦ **'The Fairy':** Pink polyantha
- ❦ **'Watermelon Ice':** Pink shrub

Picking a Pot for the Rose

You can choose from a ton of different types of containers. If you don't believe us, go to a large nursery or garden center and compare pot sizes, shapes, and materials.

The first criterion in choosing a container is to make sure that you like how it looks. If you want to grow roses in old coffee cans, fine; just don't invite us over to take pictures. A nice-looking pot can really turn a healthy rose into something special. A pretty pot also makes everything else around it look better. A few nice pots can turn a patio into a perfectly ornamented garden room. Or they can turn a front porch into an entry that elegantly says, "Welcome."

After you decide what looks good to you, start looking at some of the other characteristics of containers. These variables may or may not sway your decision about what to buy, but some kinds of containers last longer than others; some are heavy, some are light; and some dry out faster than others.

Some common container types and their characteristics:

- **Clay pots** (shown in Figure 7-1) are attractive, relatively inexpensive, and come in a variety of styles. They break easily, though, and the larger ones can be quite heavy. The most common type is the familiar terra cotta, which is porous and allows the soil to dry out quickly. However, you can get glazed clay or ceramic pots, which are not only colorful but also hold on to water longer. But you pay a price for their staying power as these pots are more expensive.

- **Plastic pots** come in many styles, colors, and sizes. Some are even made to look like wood or clay pots. They're lightweight, inexpensive, and keep soil moist longer than clay pots. Some kinds become brittle after being in the sun for a year or two; after they break, about all you can do with them is to ship them off to a landfill, where they stay for eternity.

- **Wooden pots** are attractive, relatively inexpensive, and come in many styles, sizes, weights, and shapes. They include the very popular and inexpensive wine and whiskey half-barrels (shown in Figure 7-2). With a little carpentry skill, you can even build your own wooden container.

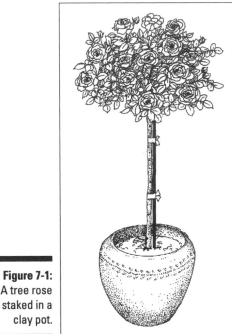

Figure 7-1:
A tree rose
staked in a
clay pot.

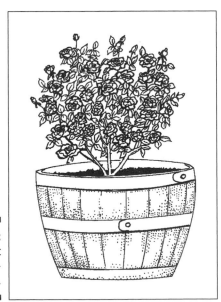

Figure 7-2:
A rose plant
in a half-
barrel.

The one downside of wooden containers is that they tend to be short-lived — the wood often rots quickly from being in constant contact with wet soil. But you can do a few things to prolong the life of wooden containers:

- Use containers made of a rot-resistant wood such as redwood or cedar. If you're building your own containers, don't use pressure-treated woods without checking them out first.

  The preservatives forced into pressure-treated woods make them quite long-lived, but are also often toxic. So ask someone at the lumber yard about safety techniques to follow when handling pressure-treated wood before you buy it.

- Treat the inside of the container. You can significantly prolong the life of a wooden container by painting the inside with the black asphalt-like goop used to patch roofs. Ask your hardware clerk; he or she will know the stuff. Use the goop liberally and let it dry thoroughly before filling the pot with soil. The roof patch is safer for you and the plants and is much longer-lasting than other wood preservatives.

- Raise containers off the ground. Set wood containers on small pieces of wood or bricks to create an air space under the pot. This space helps the barrels dry out and slows the rotting process of the wood.

- **Hanging baskets** are what they sound like — pots that hang in the air (see Figure 7-3). Some gardeners build or buy hanging baskets lined with sphagnum moss, but you don't want to do that with roses. The darn things dry out way too fast. Instead, stick to baskets made of wood, clay, or plastic.

Other types of containers exist, including heavy ones made of concrete and very inexpensive but short-lived ones made of pressed fibers. But those detailed in the preceding list are the most common and are the best choices for roses.

Bigger is (usually) better

Obviously, containers come in many sizes. Their sizes are usually described by their diameter at the top — 6-inch, 10-inch, 12-inch, on up; or by how much soil they hold, in gallons — 1-gallon, 5-gallon, 15-gallon, and so on. A 6-inch pot is close to a 1-gallon pot in size but that's about as far as easy comparisons go. (You folks in countries that use the metric system may run into different sizes.)

Figure 7-3:
A rose plant
in a hanging
basket.

As a general rule, bigger is better. The more soil a container holds, the more root space your rose has, and the easier the rose is to care for. But bigger also means heavier and more expensive, so you often have to compromise. Small roses like miniatures need at least a 12-inch or 2-gallon container. Large plants like shrubs, floribundas, polyanthas, and hybrid teas can go for a year or two in a 5-gallon or 14-inch pot, but a 15-gallon container or half-barrel is much better. In fact, half a wine or whiskey barrel is great for growing roses, especially if you want to include other flowers, or more than one rose plant.

Accessories for your pots

When shopping for pots, consider two other accessories:

✔ **A saucer for underneath the pot:** Saucers collect the water that runs out of the holes in the bottom of the pot and prevent the pot from staining whatever it's sitting on. Plastic saucers are least likely to stain, and you can get invisible, clear plastic saucers, or saucers made of the same or similar material as your pot. Saucers can also help you water your pots, but we'll get to that in a bit. Just make sure that you don't let water stand too long in the saucer; water can rot roots and wooden pots. Put small pieces of wood or brick in the saucer to raise the bottom of the pot out of the saucer, so that the soil drains and dries quickly.

> ✔ **Wheels for mobility:** Most nurseries and garden centers sell wheeled platforms on top of which you can set pots. Mobility is freedom, so take a close look at these accessories. Otherwise, you'll have to lift heavy pots or cart them around on a dolly.

Potting Soil Simplified

No nonsense here. Potting soil rule one and only: Don't fill your pots with soil from your garden. It's too heavy and too dirty (you know, weed seeds, bugs, bacteria — stuff you don't want in your pots), and it may not drain properly after it's in a pot.

Instead, use potting soil. Now, we could tell you a lot about potting soils: how they're supposed to be well aerated, sterile, lightweight, and made of a good balance of organic matter and mineral particles like sand or perlite. We could even give you a recipe to make your own. But you'd nod off in a second. Either that or you'd hurt your back mixing up a batch.

Trek to your local nursery or garden center and buy whichever packaged potting soil is cheapest or comes in the prettiest bag. If you need a lot, many nurseries sell soil in bulk quantities.

Yes, many potting soils are out there, and they have different qualities. So you may want to try different brands over time to see which you like best in terms of ease of wetting and moisture-holding capacity. But don't have a personal crisis over which one to buy. Caring for a rose properly after you plant it is more important than choosing the perfect potting soil.

Proper Planting in Pots

Proper pot planting is a piece of cake. Just a few things to remember: Plant an inch deeper than you normally would, because potting soil settles quite a bit, and don't fill the container to the very top with soil. Leave at least 2 inches of space at the top of the pot (more in large containers) for easy watering.

Here are the basic steps:

1. **Check for drainage holes.**

   Your pots must, and we mean *must,* have holes in the bottom so that water can drain out. Otherwise, the roots will drown. Most pots come with holes in the bottom. But if you build your own wooden container or buy half a wine or whiskey barrel, you probably need to drill holes in the bottom. Use a ½- to 1-inch drill bit. Five to seven evenly spaced holes are usually enough for a half-barrel, but more are better than fewer.

2. **Fill the container halfway with potting soil and then thoroughly wet the soil.**

3. **Place the rose plant in the pot on top of the soil.**

   Check to see whether the bud union (covered in Chapter 2) or original planting depth is about the right level in the pot — it should be a few inches below the rim of the pot and at or below the actual soil line. Add or remove soil as necessary.

4. **Fill the container with soil so that the bud union is about an inch above the surface and there are a few inches between the lip of the pot and the top of the soil. Own-root roses should be planted so that the uppermost roots are an inch below the surface.**

5. **Water and check for settling.**

   Wet the soil thoroughly, let the pot drain, and then repeat. Now check the planting depth. If you need to, add or remove soil around the base of the plant so that it's not planted too high or too deep. But make sure to leave a few inches between the top of the soil and the top rim of the container so that it has plenty of room to hold water.

Caring for Container Roses

Roses grown in containers need different care than roses grown in the ground in a few important ways:

- **More frequent watering:** Potting soils dry out faster than regular garden soil, so you must water roses growing in potting soil more often. In really hot weather, your roses may need water more than once a day.

  You can check to see whether a container is getting dry several ways. First, you can stick your finger in the soil. If the top few inches are bone dry, you should water. You can also check soil moisture by lifting or tipping a container on its side. If the container is on the dry side, it will be very light. Never let your roses dry out completely.

- **More thorough watering:** Wetting dry potting soil can be tricky. Sometimes the *rootball* (the soil held together by the roots) of the rose shrinks a bit and pulls away from the sides of the pot as it dries. So when you water, all the water rushes down the space along the side of the pot without wetting the soil. To overcome this problem, make sure that you fill the top of the pot with water more than once so that the rootball can absorb water and expand. In fact, you should do so anyway to be sure that the rootball is thoroughly wet with each watering.

If you still have trouble wetting the rootball, place the pot in a saucer and fill the saucer repeatedly with water. The water soaks up into the rootball and slowly wets all the soil. You can also try adding a bit of loose potting soil down the side of the pot to prevent water from going down the sides. Otherwise, it's probably time to move the rose into a bigger pot. If it's in a big pot already, pull the rootball out and slice off the outside inch or two with an old knife. Then place the rose back in the pot, add fresh soil around the outside, and water thoroughly. This process is called *root pruning* and does a great job of rejuvenating a rose that has been in a pot too long.

✔ **More frequent fertilizing:** The frequent watering that container-grown roses need leaches nutrients from the soil, so you need to fertilize container roses more often than in-ground roses — at least every two weeks. Liquid or water-soluble fertilizers are easiest to use and get the nutrients right down to the roots. A complete fertilizer, including chelated iron and other micronutrients, is best. For more on fertilizing roses, see Chapter 18.

So, you see, growing roses in containers isn't all that different from growing them in the ground — you just need more water and fertilizer. No big deal.

Growing Roses in a Raised Bed

Raised beds are just what they sound like — planting beds raised above the surrounding soil level. A raised bed can be a simple as a mound of soil, or it can have sides, made of wood, brick, stone, or whatever. Raised beds with sides are really nothing more than big containers — you fill them with good potting soil and grow the roses like you would in a pot.

The big advantage of raised beds is that they improve soil drainage. And if you live in an area where it rains all summer, or where you have to garden in heavy clay (Chapter 16 tells you more about soil), improved drainage is a big deal. Soggy soil is bad news for rose roots: It causes them to rot.

To make a simple mounded raised bed, follow these steps:

1. **Measure out a 2- to 3-foot-wide planting bed.**

   That size is wide enough for one row of roses. Make the bed as long as you want.

2. **Spread 3 to 4 inches of good organic matter, like compost or leaf mold, over the area and work it into the soil with a shovel.**

   This is also a good time to blend in any other soil additives like those described in Chapter 16.

3. **Shovel soil from along the sides of the bed on to the top so that your newly "raised" bed is 10 to 12 inches above the original soil level.**

   Add another few inches of organic matter to the planting area and work it in.

4. **Fill the sunken areas along the sides of the bed with a coarse mulch — like bark chips.**

   Now when it rains, the water will drain out of the raised bed and away from your rose roots. If water accumulates in the low spots, the mulch will keep your roses high and dry.

To find out how to build a raised bed with sides — which can be a very handsome addition to your garden — see *Landscaping For Dummies,* by Philip Giroux and Bob Beckstrom, along with the authors of this book (IDG Books Worldwide, Inc.).

Part III

All the Roses You Need to Know

The 5th Wave   By Rich Tennant

"Would you ask the men with the pink 'Simplicity' boutonnieres not to group around the 'Butterscotch' rose bush? It plays havoc with the entire color scheme of my garden."

In this part . . .

*I*t's a big, wide, wonderful world of roses out there — there are more to choose from than you can imagine. In this part, we tell you about the best varieties, organizing them by type and flower color. Everything you need to know about each bloom and plant is here. We also note varieties that have been designated as All-America Rose Selections (AARS). These varieties were evaluated at test gardens throughout the United States and judged to be the best of the new introductions for a particular year.

If you can't find a rose you like here, you'd better check your pulse.

One other bit of information provided for every rose variety described in this part is the year the rose was introduced — but don't bet your life on the accuracy of these dates. Published information on that topic is inconsistent, to say the least. Sometimes, for example, it's unclear whether the date given is when the rose was created or when it was formally introduced for sale. All you really need is an idea of when a rose was introduced. If it's a new variety, it probably possesses all the latest trendy characteristics, such as disease resistance. If the variety is old and still around, it has probably stood the test of time and deserves consideration.

Chapter 8

Hybrid Teas

• •

In This Chapter

▶ Why hybrid teas are the world's favorite roses

▶ Growing hybrid teas

▶ Landscaping with hybrid teas

▶ The best hybrid tea roses — in every color of the rainbow

• •

*H*ybrid teas are the royalty of the rose family — by far the most popular type of rose, and probably the most popular flower in the world, period. Gardeners everywhere purchase and plant millions of hybrid tea rose plants every year. And sales of hybrid teas as cut flowers far surpass the sales of any other cut flower. Hybrid teas are *the* florist roses.

The popularity of hybrid teas is well earned. The blossoms are exquisite, slowly rolling open petal by petal from beautifully formed buds. Each flower may have as many as 60 or more petals and is often more than 5 inches wide. Supported by long, strong stems, hybrid teas are unmatched as cut flowers, whether you buy them in the dead of winter or grow them in your own backyard. And the fragrance, oh the fragrance — not always powerful but, in some varieties, strong enough to carry you away.

What Makes a Hybrid Tea a Hybrid Tea?

The way in which hybrid teas grow distinguish them from other roses. As shown in Figure 8-1, hybrid teas produce their flowers mostly one bloom to a long stem instead of in clusters. Most hybrid tea plants grow about 3 to 6 feet high and tend to be open rather than bushy, with long, straight, upright canes. Virtually all hybrid teas are repeat bloomers, producing flowers throughout the growing season.

Figure 8-1: Hybrid tea flowers are typically borne one to a stem and have more than 25 petals. The buds are pointed and the petals unfurl in a spiral around a high center.

The hybrid tea rose plants available for purchase are always budded onto hardy rootstock. Commercial rose growers have found that these plants are more vigorous and reliable to propagate when they are budded. The *bud union* (the point at which the plants are budded) grows to almost the size of a fist as the plant matures. The bud union is the magic place at the base of the plant where new canes sprout and grow. Although the bud union is a truly amazing part of the rose plant, it's also the most vulnerable part. If grown without winter protection where winter temperatures reach 10°F (–12°C) or lower, the bud union is the first part of the plant to be damaged or killed by cold and wind.

People who don't grow roses often think that hybrid teas require mysterious culture practices. But the truth is that although hybrid tea roses may require a little extra work, especially in cold climates, nothing is really difficult or mysterious about them. Hybrid teas are no more or less pest- or disease-resistant than any other classification of roses. But as the 21st century approaches, you must be politically correct and not judge a rose by its race, but by its individual traits. And every variety of hybrid tea is an individual, demonstrating a character all its own. Any given hybrid tea may be more or less floriferous, more or less disease-resistant, or more or less winter hardy than other varieties of hybrid teas.

Hybrid teas are available in almost every color but true green and blue. Some red varieties are so dark that they're almost black. And the mauves are the closest any rose gets to blue. Many of the loveliest hybrid teas are bicolors or blends. See the section "A Secret and the President's Wife: Hybrid Tea Types by Color" for a color-by-color breakdown of the different varieties of hybrid tea roses.

Although gardeners may grow hybrid teas for their fragrance or their color, the characteristic that makes rose growers' hearts sing is the form. A hybrid tea's perfection of form, or *exhibition form,* is a trait that must be present in the variety's genetic makeup to begin with, but excellent culture is required to encourage the form to reach its pinnacle of perfection.

Hybrid tea flowers with excellent form have long, pointed buds that unfurl in a perfect spiral around a high, pointed center. When viewed from the side, the flowers have a triangular shape, with the outside, or lowest petals, remaining horizontal rather than falling below the horizontal plane. Because great form is always associated with the hybrid teas, other classifications of roses that have really good form are often described as having hybrid tea form.

Flowers with great form usually have substance as well. *Substance* is the thickness, or leathery rigidity, of the petals. Roses with substance are usually better able to withstand the vagaries of weather and last longer in the vase after being cut. A rose's capability to maintain its beauty for a length of time after it's cut is called *vase life.* Generally, a rose variety's vase life is more important to commercial cut flower growers than to rosarians.

For more information about rose flowers, see Chapter 2.

Some royal tea history

The first hybrid tea, 'La France', was born in 1867 when a French nurseryman, Jean-Baptiste Guillot, cross-bred two old garden roses and came up with a whole new kind of a rose. Because one of the roses Guillot used for cross-breeding, or *hybridizing,* was an old garden rose of the tea subclass, the classification "hybrid tea" was used to describe this new group. 'La France' and several of the early hybrid teas survive and can be found at nurseries specializing in old garden roses. But as unique as the first hybrid teas were at the time, they have been improved by judicious hybridizing over the years.

Some hybrid tea varieties have become so popular that they are synonymous with an era. For example, the 'Peace' rose, hybridized in France just prior to World War II, was reportedly (you can read the real story of 'Peace' in Chapter 27) sent to the U.S. on the last plane that was able to leave freely before the Germans invaded. Nurtured and propagated by the Conard Pyle Company during the war years, 'Peace' was introduced to the world in 1945 and is still a favorite symbol of hope for the future. Called 'Gloria Dei' in Europe, 'Peace' celebrated its 50th anniversary in 1995.

Planting Hybrid Teas: Line 'Em Up or Cover Their Feet

Hybrid teas are often grown in rows in a traditional rose cutting garden. Although hybrid teas can be nicely integrated into a perennial border and in landscape plantings, they are easier to care for when they're in beds by themselves. They should be planted 18 to 36 inches apart, depending on growth habit. (Growth habits are included in the variety descriptions later in this chapter. Upright varieties can be planted a little closer than spreading ones).

Because hybrid teas have little foliage near the base of the plants (see Figure 8-2), and spindly growth in that area should be removed, they may look a little more naked than other types of roses when used in the landscape. However, if you plant low-growing perennials or herbs at their base, hybrid teas can be attractive in flower beds (see Chapter 5 for more information about landscaping with roses). Hybrid teas also combine beautifully with other plants in large containers.

Figure 8-2:
Hybrid tea
rose plants
usually
grow
between 3
and 6 feet
high with
upright
stems.

Shear brutality

Growing hybrid teas takes little more effort on your part than growing most other kinds of roses. They need water, fertilizer, and possibly an occasional spray with a good fungicide. They are, however, usually pruned more severely (see Chapter 19 for pruning information) in late winter or spring than are other classifications of roses. Pruning hybrid teas involves cutting out spindly canes and leaving only the strongest canes to grow. The strong canes should be pruned to about 12 to 24 inches in height, but the plant will still do well if winter damage dictates lower pruning. Drastic pruning encourages the plant to produce larger flowers and longer, stronger stems, while less severe spring pruning results in more but smaller flowers often on weak stems. Translation — prune hybrid teas harder than other roses to get perfect cut flowers.

So why grow 'em, anyway?

Grow 'em for the pure joy of it! Chances are, if you buy one hybrid tea, you'll buy another and then another. Rose gardening is a wonderful hobby that can be fun and challenging. Few things in life are more satisfying than growing a perfect hybrid tea rose. And even fewer things are as stunning or say "I love you" better than a fragrant bouquet of freshly cut hybrid teas.

A Secret and the President's Wife: Hybrid Tea Types by Color

You can choose among hundreds of hybrid tea roses. You can go for color, fragrance, cut flowers, or even a wacky name. Roses are named after presidents ('Mister Lincoln', 'John F. Kennedy'), their wives ('Barbara Bush', 'Nancy Reagan', 'Pat Nixon'), somebody's old car ('Chrysler Imperial'), and one we're not sure about ('Secret'). There are even thornless varieties (look for "smooth" in the name) that take the *ouch* out of growing roses. But most people choose by color, so that's how we break them down.

Red hybrid teas

Every garden needs at least one good red hybrid tea. Trust us: You need them in vases, you need them for their form and fragrance, and besides, what are you going to give that special someone when you want to say "I love you"?

Red roses are by far the most popular, but no single variety today can be considered the "perfect" red rose. Some red roses turn bluish as the flowers age, some have so many petals that they don't want to open properly when the weather is cool (see Chapter 4 for more on the effects of climate), and some are too small to be considered perfect. If you want to make your everlasting fortune, read Chapter 22 on propagating roses and hybridize a red rose that's big, fragrant, has perfect form, great substance, and is disease resistant. Oh — and it should be very winter hardy and have great-looking foliage, too.

In the meantime, you can't miss with these favorites: 'Mister Lincoln' and 'Chrysler Imperial' for their fragrance, and 'Olympiad' for its pure energy and all-weather performance. Each of these roses has won the coveted All-America Rose Selection (AARS) award.

Here is a list of our favorite red roses for you to consider:

- **'American Spirit':** Lightly fragrant, large, double (30 to 35 petals), bright velvety red blooms open from nicely formed, pointed buds. Their long stems help make this a good cut flower, plus, it reblooms well. The plant has a vigorous, upright habit with dark green leaves with good hardiness, but it is prone to mildew. Introduced in 1988.

- **'Christian Dior':** AARS 1962. Handsome, deep red buds open into large, double (50 to 55 petals), long-lasting, medium red blooms with very little fragrance. The vigorous, upright bush has leathery, glossy green leaves.

- **'Chrysler Imperial':** AARS 1953. This prize-winning hybrid tea is much loved for its classic flower form, deep red color, and intense, spicy fragrance. Beautifully formed buds open into large, double (40 to 50 petals), velvety red blooms. Winner of the James Alexander Gamble Rose Fragrance Award in 1965. Long, strong stems are excellent for cutting. Bushy, medium-sized plant has dark green leaves performs best in warm-summer climates. A breeding parent for many modern red roses, the 'Chrysler' is also available in a climbing form. You can see a photo of this fragrant beauty in Fragrant Favorites in the color section.

- **'Crimson Glory':** Probably the first great red hybrid tea, prized for its intense color and powerful fragrance, this rose won the James Alexander Gamble Rose Fragrance Award in 1961. Pointed blackish red buds open into large, double (30 to 35 petals), velvety red blooms. The plant shows vigorous, spreading growth with leathery, dark green leaves and is a breeding parent for many modern red roses. It performs best in areas with hot summers. Introduced in 1935.

- **'Dublin':** Large, smoky red, double blooms (35 to 40 petals) have a unique raspberry fragrance. Long stems are great for cutting. The medium-sized, upright plant does best in warm weather. Introduced in 1982.

- **'Ingrid Bergman':** Large, bright red, double blooms (35 to 40 petals) have a velvety texture and a light fragrance. The long stems are good for cutting. The medium-sized plant has a bushy habit, dark green foliage, and is disease-resistant. Introduced in 1985.

- **'Kentucky Derby':** Large, dark red, double blooms (35 to 45 petals) have a light fragrance. The vigorous, upright plant has semi-glossy leaves. Introduced in 1972.

- **'Legend':** Large, wine-red, double flowers (30 petals) with especially long stems are ideal for cutting. Blooms on this tall, upright plant are moderately fragrant. Introduced in 1993.

- **'Mister Lincoln':** AARS 1965. One of the truly great fragrant red roses, You can see Mister Lincoln pictured in the colored section under Fragrant Favorites. This easy-to-grow wonder has lovely, deep red buds that open into large, velvety red, double blossoms (30 to 35 petals) with a heady rose fragrance, and makes an excellent cut flower. The tall, vigorous plant has deep green leaves. It performs well in all climates.

- **'Oklahoma':** One of the deepest, darkest red roses available. Nicely formed buds of the darkest red open into large, blackish-red, double blooms (40 to 55 petals) with a strong musky aroma. It makes a good cut flower. Vigorous, bushy plant has dull green leaves that are prone to mildew. It does best in areas with warm summers. Introduced in 1964.

- **'Old Smoothie':** Unique because of its thornless stems, 'Old Smoothie' produces large, deep red, double blooms (45 to 50 petals) on long, straight stems. This lightly fragrant bloom is the ideal cut flower for those who don't like to get stuck. The vigorous, tall plant needs warm summers for best performance. Introduced in 1970.

  Other thornless varieties are also becoming more widely available. Look for names like 'Smooth Perfume' (pink), 'Smooth Angel' (apricot yellow), 'Smooth Velvet' (red), or any rose with *smooth* in the name.

- **'Olympiad':** AARS 1994. One of the best red roses for gardeners in areas with cool summers. The large, brilliant red, double flowers (30 to 35 petals) have a light, fruity fragrance and make excellent cut flowers. Tall, compact plant has good disease resistance and hardiness, and is an excellent choice for a beginning gardener. See it pictured under Red Favorites in the color section.

- **'Opening Night':** AARS 1998. These large, dark red, double blooms (25 to 30 petals) on strong stems have a slight fragrance. Long lasting both on the plant and in the vase. The bush has dark green, semi-glossy foliage with good disease resistance.

- **'Papa Meilland':** Deep velvety red, double flower (about 35 petals) has a strong fragrance. Winner of James Alexander Gamble Fragrance Award in 1974 and World's Favorite Rose in 1988. Medium-size plant has leathery, olive-green leaves.

- **'Proud Land':** Large, bright red, double flowers (55 to 60 petals) with long, strong stems that make them ideal for cutting. The blooms have a moderate to strong fragrance and grow on a medium-sized, upright plant which performs best where summers are hot. Introduced in 1969.

- **'Red Masterpiece':** Perfectly formed, deep red buds open into large, dark red, double flowers (35 to 40 petals) with the heady fragrance of old-fashioned roses. The tall plant has dark green leaves. Introduced in 1974.

- **'Swarthmore':** Large, rose-red, double flowers (45 to 50 petals) are darker near the outside of the petals and have a mild, spicy fragrance. The tall, upright plant performs best in areas with hot summers. Introduced in 1963.

- **'Taboo':** Large, deep, dark velvety red, double flowers (30 petals) on long, strong stems are moderately fragrant. The tall, vigorous plant has glossy, deep green leaves. Introduced in 1993.

- **'Traviata':** This bright red, many petaled (up to 100) flower is one of the new Romantica series of roses from France. All the plants in the series share old rose character (often cupped or quartered blooms) and fragrance combined with modern disease resistance. Other Romantica hybrid teas to look for include 'Jean Giono', with yellow flowers; 'Abbaye de Cluny', with apricot blooms; light pink 'Frederic Mistral'; and pink 'Auguste Renoir'.

- **'Veterans' Honor':** A dark red hybrid tea introduced to honor individuals in the American armed forces whose contributions established and protect the United States of America. Portions of the proceeds from sales of the rose are earmarked for the Department of Veterans Affairs. The bush has dark green, glossy foliage, and blooms with a light raspberry fragrance. Introduced in 1999.

Pink hybrid teas

You need pink roses, if for no other reason than they go so well with red roses in a garden and in a vase.

Need a hint on what to plant? You can't miss with 'First Prize', 'Dainty Bess', or any of the pink roses whose name includes the words *sheer* or *perfume*. 'Tiffany' and 'Touch of Class' are also proven pink roses.

Popular pink roses include the following:

- **'Breathless':** Huge, dark pink, double flowers (20 to 25 petals) have a sweet fragrance. Large, upright plant has semi-glossy foliage. Introduced in 1993.

'Billy Graham': Light pink blooms are especially beautiful in the bud. Large, double (25 to 30 petals) flowers emit a light, sweet fragrance. The bush has dark green, glossy foliage. Introduced in 1999.

'Brides Dream': Slightly fragrant, creamy pastel pink, double (25 to 35 petals) flowers make great cut flowers. Tall, upright plant has good disease resistance. Introduced in 1984.

'Century Two': A free-blooming, deep pink, moderately fragrant flower produces very large, double blooms (30 to 35 petals) from a medium-sized, bushy plant with leathery leaves. Introduced in 1971.

'Charlotte Armstrong': AARS 1941. A longtime favorite rose admired for its shapely reddish-pink buds and large, sweetly fragrant, pink, double flowers (25 to 30 petals), 'Charlotte Armstrong' is a prolific bloomer and makes a nice cut flower. The medium-sized, slightly spreading plant blooms best in cooler weather. Also available in a climbing form.

'Color Magic': AARS 1978. The apricot-pink buds open into large, salmon-pink, double blooms (25 to 30 petals) that gradually fade to deep pink. They show their best color in cool weather. The blooms have a nice, fruity fragrance. Medium-sized, upright plant bears dark green leaves, but is less winter-hardy than most hybrid teas.

'Dainty Bess': An elegant, free-blooming rose with clusters of single (5 petaled) pink blossoms centered with maroon stamens. The lightly fragrant flowers resemble the blooms of a dogwood and make a distinctive cut flower. Dense, medium-sized plant has dark green leaves. This very hardy and widely adapted plant has good disease resistance and is easy to grow, but is prone to rust in some regions (see Chapter 21 for more on rose pests and diseases). You can see it pictured in the color section. Also available in a climbing form. Introduced in 1925.

'Dream Pink': Soft pink flowers with about 20 petals have a mild musk fragrance. Good repeat bloom on a compact, full-foliaged plant with good disease resistant. One of the new Dream series of roses which combine hybrid tea-like flowers with full-foliaged, shrubby plants, ideal for landscape use. Other varieties include 'Dream Yellow', 'Dream Red' and 'Dream Orange'. Introduced in 2000 (You can order it from your spring 2000 catalog).

'Duet': AARS 1961. This beautiful, two-toned hybrid tea has petals that are light pink on top and darker pink on the bottom. The blossoms are large, double (25 to 30 petals), sometimes ruffled, and carry a light fragrance. It makes a good cut flower. The vigorous, dense, upright plant has deep green, disease-resistant foliage. One of the better hybrid teas for landscape use, especially as a hedge.

'Elizabeth Taylor': Elegant, large, dark pink, double (30 to 35 petals) blooms with even deeper pink edges put out a slight, spicy fragrance. Long stems make this a good cut flower. Vigorous, upright plant has deep green foliage and does best in warm weather. Introduced in 1986.

◉ **'First Prize':** AARS 1970. The lovely silvery pink color of these perfectly formed flowers develops best in cooler weather. The large blooms are double (25 to 30 petals) and mildly scented. The plant is medium-sized, slightly spreading, and generally lacks winter hardiness. The dark green, leathery foliage is susceptible to black spot and mildew. Also available in climbing form.

◉ **'Fragrant Memory':** Also known as 'Jadis', this hybrid tea has light rose-pink, double flowers (25 to 35 petals) with a strong old-rose fragrance growing on a vigorous, medium-sized plant. Introduced in 1974.

◉ **'Friendship':** AARS 1979. Large, double (25 to 30 petals), deep pink blooms with a touch of red at the petals' edges are sweetly fragrant. Vigorous, upright plant performs well in a variety of climates and has good disease resistance.

◉ **'Great Century':** Huge (up to 8 inches across in temperate climates), light crystal-pink and cream, double blooms (25 to 30 petals) with deep red stamens in the center are mildly fragrant. Long stems make it ideal for cutting. Medium-sized plant spreads slightly. Also known as 'Grand Siecle'. Introduced in 1987

◉ **'Helen Traubel':** AARS 1952. An old-time favorite, this peachy-pink rose has a touch of orange in the bud. The large flowers are double (25 to 30 petals) and have a moderately strong, fruity fragrance. The plant is vigorous and upright with abundant bloom, but the flowers are weak-stemmed and often droop. You get the best color in cool weather.

◉ **'Keepsake':** Usually a beautiful blend of dark and light pinks, this flower often has peach and yellow tones also. The large flowers are double with 35 to 40 petals and have moderate, sweet fragrance. The plant is upright, vigorous, and hardy, and has dark green foliage. It blooms well in all climates. Introduced in 1981.

◉ **'Miss All-American Beauty':** AARS 1968. Large, rich deep pink, double flowers (50 to 55 petals) have a strong rose fragrance. Large, deep green leaves adorn a bushy plant. Performs best in areas with hot summers.

◉ **'New Zealand':** A lovely, soft pink rose with a wonderful honeysuckle-like fragrance has large, double (30 to 35 petals) blossoms with strong stems ideal for cutting. Cooler weather promotes even bigger flowers. Good-looking, glossy, deep green leaves grow on a medium-sized, upright, disease-resistant plant. Introduced in 1991.

◉ **'Perfume Delight':** AARS 1974. This large, deep rose-pink, double blooms (about 30 petals) with a wonderfully intense fragrance. Strong stems are ideal for cutting. Full-foliaged, upright plant has good disease resistance.

◉ **'Pink Peace':** This deep pink, double rose (50 to 60 petals) with a strong rose fragrance was developed from 'Peace' but has never been as popular. The medium-sized, upright plant is prone to rust. Introduced in 1959.

◉ **'Royal Highness':** AARS 1963. A delicate pastel pink rose with exceptional flower form and a sweet fragrance produces large, double blooms

(45 to 50 petals) in abundance. Strong stems make the rose ideal for cutting. Bright green foliage adorns the medium-sized, upright plant. You get the best color in cool weather, but the plant lacks winter hardiness and is subject to rust and mildew.

'Seashell': AARS 1976. A clean-looking blend of salmon-pink, pinkish cream, and soft orange, the flowers are large and double (45 to 50 petals) with a soft, fruity fragrance. This free-blooming plant produces a good cut flower. The vigorous, upright plant has glossy, dark green leaves.

'Sheer Elegance': AARS 1991. Light but rich pink, double blooms (30 to 35 petals) are lightly dusted with creamy pink, have a light fragrance, and make a great cut flower. Glossy, dark green leaves on a medium-sized, upright plant. Excellent disease resistance.

'Signature': Beautifully formed, deep pink, double blossoms (30 to 35 petals) have swirls of cream and darker pink dancing on the petals. Light fragrance and strong stems make this ideal for cutting. Vigorous, upright plant has deep green, disease-resistant foliage. Introduced in 1996.

'Sweet Surrender': AARS 1983. The large, silvery pink, double blossoms (45 to 50 petals) have that full-petaled, old cabbage rose appearance (for more specifics on old roses, including the cabbage rose, see Chapter 14). Heady fragrance and long stems help make this ideal for cutting. The medium-sized, upright plant with dark green leaves performs best in warm summer areas, and is typically not very winter hardy.

'Tiffany': AARS 1955. A longtime favorite hybrid tea with large, soft pink, double blooms (25 to 30 petals), the flower is touched with yellow at the base of the petals and gives off a wonderfully strong, fruity fragrance. Winner of the James Alexander Gamble Rose Fragrance Award in 1962, 'Tiffany' makes an outstanding cut flower. Dark green foliage adorns a medium-to-tall plant with good disease resistance. It produces its best color in areas with hot summers. Although classified pink, because of its yellow touches, you can see it pictured in the color section under "Multicolored Favorites."

'Timeless': AARS 1997. Long-lasting, deep pink to almost red, double blooms (25 to 30 petals) have a slight fragrance and long stems, ideal for cutting, although the flowers tend to bloom in clusters. Medium-sized plant has shiny, dark green leaves and good disease resistance.

'Touch of Class': AARS 1986. Beautifully formed, coral-pink, double blossoms (about 30 petals) with hints of cream and orange (especially in cool weather) carry a slight fragrance. It makes a beautiful cut flower. Medium-sized plant has dark green leaves.

'Ultimate Pink'. Shapely, light pink, double flowers (about 30 petals) with a light, rich fragrance make for a nice cut flower with long stems. Upright plant has dark green, disease resistant foliage. Introduced 1999.

'Unforgettable': Large, clear pink, double blooms (about 35 petals) emits a light fragrance. Tall, vigorous plant produces an abundance of flowers. Introduced in 1992.

Orange hybrid teas

Orange is a strong color; if you're not careful, it can really mess up the mix of other colors you choose for your garden or bouquets. Mix orange with reds, whites, and yellows or use it by itself, but watch out if orange gets around pink or lavender. Yuck!

Our favorite orange roses include 'Artistry', 'Fragrant Cloud', 'Just Joey', and 'Medallion'. Here are more orange (or almost orange) hybrid teas that you can find at the nursery or in catalogs:

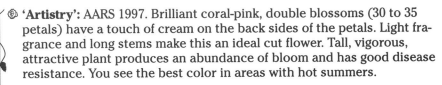

- ❀ **'Artistry':** AARS 1997. Brilliant coral-pink, double blossoms (30 to 35 petals) have a touch of cream on the back sides of the petals. Light fragrance and long stems make this an ideal cut flower. Tall, vigorous, attractive plant produces an abundance of bloom and has good disease resistance. You see the best color in areas with hot summers.

- ❀ **'Brandy':** AARS 1982. Beautifully formed, double blossoms (25 to 30 petals) bloom in rich shades of light apricot-orange. 'Brandy' makes a fine cut flower with a mildly sweet fragrance. Medium-tall, upright plant has semi-glossy, bright green leaves, and lacks winter hardiness.

- ❀ **'Cary Grant':** Luminous orange, double blooms (35 to 40 petals) with rich shadings of gold and copper have a wonderful spicy fragrance, and make good cut flowers. The vigorous, medium-sized plant with glossy, dark green leaves gives its most intense color in cooler, fall months. Introduced in 1987.

- ❀ **'Dolly Parton':** Bright, coppery, reddish orange, double blossoms (35 to 40 petals) have an alluring, strong, spicy clove fragrance. 'Dolly Parton' is a long-lasting cut flower. The bushy, medium-sized plant produces its best color where the nights are warm. Introduced in 1984.

- ❀ **'Fragrant Cloud':** Large, rich coral-orange flowers have an intoxicating, spicy aroma, and make an excellent cut flower. Won the James Alexander Gamble Rose Fragrance Award in 1970. Prone to mildew, the vigorous, medium-sized plant has glossy, deep green foliage and gives its deepest color in areas with cool summers. Introduced in 1968.

- ❀ **'Fragrant Hour':** Pink, double (30 to 35 petals) blooms with orange centers are very fragrant, with hints of spice and fruit. Winner of the James Alexander Rose Fragrance Award in 1997, it makes a good cut flower. The medium-size, upright plant produces its best color when nights are cool and days are warm. Introduced in 1973.

- ❀ **'Just Joey':** Rich apricot, double flowers (25 to 30 petals) emit a strong, fruity fragrance. The free-blooming, easy-to-grow, medium-sized plant has glossy green leaves and produces its best color in areas with hot summers. The plant has good disease resistance. Introduced in 1972.

- ❀ **'Magic Lantern':** Beautifully formed, coppery orange, double blooms (about 30 petals) produce a light fragrance, and make good cut flowers. The plant is tall and vigorous. Introduced in 1989.

- ❀ **'Medallion':** AARS 1973. Huge, creamy, light apricot, double flowers (30 to 35 petals) carry a strong, sweet licorice fragrance, and makes a excellent cut flowers. Medium-to-tall plant has deep green leaves. In cooler climates, the blooms pick up some pink hues. The plant lacks hardiness.

- ❀ **'Spice Twice':** Perfectly formed, bright coral-orange, double blossoms (about 30 petals) with a lighter cream-orange on the back side of the petals have a slight fragrance, and make an excellent cut flower. Tall, upright plant is vigorous and disease resistant. Introduced in 1997.

- ❀ **'Sunset Celebration':** AARS 1998. Introduced in the U.S. to commemorate the 100th anniversary of *Sunset Magazine,* the large, double blooms (35 to 40 petals) range from orange touched with cream, to orange blushed with pink, to rich peach depending on the climate. You get deeper colors in cool summer areas. This nice cut flower has a moderate fruity fragrance. The medium-sized, upright plant has dark clean leaves.

- ❀ **'Tropicana':** AARS 1963. Long one of the most popular hybrid teas, 'Tropicana' produces rich coral-orange, double flowers (30 to 35 petals) with a strong, fruity fragrance, and makes an excellent cut flower. However, it is now losing favor to some of the newer, more disease-resistant orange roses. The vigorous, tall plant with glossy, dark green leaves is prone to mildew.

- ❀ **'Voodoo':** AARS 1986. A blend of orange and yellow with a touch of scarlet, these large, double flowers (30 to 35 petals) have a strong, fruity fragrance. The very vigorous, tall plant with glossy, deep green leaves has good disease resistance and produces its best color in areas with warm summers.

Yellow hybrid teas

Yellow roses are about as sunny as you can get — and they look so good with green-foliaged plants. Our favorite yellow hybrid teas include 'Celebrity', 'Elina', 'Graceland', 'Midas Touch', and almost anything in this list after that:

- ❀ **'Celebrity':** Beautifully formed, deep yellow, double blossoms (30 to 35 petals) are borne in abundance. The flowers sometimes pick up a slight reddish blush and have a light, fruity fragrance. The vigorous, easy-to-grow, medium-sized plant with deep green leaves is widely adapted to many climates. Introduced in 1989.

- ❀ **'Elina':** A soft pastel yellow, double flower (30 to 35 petals) with a light fragrance is an excellent cut flower. The full-foliaged, tall plant produces a lot of blossoms. 'Elina' grows well in many climates and has dark green, disease-resistant foliage. Introduced in 1984.

- ❀ **'Golden Masterpiece':** Huge, golden yellow, double flowers (30 to 35 petals) with a strong licorice-like fragrance make fine cut flowers. The vigorous, bushy plant with shiny, deep green leaves performs well in a variety of climates. Introduced in 1954.

- ❀ **'Houston':** Large, intense yellow, double blooms (35 to 40 petals) have a nice, fruity fragrance. Strong-growing, bushy plant with leathery, dark green leaves produces its deepest color in cool climates: The color fades when exposed to intense sun and heat. Introduced in 1980.

- ❀ **'King's Ransom':** AARS 1962. Large, deep golden yellow, double blooms (35 to 40 petals) with a sweet, fruity fragrance make a great cut flower. Medium-to-tall plant with an upright habit has glossy, dark green leaves and performs well in a variety of climates but is prone to mildew.

- ❀ **'Midas Touch':** AARS 1994. A fine plant deserving of the first AARS award for a yellow rose in 19 years. Bright yellow, double flowers (25 to 30 petals) are produced in abundance. 'Midas Touch' has a moderate, fruity fragrance and makes an excellent cut flower. The vigorous, easy-to-grow, medium-to-tall plant with dark green leaves performs well in a variety of climates, but best size occurs in areas with cool summers.

- ❀ **'New Day':** Sunny yellow, double blossoms (30 to 35 petals) with a slight spicy fragrance make good cut flowers. Vigorous, medium-to-tall, upright plant has unusual gray-green foliage. Introduced in 1977.

- ❀ **'Oregold':** AARS 1975. Large, deep golden yellow, double flowers have exceptional form and a slightly fruity fragrance. 'Oregold' makes a fine cut flower. The medium-sized, upright plant has glossy, dark green leaves.

- ❀ **'St. Patrick':** AARS 1996. An unusual light yellow, double rose (30 to 35 petals) has hints of green when grown in areas with hot summers. Long-lasting cut flower has a slight fragrance. Vigorous, medium-to-tall plant has gray-green foliage and produces its best color in areas with hot summers. Only the second AARS winner to be developed by an amateur.

- ❀ **'Summer Sunshine':** Bright, deep yellow, double flowers (24 to 30 petals) have a light, fruity fragrance. The medium-sized, rounded plant with deep gray-green foliage performs best in areas with cool summers and may lack winter hardiness. Introduced in 1962.

White hybrid teas

White hybrid teas light up the garden or a bouquet, making every other color look brighter. Our favorites include 'Honor', 'John F. Kennedy', and 'Pascali', but all the varieties in the following list are good choices:

- ❀ **'Crystalline':** Pure white, double flowers (30 to 35 petals) with classic form produce a moderately strong, sweet fragrance and makes an excellent cut flower. Vigorous, tall plant has dark green foliage. Introduced in 1987.

'Garden Party': AARS 1960. Creamy white, double blooms (25 to 30 petals) with a touch of pink on the outside petals boast a light fragrance. The fine cut flower with excellent form grows on a medium-sized, slightly spreading plant with semi-glossy green leaves. It gives its best performance in areas with hot summers.

'Grand Finale': Beautifully formed ivory white, double (about 30 petals) blooms with moderate, honeysuckle-like fragrance make fine cut flowers. Dark green semi-glossy foliage adorns the medium-sized plant. Introduced in 1998.

'Honor': AARS 1980. Large, clear white, double flowers have exquisite form and substance. Lightly fragrant, 'Honor' makes a great cut flower. Tall, upright plant with dark green, disease-resistant foliage has its best form in areas with cool summers. You can see this beauty in the color section under "White Favorites."

'John F. Kennedy': Interesting double rose (40 to 45 petals) that starts out greenish white in the bud and gradually turns clean white as the flower opens. Blooms have a moderate-to-strong fragrance and grow on a medium-sized plant with leathery green leaves. It grows best in areas with hot summers. Introduced in 1978.

'Louisiana': Medium-to-large, double blossoms (35 to 40 petals) are greenish in the bud, opening to creamy white with a touch of green in the center. This interesting cut flower has a light fragrance. Tall, slightly spreading plant with dark green leaves performs best in warm-summer climates. Introduced in 1969.

'Pascali': AARS 1969. A longtime-favorite white rose, loved for its generous production of well-formed, double flowers (30 to 35 petals), 'Pascali' has a light fragrance. Vigorous, upright plant with dark green leaves is easy to grow and has good disease resistance. Introduced in 1968, this rose was granted the World's Favorite Rose Award in 1991.

'Polar Star': Medium-sized, creamy white, double blooms (30 to 35 petals) have a slight licorice aroma and the long stems that make them fine cut flowers. Widely adapted, this vigorous plant with gray-green leaves has excellent disease resistance. Introduced in 1982.

'Pristine': Bright white, double blooms (25 to 30 petals) are blushed with soft pink, and are mildly fragrant, 'Pristine' makes a beautiful cut flower, although the vigorous, slightly spreading plant lacks hardiness. Introduced in 1978.

'Sheer Bliss': AARS 1987. Soft, creamy white with a blush of pink, the double flowers (about 35 petals) have a strong, sweet fragrance. Dark green, glossy foliage adorns a medium-sized, upright plant.

Lavender hybrid teas

As much as people want to call these roses blue, they are really lavender or purple. Of these, we especially like 'Paradise', 'Purple Passion', and 'Stainless Steel'. Each rose in the following list can add a delicate color accent to your garden:

- **'Blue Girl':** Large, light lavender, double blooms (30 to 35 petals) put out a moderate, spicy fragrance. The medium-sized, rounded bush has dark green foliage. Introduced in 1964.

- **'Blue Nile':** Large, dark purplish lavender, double flowers (25 to 30 petals) with a fruity fragrance grows on a tall plant with large, dark green leaves. Introduced in 1981.

- **'Heirloom':** Deep lilac, double blooms (30 to 35 petals) are darker purple on the edges of the petals and have a strong, sweet fragrance. The medium-sized plant has dark green leaves. Introduced in 1972.

- **'Lady X':** Well-formed, lavender-pink, double flowers (35 to 40 petals) with a mild fragrance make a nice cut flower. Tall, vigorous plant with medium green leaves produces the best color in areas with cool summers. Introduced in 1966.

- **'Moon Shadow':** These strongly fragrant, nicely formed, deep lavender, double blooms (30 to 35 petals) are borne in clusters. Tall, upright plant has glossy, deep green leaves. Introduced in 1996. You can see it under "Lavender Favorites" in the color section.

- **'Paradise':** AARS 1979. Large, lavender, double flowers (25 to 30 petals) are edged with deep red along the outside of the petals. The plant produces many blossoms with a moderately fruity fragrance which are excellent for cutting. Medium-sized, vigorous plant with glossy, deep green leaves has good disease resistance. You can see it on the front page of the color section.

- **'Purple Passion':** Dark purple, double flowers (about 30 petals) with strong lemony fragrance make a unique cut flower. The plant grows upright and has dark green leaves. Introduced in 2000.

- **'Stainless Steel':** An improved version of 'Sterling Silver' with paler silvery lavender, double blooms (25 to 30 petals), this plant produces more flowers and is easier to care for. Strongly fragrant, 'Stainless Steel' makes a good cut flower. Tall, upright plant with dark green leaves produces its best color where summers are cool. Introduced in 1997.

- **'Sterling Silver':** Silvery lavender, double blooms (about 30 petals) with a fruity fragrance make a nice cut flower. Medium-sized plant with dark green leaves produces its best color in areas with cool summers. The plant lacks winter hardiness and vigor (see Chapter 25). Introduced in 1957.

Multicolored hybrid teas

These whirlwinds of color change complexion on a daily basis. How distinct their colors are usually depends on where they're grown. Before you buy a variety, check it out at a local rose garden to make sure that you're getting what you want.

Of these roses, several stand out. Our favorites include 'Double Delight', 'Granada', 'Peace', 'Secret', and 'Sutter's Gold'. Any selection from the following list will make a splash in your garden:

- ✿ **'Barbara Bush':** Large, coral-pink and soft white, double flowers (30 to 35 petals) have a light to moderate fragrance, and long stems — ideal for cutting. Vigorous, tall plant has dark green leaves. Introduced in 1991.

- ✿ **'Brigadoon':** AARS 1992. Nicely formed, double blossoms (25 to 30 petals) start out creamy white to pink in the bud and then darken to pinkish red around the edges, with a creamy pink center. Giving its best color in warm-summer areas, the blooms are lightly fragrant and make an excellent cut flower. The plant is medium to tall with a slightly spreading habit and dark green, disease-resistant foliage.

- ✿ **'Broadway':** AARS 1987. Large orange-yellow, double blossoms (30 to 35 petals) edged with red emit a strong, spicy fragrance. Medium-sized plant with dark green, leathery leaves has good disease resistance and produces its best color in cool weather. Introduced in 1986.

- ✿ **'Chicago Peace':** A mutation of 'Peace' with darker pink edging set off by a bright yellow center, this double flower (40 to 45 petals) has a light, fruity fragrance. The medium-sized, bushy plant with dark green leaves is very susceptible to black spot. Introduced in 1962.

- ✿ **'Diana, Princess of Wales':** A recent introduction in memory of the Princess of Wales, this promises to be one of the more popular hybrid teas. Creamy white petals are gracefully touched with a clear pink blush. Large, double flowers (30 to 35 petals) have a sweet fragrance. The plant has dark green foliage. A portion of the proceeds from the sales will be donated to the Princess of Wales Memorial Fund. Introduced in 2000.

- ✿ **'Double Delight':** AARS 1977. One of the most popular bicolored roses, the large, creamy white, double flowers (30 to 35 petals) are edged with bright red and make an excellent cut flower. The strong, spicy fragrance earned the James Alexander Gamble Rose Fragrance Award in 1986. This easy-to-grow, medium-sized, rounded bush with dark green leaves produces its best color with warm days and cool nights. Also available in a climbing form.

- ✿ **'Gemini':** AARS 2000. Large double flowers (25 to 30 petals) of blended shades of coral pink and cream have a mild fragrance and make a good cut flower. The plant has deep green, disease-resistant leaves.

‘**Granada**’: AARS 1963. Swirling, ever-changing shades of gold, yellow, pink, and red adorn these double blossoms (18 to 25 petals) with a strong, spicy fragrance. ‘Granada’ is a long-lasting cut flower. Medium-to-tall, upright plant with crinkled, dark green leaves gives its best color in cool climates, but does tend to get mildew.

‘**Las Vegas**’: Glowing orange-red, double blooms (about 25 petals) with a golden-yellow reverse have a light fragrance. The medium-to-tall plant has glossy, dark green leaves. Introduced in 1981.

‘**Lynn Anderson**’: Large, creamy white, double blossoms (25 to 30 petals) are edged with bright pink and give off a light fragrance. Tall, upright (almost a climber) plant has large, dark green, disease-resistant leaves. Roses have their best color in cool climates. Introduced in 1995.

‘**Mikado**’: AARS 1988. Deep scarlet red, double blooms (25 petals) with yellow at the base of the petals have a light, spicy fragrance. ‘Mikado’ makes an excellent cut flower, and its colors intensify in cool weather. Medium-sized, upright plant with glossy, dark green leaves has good disease resistance.

‘**Mon Cheri**’: AARS 1982. Large, deep red, double flowers (30 to 35 petals) with a creamy pink center are lightly fragrant and make a good cut flower. Medium-sized, dense plant has dark green, disease-resistant leaves. Introduced in 1982.

‘**Monet**’: Huge, double rose (30 to 35 petals) in blended shades of pink, yellow, peach, and apricot makes a good cut flower and is moderately fragrant. Vigorous, medium-sized plant with medium green leaves is disease-resistant. Introduced in 1996.

‘**Moonstone**’: Very large, pearly white, double blooms (30 to 35 petals) are edged in pink. Mildly fragrant, this great cut flower does best in warm summer climates. Medium-sized, upright plant has dark green leaves. Introduced in 1999.

‘**Party Time**’: A hot blend of bright yellow edged with red, this double flower (30 to 35 petals), with the licorice-like fragrance makes a fine cut flower. Medium-sized, round plant with medium green leaves does best where summers are warm. Introduced in 1986.

‘**Peace**’: AARS 1945. This award-winning rose is one of the most popular flowers of all time. Large, perfectly formed, double blossoms (40 to 45 petals) are bright yellow edged with pink and emit a light, fruity fragrance. You get the best color where summer temperatures are mild. The medium-sized plant with glossy, dark green leaves is prone to black spot.

‘**Perfect Moment**’: AARS 1991. Large, deep yellow, double flowers (25 to 30 petals) are heavily edged with red and have a light, fruity fragrance. Best color comes in mild-summer areas. Medium-sized, upright plant with dark green leaves has good disease resistance.

TIP

Seeing roses before you plant

One way to whet your appetite for rose growing and get your imagination off and running is to see roses in person. The All-America Rose Selections World Wide Web site (www.rose.org) has a clever mechanism for finding rose gardens (primarily commercial and botanical gardens) in a particular state — just type in the state name, and the program fires back a list of the rose gardens in that state. You can also locate public and private rose gardens by using the search features at www.helpmefind.com/roses.

The Canadian Rose Society offers event listings on its Web site (www.mirror.ofg/groups/crs), and membership allows access to a number of publications, rose events, and even private gardens throughout Canada.

You can find an attractive site on English rose gardens at www.ostavizn.com/site/gardens.HTML, which offers a brief description of and tour information for lovely rose gardens in the UK.

And the Australian Rose Festival has its own Web site at www.visiblemgt.com.au/rosefest/. This site offers historical information about roses, discussion of the festival and its roses, and tour details.

PHOTO OP

PHOTO OP

- **'Rio Samba':** AARS 1993. Bright yellow, double flowers (about 25 petals) are edged with orangish red and have a light fragrance. Medium-sized, bushy plant with dark green leaves has good disease resistance and gives its best color in cool weather.

- **'Rosie O'Donnell':** This nice cutting flower bears velvety red, double flowers (30 to 35 petals) with a creamy yellow reverse and a mild fragrance. The moderately upright to spreading plant has dark green leaves. Introduced in 1998.

- **'Secret':** AARS 1994. Lovely, creamy white, double flowers (30 to 35 petals) are edged with soft pink and carry a strong, spicy fragrance. An excellent cut flower, 'Secret' produces larger flowers in cool weather. Medium-sized plant with dark green leaves has good disease resistance.

- **'Sutter's Gold':** AARS 1950. A much-loved, beautifully formed golden-yellow rose blushed with orangish red, the large, double flowers (25 to 30 petals) have an intense, spicy fragrance. Winner of the James Alexander Gamble Rose Fragrance Award in 1966, it gives its best color where summers are mild, and makes an excellent cut flower. Medium-sized, bushy plant with leathery, dark green leaves has good disease resistance.

- **'Tropical Sunset':** This striped beauty has orange and yellow markings fading to pink. The double flower (about 35 petals) has a light fragrance, and the bush has dark green, glossy foliage. Introduced in 2000.

The name is Barbra

Roses often get named after famous people. This year, a rose named after Barbra Streisand is predicted to be a big hit. Rayford Reddell was one of the testers of the rose at his Garden Valley Nursery (you can find the address in Appendix C), and he gives this rose an A+. We love the description he posted on his Web site, which we excerpt with his permission:

"Barbra Streisand has agreed on a rose to bear her name that's a doozy and sure to weather the test of time. I've grown it under test conditions for three years and can attest to its many attributes.

"Tom Carruth of Weeks Roses hybridized the stunning Hybrid Tea, thereby adding yet another rose to his list of winners ('Scentimental', 'Betty Boop', and 'Fourth of July').

"An unnamed sister seedling of 'Lagerfeld' was used to mother the offspring and 'New Zealand' was the dad. Both roses are known for their fine fragrance, but their daughter handily outdoes them both. Fragrance is ravishing and as deeply scented of pure rose as any variety I know.

"Ms. Streisand inherited other good qualities from her parents. Like her mother, she's exquisitely formed with 30-35 petals that unfurl symmetrically around a bull's-eye center (expect to see her on the winners table at many a rose exhibition). Like her father, plants have an agreeable shape and good growth habits. Foliage is dark green, glossy, and plentiful. Immature growth is an especially appealing shade of clear red.

"Streisand is being registered as a mauve blend, which indeed it is although that classification alone doesn't do justice to how finely it's colored. Unlike many modern mauve roses that have too much red or, worse, too much blue in their petalage, Streisand got it just right and colors remain pure from start to finish, never graying.

"Considering how masterfully she's managed her career, in retrospect, it's no wonder that Streisand waited for the right rose to come along before committing to it. From what I understand, she not only knows roses well, she appreciates fully the differences between great, good, and mediocre ones. Her selection bears testament to such judgment."

Thanks, Rayford. We're going to try this one ourselves.

Chapter 9

Grandifloras

• •

• •

*G*randiflora roses always seem to be having some type of identity crisis. The class was created around 1954 to accommodate 'Queen Elizabeth', a tall, vigorous hybrid that has large flowers — like a hybrid tea — but long stems that grow in clusters — like a floribunda. 'Queen Elizabeth' was named for Elizabeth II, the young Queen of England (what's in that purse, anyway?), and won nearly every international award for roses. In 1978, the World Federation of Rose Societies named it one of its "World Favorite Roses."

Although the 'Queen' is still very popular, grandifloras as a class haven't really made the big time in the rose world yet. In fact, England doesn't even recognize grandifloras as a true class of roses. Instead, they call them *clustered-flowered* and include them with floribundas.

Anyway, Americans are going to keep calling them grandifloras and, in fact, the future is starting to look pretty darn good for grandifloras. The last few years have seen some great new varieties. They include 'Fame!', a 1998 All America Rose Selection (AARS); 'Candelabra', a 1999 AARS; and 'Crimson Bouquet', an AARS for 2000. That's three in a row. And there are some other good new ones listed here as well. Get the feeling something good may be happening?

As a class, grandifloras bear large, long-stemmed, hybrid tea-like flowers (see Figure 9-1), either in clusters or one to a stem.

Generally, grandiflora plants are tall, hardy, and vigorous, as shown in Figure 9-2, but plant habits can vary a bit. Some of the new award winners we just listed are smaller, more compact plants.

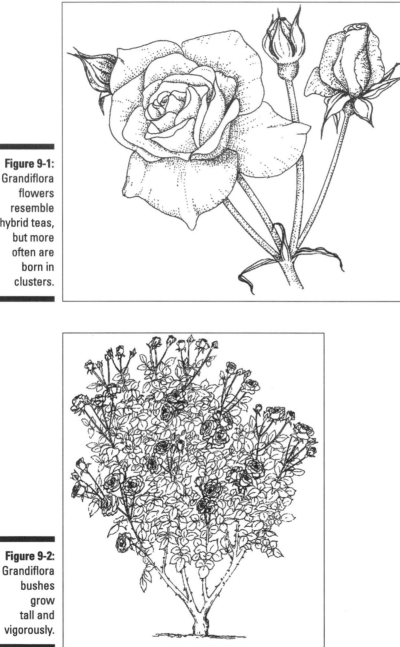

Figure 9-1:
Grandiflora
flowers
resemble
hybrid teas,
but more
often are
born in
clusters.

Figure 9-2:
Grandiflora
bushes
grow
tall and
vigorously.

Treat Them Like Hybrid Teas

Care for grandifloras as you would hybrid teas — watering, fertilizing, winter protection, pruning practices, and so on are pretty much the same. (Part IV, "Growing Healthy Roses," fully describes all that.)

You may want to prune 'Queen Elizabeth' a touch higher (don't cut it as far back) in winter, especially if you're using her for a tall hedge. And if that's the case, don't be afraid to use hedge shears for pruning a large planting, that is if you can shear through those thick canes. You can find more on pruning roses in Chapter 19.

Grandifloras are often used like hybrid teas and planted in rows for cut flowers. However, they tend to put on a better show of color than many hybrid teas do, so don't hesitate to use them in the landscape. Tall varieties, like 'Queen Elizabeth', make useful hedges or background plants. Lower-growing types, like 'Crimson Bouquet' can be mixed with other flowers in perennial borders. You can find more on landscaping with roses in Chapter 5.

Grandifloras by Color

Grandifloras come in many colors and sizes. The following sections list some of our favorites.

Red grandifloras

Of the few red grandifloras to choose from, 'Love' has always been a favorite, but 'Crimson Bouquet' is coming on strong.

- ✹ **'Candy Apple':** Lustrous apple-red blossoms with a slight fragrance and lots of petals bloom in a cupped form. Olive-green foliage decorates the upright bush. Introduced in 1966.

- ✹ **'Crimson Bouquet':** All-America Rose Selection (AARS) 2000. Large, double (20 to 25 petals), bright-red blooms have a slight fragrance and long, strong stems good for cutting. Good-looking rounded plant, slightly smaller than many other grandifloras has glossy deep green foliage with excellent disease resistance and good hardiness.

- ✹ **'Love':** AARS 1980. Part of a trio of roses introduced in 1980: 'Love', 'Honor', and 'Cherish' ('Love' and 'Honor' are great; 'Cherish' is sort of blah). True to the name, the flowers are bright red with a silvery reverse and 35 petals. It has a slight, spicy fragrance and is a good cutting flower. The bush is compact and of medium height.

Pink grandifloras

If you can't make up your mind on a pink grandiflora, go with 'Queen Elizabeth', 'Tournament of Roses', or 'Fame!'.

- ✿ **'Camelot':** AARS 1965. The largest of the grandiflora flowers, it can measure up to 5 inches across. The light to moderately fragrant blooms are pale salmon in color with 50 to 55 petals, opening in a cup shape. The color changes with the weather from salmon, when it's cooler, to orange, when it warms. The tall and spreading bush is a vigorous grower; likes hot weather. Leaves are large, heavy, and glossy.

- ✿ **'Fame!':** AARS 1998. Large, beautifully formed, deep pink, double blossoms (30 to 35 petals) are lightly scented. Tall, bushy, vigorous plant has dark green leaves and abundant blooms. Best flower form for areas with mild summers.

- ✿ **'Pink Parfait':** AARS 1961. Petite buds open into well-formed flowers, colored with a blend of deep pink and cream with 20 to 25 petals. Flowers grow singly on narrow stems and have a slight fragrance. This profuse bloomer makes a good cutting flower, though the color may fade in hot weather. The plant is of medium height, upright, and bushy with lots of branches and leathery, semi-glossy green leaves. It is also disease resistant.

- ✿ **'Prima Donna':** AARS 1988. Deep, fuschia-pink flowers have 27 petals and a light fragrance. Foliage is large, glossy, and medium green on a spreading bush. Plant lacks hardiness and disease resistance. Introduced in 1984.

- ✿ **'Queen Elizabeth':** AARS 1955. The first grandiflora, and still the finest, has received top honors in many countries over the years. Clear pink, ruffled blooms adorn the stately, tall bush in long-stemmed clusters. The abundant blooms are high-centered or cup-shaped, moderately fragrant, vigorous, and bushy. Leaves are dark green and glossy on this easy-to-grow plant that is disease resistant and winter hardy.

- ✿ **'Sonia':** A popular florist's rose in the United States and Europe, 'Sonia' grows pretty well in the home garden, too. Delicate, long buds give way to shapely, pastel pink flowers on long stems with 30 to 35 petals which have a sweet, fruity fragrance. The bush has glossy green leaves and medium height, and is bushy and disease resistant. Introduced in 1974.

- ✿ **'Tournament of Roses':** AARS 1989. Flowers profusely in clusters of two-toned pink blooms with 25 to 30 petals and a light fragrance. Medium, upright bush with glossy green leaves is highly disease resistant and easy to grow.

Orange grandifloras

Our favorite orange grandiflora? It's a tough choice, but many rose growers love 'Caribbean', and 'Reba McEntire' and 'Candelabra' can't be ignored.

- **'Caribbean':** AARS 1994. This luscious, bright orange-yellow blend has spiral-shaped flowers growing on long stems with bright green foliage and 30 to 35 petals. The mildly fragrant flower grows on a medium-sized, upright bush which is vigorous and productive. It produces its best form and color in the fall.

- **'Candelabra':** AARS 1999. Glowing coral orange, double flowers (about 25 petals) have exceptional form and a slight fragrance. The plant has a bushy, upright habit with dark green foliage and good disease resistance, making it a fine landscape shrub. You see the best size and color in cool summer climates.

- **'Montezuma':** Produces loads of long-stemmed, reddened coral-orange flowers with 30 to 35 petals and a light scent. The plant is tall, bushy, and slightly spreading with dark green, leathery foliage. Disease-resistant and winter hardy, this plant does well in cool climates. Warm night temperatures help flower color remain stable. Introduced in 1955.

- **'New Year':** AARS 1987. A colorful blend of yellow and orange with hints of gold and 20 petals and a light, fruity fragrance. The upright plant has deep green, glossy foliage and excellent disease resistance.

- **'Olé':** These long-lived, ruffled flowers suggest a flamenco dancer's vibrancy with their brilliant orange-red tones that do not fade. The blooms have 40 to 45 petals and a slight fragrance. The medium, rounded, bushy plant with holly-like, glossy green leaves achieves the best size in cooler coastal conditions, such as in the North American Pacific Northwest. Introduced in 1964.

- **'Prominent':** AARS 1977. Star-shaped, hot orange flowers with 25 to 30 stiff petals that curve under bloom continuously. The flowers are small (2½ to 3½ inches) compared to most grandifloras. The color of the lightly fragrant blooms does not fade. Stately, upright, tall plant has matte green foliage, and is disease resistant and winter hardy. Introduced in 1971.

- **'Reba McEntire':** Bright orange red, double blooms with about 30 petals are borne in clusters and have a slight fragrance. Vigorous, upright plant with deep green, glossy, disease-resistant foliage. It achieves its best size in cool summers. Introduced in 1998.

- ❀ **'Shreveport':** AARS 1982. Named for the city in Louisiana that is home to the American Rose Center. Full flowers (45 to 50 petals) of warm, blended salmon and yellow tones bloom all season. Cut flowers have a long vase life and a mild scent. Tall, upright plant is covered with dark green, shiny foliage. Fall conditions bring out the best color in this easy-to-grow rose.

- ❀ **'Solitude':** AARS 1993. Brilliant bright orange blooms with hints of yellow and gold and 30 to 35 petals show their best color with heat. The flower has a mild, spicy fragrance. Upright plant has bright green leaves and good disease resistance.

- ❀ **'Sundowner':** AARS 1979. A distinctive, warm apricot color marks these cup-shaped flowers. The bloom have a moderate fragrance and 35 petals. 'Sundowner' blooms well all season in clusters and singly. Plant is tall, upright, and vigorous. Leaves are large, leathery, and medium green. Disease-resistant and winter hardy, but susceptible to mildew in cool, wet climates.

Yellow grandifloras

We like the following yellow grandiflora roses, but 'Gold Medal' stands above the rest.

- ❀ **'Gold Medal':** Gives a nearly constant supply of dark gold buds and richly fragrant, golden-yellow flowers with a flirtation of red at the tips and 30 to 35 petals. The stems of this very tall plant (which easily reaches more than 5 feet high) have few thorns. The plant has deep green foliage and is disease resistant. This rose is a bit more cold-sensitive than most, so we advise that you provide winter protection. (See Chapter 20.) Introduced in 1982.

- ❀ **'Shining Hour':** AARS 1991. Deep yellow, cup-shaped flowers grow singly and in clusters or sprays with 33 petals and have a moderate fragrance. Upright, bushy, medium-height plant has shiny, dark green leaves.

White grandifloras

Of these two white grandifloras, only 'White Lightnin' has stood the test of time.

- ❀ **'Mt. Hood':** AARS 1996. Masses of ivory-white flowers on a bushy plant resemble snow-capped Mount Hood. Flowers are full and fleshy with 40 to 45 petals and have a light fragrance. Full-branching, tall bush has deep, glossy green foliage and is disease resistant. Flowers open better in warmer temperatures. This variety has actually been recategorized as a hybrid tea but is still sold as a grandiflora. See this pictured among our favorite white roses in the color section.

- ❀ **'White Lightnin':** AARS 1981. Small, white clusters of cupped, very fragrant flowers with 26 to 32 petals burst forth all season on the low growing, robust bush. The plant is winter hardy and disease resistant with dark green, glossy leaves.

Lavender grandifloras

Several great lavender (or mauve) grandifloras exist in the rose world. Take your pick of these beautifully fragrant varieties::

- ❀ **'Cologne':** Light lavender, double flowers with 17 to 25 petals are intensely fragrant. Upright plant has matte green leaves. Introduced in 1998.

- ❀ **'Fragrant Plum':** This elegant, deep plum flower has perhaps more true blue than any rose to date. Vigorous, tall plant has lush, deep green foliage. The buds are long and pointed; flowers have good form and a strong, fruity fragrance. Color brightens in heat; best form comes in spring and fall. Introduced in 1990.

- ❀ **'Lagerfeld':** Light silvery lavender, double flowers (30 to 35 petals) have a strong fragrance and make good cutting flowers. Tall, vigorous plant has medium green leaves. Introduced in 1986.

- ❀ **'Melody Parfumée':** Deep purple buds open into lovely lavender blooms gradually fading with a silvery sheen. A double with about 30 petals and a sweet, spicy fragrance, this tall plant has deep green leaves. Introduced in 1995.

- ❀ **'Spellcaster':** A flower with substance, the blooms are deep mauve and lavender with 26 to 40 petals and intense fragrance. The bush is full, upright, and uniform in growth. Leaves are large, glossy, and dark green. Introduced in 1991.

Multicolored grandifloras

All these are good, but 'Octoberfest' really shines.

- ❀ **'Arizona':** AARS 1975. High-centered blooms with 35 to 40 petals are full of powerful perfume. Colors are blended tones of bronzy orange and mellow pink. Tough, tall, slender plant has glossy emerald-green leaves and is disease-resistant. Color does not fade. Disease-resistant.

🌺 **'Heart O' Gold':** Deep golden-yellow blooms are edged with soft pink. Flowers have 30 to 35 petals and a strong, fruity fragrance. Long stems make for good cutting flowers. Tall, upright plant has dark green foliage. Warm weather brings out the best color, but the flowers are larger in cool-summer climates. Introduced in 1997.

🌺 **'Octoberfest':** Beautiful autumn shades of red, orange, and yellow bloom in large clusters of double blooms with about 17 to 25 petals and a pleasing, fruity fragrance. You can see it among our orange favorites in the color section. It makes a nice cutting flower. Glossy, dark green leaves adorn a tall, upright plant. Introduced 1999.

🌺 **'Quaker Star':** The double flowers with 35 to 40 petals are dark pink with orange tips and orange reverse. This plant is very free blooming but has no fragrance. The bush has medium green leaves and excellent disease resistance. Introduced in 1991.

Chapter 10

Polyanthas and Floribundas

. . . .

In This Chapter

▶ The origin of polyanthas and floribundas

▶ Using polyanthas and floribundas in the landscape

▶ Caring for polyanthas and floribundas

▶ Polyantha and floribunda varieties

. . . .

*P*olyanthas and floribundas are the workhorses of the rose garden. Of all the different kinds of roses, they're the most prolific bloomers, plus they're useful in the landscape, in perennial borders, and in large group or mass plantings. Most varieties need winter protection in areas where temperatures fall below 10°F (−12°C), but the springtime bloom makes it all worth it. If you can't find a floribunda you love, you'd better get your eyesight checked!

Polyanthas originated in France in the late 1800s, and only a few varieties are still widely grown. But polyanthas are important, not only because they're excellent roses, but also because they're the forerunners of the very popular and useful floribundas. For that reason, we group the two together in this chapter.

To France, Late 19th Century

The origin of polyantha roses is a bit fuzzy, but they are believed to have shown up in France in the late 19th century — about the same time as the first hybrid tea rose. They can probably claim *Rosa multiflora* and *Rosa chinensis* as their parents, but some kind of hanky-panky must have been going on somewhere, because no one really wants to admit who mom or dad is.

Anyway, polyanthas are compact plants that usually grow about 2 to 3 feet high. And do they ever bloom! They virtually cover themselves in large, flat clusters of small flowers (usually about an inch wide) in shades of white, pink, red, orange, and yellow. (See Figure 10-1.) Plus, they bloom and bloom again, all season long.

Figure 10-1:
Polyanthas
bear small
flowers in
large
clusters.

Polyantha leaves are small and narrow and the plants are fairly hardy, at least more so than hybrid teas. The most common polyantha, 'The Fairy,' is one of the hardiest and most reliable, thriving without winter protection even to –25°F (–31°C).

Floribundas: Workhorses of the Garden

Early in the 20th century, someone got the bright idea to cross the generous-blooming polyanthas with the larger-flowering hybrid teas. The results are what we now call the floribundas, which, as their name suggests, offer flowers in abundance.

Today, floribundas are one of the most useful types of roses. The flowers emerge in large clusters like polyanthas, but the individual blooms are bigger, often with that beautiful hybrid tea form, and most are great cutting flowers. They really shine in the landscape, where they can brighten a dreary corner of the yard, highlight a garden ornament, or keep a perennial border wonderfully colorful all season long.

Floribundas come in all the hybrid tea colors, which is probably almost any flower color you can think of except blue and true green. The plants grow from 3 to 5 feet high and may be upright or low and spreading — or anything in between. Figure 10-2 shows a shrubby bush. Their range in plant shape makes them versatile landscape plants.

Figure 10-2: Generally compact, shrubby plants about 3 to 5 feet high, floribundas are top-notch landscape plants with a long season of bloom.

Some floribunda varieties have compact growth habits and are very "tuckable" into small areas of the garden. Others grow tall and wide and exhibit many of the characteristics of modern shrubs. "Grow as shrub" is a common description in rose catalogs. Choose varieties that suit the area in which you want to plant them.

The amount and persistence of bloom are what really make floribundas so great. Some varieties, like 'Iceberg', have almost cult-like followings because of their generosity of bloom.

Try 'em; you'll like 'em.

All This and Easy to Grow, Too

Floribundas and polyanthas are among the easiest roses to grow. Most have good disease resistance and need little care other than water and fertilizer.

Removing spent flowers during the growing season is important if you want a bush to keep producing flowers. You can just get out your hedge shears to cut off faded flowers. In warm climates, you may need to whack off a cane or two during the season to keep the plant within bounds, and then cut back the whole plant 25 to 50 percent in winter. But in cold climates, floribundas need pruning only in early spring. Cut off any part of the plant that was damaged over the winter.

Today's rose hybridizers are working very hard to breed disease resistance into new varieties of roses. Therefore, many of the newer floribunda varieties are naturally resistant to the diseases that attack our favorite flower. Rose culture, especially for the new floribundas, is getting simpler every year. If a floribunda variety excels in the disease resistance department, you can bet that the rose catalogs will say so. So if you don't care much for spraying for black spot and powdery mildew, choose disease-resistant varieties. On the other hand, as is always the case, many of the most distinctive and desirable varieties are susceptible to disease but respond nicely to disease-control measures. It just goes to show you: If it's not one thing. . . .

Even though these plants tend to be slightly hardier than hybrid teas, you may still need to provide winter protection if you live where winter temperatures fall to 10°F (−12°C) or lower. But protecting roses in winter is no big deal; see Chapter 20 to find out how.

Don't Plant Just One!

If you haven't already guessed, we really like polyantha and floribunda roses. The reasons are simple: The amount of bloom, the clean-looking foliage, and the ease of care make these roses top-notch landscape plants.

We cover using specific varieties for specific landscape purposes in Chapter 5, but one piece of advice is worth repeating here: Polyanthas and floribundas are best used in mass plantings. Don't buy just one or two plants; get a bunch and line them up as a hedge or as edging for other plants. Or plant several of them in a bed all by themselves: Their season-long color will knock your neighbors' socks off! Some of the lower-growing varieties, such as 'Sarabande', can even be grouped as ground covers. Or you can spread them throughout your garden to tie everything else together. These babies are workhorses; they can carry an entire garden.

There's another reason to buy these roses in quantity: Many of the mail-order catalogs listed in Appendix C offer discounts when you buy more than one of any variety.

Oh yeah, floribundas, and especially polyanthas, are also great planted in containers.

A Few of Our Favorite Things

The following sections list our favorite floribunda varieties. Also described are our favorite pink polyanthas, 'Cécile Brünner' and 'The Fairy'. You may also find the pink polyanthas 'China Doll' and 'Margo Koster', though they're less common.

Red roses

Here are four great red floribundas. You can't lose with any of them, especially the first three:

- 'Europeana': All-America Rose Selection (AARS) 1968. This top exhibition rose produces large clusters of dark crimson, long-lasting blossoms with 15 to 20 petals. Slightly fragrant flowers bloom abundantly throughout the season. Young, red leaves mature to a dark, glossy green. The bush is disease resistant and hardy in winter. Introduced in 1963.

- 'Frensham': A glorious red rose that bursts open to reveal feathery, golden stamens, 'Frensham' has a light scent and is an excellent midseason and repeat bloomer. Vigorous, bushy, spreading plant with dark green, semi-glossy leaves is disease-resistant. Winner of the American Rose Society Gold Medal in 1955, awarded to roses that show the best performance over a five-year period. Introduced in 1946.

- 'Lavaglut': Deep, velvety red, ruffled blossoms are double (25 to 30 petals) with light fragrance and borne in never-ending clusters. The medium-sized, upright plant has deep green, disease-resistant foliage. Introduced in 1979.

- 'Showbiz': AARS 1985. An orange-red workhorse whose 29 to 30 petals are rarely out of bloom, 'Showbiz' makes an excellent ever-blooming mass of color on dark green, glossy leaves. The bush is disease resistant and winter hardy. Introduced in 1981.

Pink roses

There's not a bad rose in this batch of pink floribundas and polyanthas:

- 'Betty Prior': Charming, old-fashioned rose blooms profusely and continuously. The exuberant, five-petaled flowers are carmine pink and moderately fragrantly. When in full bloom, the plant resembles a flowering dogwood. Vigorous, tall plant has glossy leaves and excellent resistance to black spot and mildew. Introduced in 1935.

CAN'T MISS ▶

'Bill Warriner': Beautifully formed, salmon- to coral-pink blooms with 20 to 25 petals have a light fragrance and a long blooming season. Compact, disease-resistant plant has dark green, glossy leaves. Introduced in 1996.

'Bridal Pink': A florist's favorite, the long, elegant buds and creamy pink, luxurious flowers with 30 to 35 petals grow abundantly in spring and fall and have a moderately spicy fragrance. Dark green foliage decorates the medium-to-low bush. Introduced in 1967.

'Cécile Brünner': The original sweetheart rose, this lightly fragrant polyantha has little pink buds and small, perfectly formed blooms with 30 petals, which resemble diminutive hybrid teas and blanket the plant throughout the growing season. The compact, long-lived, and healthy bush can even tolerate poor soil and partial shade. It is also available in a popular climbing form. Introduced in 1881.

'Cherish': AARS 1980. Large (3 inches across) coral pink flowers, with 28 petals are slightly fragrant. Compact, spreading bush has large, dark green leaves.

'City of London': Long-lasting, pale pink, open-faced flowers with 15 to 20 petals have a strong, sweet fragrance. Tall, upright plant produces abundant blooms. Introduced in 1986.

'Columbus': Egg-shaped, pointed buds unfurl into deep, rose-pink blooms with 28 petals carried singly or in sprays of three to five. These flowers hold their color with little fading and make good exhibition roses. Medium-sized, bushy plant has large, dull green leaves. Introduced in 1991.

'Dicky': Soft salmon-pink, double (35 petals) blossoms have only slight fragrance but excellent form. Flowers are borne in large clusters and make wonderful cut flowers. The medium size, slightly spreading plant has glossy green foliage. Introduced in 1983.

'Fashion': AARS 1950. Small, red-tipped buds unfold into lustrous coral-pink flowers with a sweet and fruity fragrance and 21 to 24 petals. The medium-size, bushy, spreading shrub is always in bloom. Foliage is glossy and bronze-green, and the bush is disease resistant.

'Gene Boerner': AARS 1969. Blossoms of unflinchingly true pink grow in clusters or singly on long, strong stems — upright for all to see. Blooms have 30 to 35 petals and are slightly fragrant. A super-vigorous, tall bush (up to 5 feet) with light green, glossy leaves is disease resistant and winter hardy. Makes a good cutting flower.

'Johann Strauss': One of several floribundas (the pink 'Guy de Maupassant' and 'Leonardo de Vinci' are others) introduced as part of the Romantica series — varieties with old rose character and fragrance. This one has large, candy-pink, very double blooms (up to 100 petals) with a strong lemon verbena fragrance. Medium-sized bush has bronze-green foliage. Introduced in 1992.

- **'Nearly Wild':** The bright pink, single (5 petals) flowers have a sweet, fruity fragrance. Very hardy, the compact, rounded plant grows 2 to 3 feet high with medium green foliage. Introduced in 1941.

- **'Neon Lights':** Large, fragrant blooms, displayed in small clusters and having 15 to 25 petals, are hot magenta-pink. The plant is medium and bushy with shiny green leaves. Introduced in 1991.

- **'Origami':** Pure, pastel pink blooms brushed with coral at the tips display their best color in the heat. Flowers have 25 to 30 petals and a light fragrance. Slightly spreading and bushy plant with large, reddish green leaves may be tender in cold climates. Introduced in 1986.

- **'Playgirl':** A proven, consistent performer, 'Playgirl' flowers almost continuously with showy, large clusters of hot magenta-pink with five to seven petals and a slight fragrance. Full, rounded bush has deep green leaves. Introduced in 1986.

- **'Rose Parade':** AARS 1975. Lovely, coral-pink blooms, often with a hint of peach and 25 to 35 petals, are large and fragrant. Large, glossy green leaves grow on a compact, bushy plant with good disease resistance.

- **'Sea Pearl':** Stylish, long, pointed buds unfurl with free-blooming intensity, revealing pink blooms with creamy yellow reverses and 24 petals. Blooms tend to occur early to midseason in clusters and have a light fragrance. Upright, vigorous bush has dark green leaves. Introduced in 1964.

The *reverse* is the underside of a petal. A different color on the reverse makes for visual interest both coming and going.

- **'Sexy Rexy':** Rarely out of bloom, this rose has large clusters of rose-pink, lightly scented flowers. Vigorous, low-growing bush with small, glossy, leathery leaves is an excellent plant in groups, as a hedge, or in a container. It is resistant to mildew and black spot. Introduced in 1984.

- **"Simplicity':** Tall, dense, and free-flowering, 'Simplicity' is an excellent landscape or hedge rose. Medium pink blossoms (18 to 24 petals) appear in clusters all season long and have little to no fragrance. Medium green, semi-glossy leaves decorate the disease-resistant and winter-hardy bush. White, purple, yellow, and red forms of 'Simplicity' are also available. Introduced in 1979.

- **'The Fairy':** One of the loveliest polyanthas, 'The Fairy' bears large clusters of small, ruffled, double (20 to 25 petals) pink flowers with a mild apple fragrance. A compact, winter-hardy plant with dark green, disease-resistant foliage, it makes an exceptional, easy-to-grow landscape plant. Introduced in 1932.

Orange roses

These floribundas make a stunning statement in bright orange and apricot:

'Apricot Nectar': AARS 1966. Tight clusters sometimes obscure the beauty of this rose. Removing some of the buds enhances the large, pure apricot blooms, which have 35 to 40 very fragrant petals. Good repeat bloomer, and it does well as a cut flower. Upright bush has glossy, dark green leaves and is disease resistant and hardy.

'Brass Band': AARS 1995. A band of colors plays on the petals of these well-formed blooms, mixing bright shades of melon with subtle apricot and lemon reverses. Gives its best performances in cool weather. Large blooms of 25 to 30 petals are moderately fragrant. Medium-sized, rounded bush has bright green foliage.

'Cathedral': AARS 1976. Elegant, long-lasting flower clusters bear flowers with wavy petals of deep salmon tinted with scarlet, creating a stained-glass-window effect. The blooms have 15 to 18 petals and a light to moderate, sweet scent. Compact, low bush has glossy olive-green leaves and is disease resistant. It likes moderate temperatures. Introduced in 1975.

'Easy Going': Make the most of the generous production of rich yellow blooms with a hint of peach. Double blooms have 25 to 30 petals and a fruity fragrance. Roundish plant has bright green foliage and excellent disease resistance. It performs well in all climates. Introduced in 1999.

'First Edition': AARS 1977. Shimmering coral orange, long-lasting blooms have 20 to 30 petals and a light scent. Medium-sized, rounded bush has waxy, glossy green leaves with good disease resistance. It continually produces flowers in showy clusters. Moderate temperatures enhance the colors. 'First Edition' makes an excellent low hedge.

'Gingersnap': Long, pointed buds open into highly ruffled, pure bright orange blossoms. Large, lightly scented flowers with 30 to 35 petals bloom singly or in clusters. The bush is upright and a vigorous grower with dark green foliage. The flowers' brightest color occurs in cool conditions. Introduced in 1978.

'Impatient': AARS 1984. This is one of the best orange floribundas and is rarely out of bloom. Produces lots of deep orange blossoms with 25 petals continuously from late spring until frost. Lightly fragrant blooms are displayed in large clusters held high on the plant for all to see. Tall, upright shrub has dark green foliage with bronze-colored new growth. Heat brings out the brightest color.

'Livin' Easy': AARS 1996. The rose for the hammock gardener, 'Livin' Easy' practically grows itself. The foliage on this rounded, medium-sized bush is so glossy and green that the bush looks good without flowers. But the flowers come and come and keep coming — large apricot-orange blooms with 25 to 30 petals and a moderately fruity scent. A very consistent performer in all climates, but it is a bit cold-tender compared to others of this type. Makes a great hedge.

- **'Marina':** AARS 1981. Well-known as a greenhouse rose, 'Marina" also does very well in the garden. Produces orange blooms of 30 to 40 petals with red and gold overtones in clusters on long stems. The plant is disease resistant, vigorous, and very bushy.

- **'Outrageous':** Produces light, orangish yellow, double blooms with 25 to 30 petals and a pleasant fragrance. It is very nice in bouquets. Upright plant has dark green foliage. Introduced in 2000.

- **'Sarabande':** AARS 1960. A spectacular rose that has garnered numerous awards since its introduction in 1957, its orange-red flowers with 10 to 15 petals open to reveal bright yellow stamens. Blooms continuously in flashy clusters on low, spreading shrubs with glossy foliage. Makes an excellent low hedge or container plant. One of the most disease-resistant floribundas. Grows best in cool climates.

- **'Trumpeter':** Produces abundant and continuous brilliant orange-red flowers with 35 to 40 wavy petals. Slightly fragrant plant has dark green, glossy leaves and is disease resistant. Introduced in 1977.

Yellow roses

These yellow floribundas are as clear and bright as a sunny day:

- **'Amber Queen':** AARS 1988. The combination of the amber yellow color, sweet scent, and glossy green foliage make this rose, with 25 to 30 petals, a winner. The plant is low, bushy, and compact with a high degree of disease resistance, making it an ideal choice for the landscape. It displays its best color in cool temperatures. Introduced in 1983.

- **'Anthony Meilland':** Abundant, large, clear yellow double blooms (25 to 30 petals) with light fragrance grow on a medium-sized, rounded bush with medium-green leaves. Introduced in 1990.

- **'Brite Lites':** The buds and flowers are vivid yellow and stay that way without fading. Provides never-ending clusters of colorful, ruffled blooms (28 to 32 petals) with a moderate fragrance. The shrub is tall, upright, vigorous, and superbly disease resistant. Introduced in 1985.

- **'Singin' in the Rain':** AARS and New England Rose Trials Award 1995. A moody rose with many hues, which change with the weather. Colors can range from shades of brown- and cinnamon-pink to apricot-gold and russet-orange. Blossoms have 25 to 30 petals and a sweet scent. Rounded, bushy plant has glossy, dark leaves.

- **'Sun Flare':** AARS 1983. One of the few yellow roses that makes an excellent landscape planting, the low, mounded, bushy plant is covered with bright lemon-yellow blossoms of 25 to 30 petals in large clusters. Lightly fragrant flowers bloom all season. The bush, with its polished green leaves is highly disease resistant and winter hardy.

@ **'Sunsprite':** The best of the yellow floribundas has every quality you could ask for — nonstop bloom, fragrance, vigor, and disease resistance. The flowers are a glowing lemon-yellow with 25 to 30 petals and glossy, dark green leaves. You can see it among our "Fragrant Favorites" in the color section. Performs best in cooler temperatures. Introduced in 1977.

White roses

Two of our all-time favorite roses, 'French Lace' and 'Iceberg', are among these white floribundas. Both are top-of-the-line landscape plants.

@ **'Class Act':** AARS 1989. One of the most generous-blooming and easy-to-care-for white floribundas on the market, 'Class Act' produces continuous clusters of pure white blooms that have a mild fragrance. Semi-double flowers open flat and bloom continuously on vigorous bushes with glossy leaves. Effective as a mass planting, but equally nice mixed in a perennial garden, the plant has excellent disease resistance.

@ **'Evening Star':** Absolutely stunning, formal-appearing, white blooms have 35 petals but little scent. Profuse and continual blooms adorn an upright, medium-sized bush with large, dark, leathery leaves, which is disease resistant but not winter hardy. Sold as a hybrid tea in Europe. Introduced in 1974.

@ **'French Lace':** AARS 1982. Large, full blossoms with 35 creamy white petals bloom on cutting-length stems and have a mild, fruity scent. Upright, tall plant has dark, glossy leaves. Performs best in cooler temperatures and with lighter pruning than other floribundas. It is disease resistant but not winter hardy.

@ **'Iceberg':** One of the best white roses for landscape planting, and probably the best-known rose in the world. Though the name varies by country, wherever you go you're likely to see it. Not only is it robust, beautiful, and delightful to smell, but it also flowers freely and profusely with little care. The bush is medium to tall with dark green foliage. Introduced in 1958.

@ **'Margaret Merril':** This extremely fragrant rose won the Edland Fragrance Medal in 1978 for its perfume. The blossoms are soft white and large with a hybrid tea-type shape and 28 petals. Introduced in 1977.

@ **'Summer Snow':** So many clusters of bright white flowers (18 to 24 petals) and creamy buds blanket the plant, you may think that it snowed. And, it flowers practically all season long. Highly prized as a landscape plant, it has little or no fragrance. The bush has light green, shiny leaves and is disease resistant but not hardy in winter. Introduced in 1938.

Lavender roses

You can count the great lavender floribundas on one hand and one finger, and here they are:

- 🌸 **'Angel Face':** AARS 1969. A bit of heaven for the garden, these unusual, deep mauve flowers, with 35 to 40 ruffled petals, send out an ambrosial fragrance that permeates the air throughout the summer. The bush is vigorous, disease resistant, and winter hardy with leathery, semi-glossy leaves.

- 🌸 **'Blueberry Hill':** Clear lilac, sweetly fragrant flowers (8 to 15 petals), grow in clusters on long stems perfect for cutting. Displays all summer long. Rounded, upright plant is disease resistant and hardy. Introduced in 1997.

- 🌸 **'Cotillion':** Light lavender purple blooms are doubles with at least 40 petals and an English rose look. 'Cotillion' is pleasantly fragrant. Dark green foliage adorns a compact plant. Introduced 2000.

- 🌸 **'Intrigue':** AARS 1984. Absolutely intriguing — red-purple buds give way to velvety, plum flowers with an intense perfume and 25 to 30 petals. 'Intrigue' blooms midseason with good repeat blooms. Bushy, medium-sized plant is disease resistant but not winter hardy without protection (see Chapter 20 for more information).

- 🌸 **'Love Potion':** Deep lavender flowers, with 20 to 25 petals, have a strong fragrance. Medium-to-tall plant has shiny, dark green leaves. Introduced in 1995.

- 🌸 **'Shocking Blue':** Not blue at all, but a beautiful, clear lavender with a powerful fragrance, these blooms have 25 to 30 petals on medium-to-tall, upright bushes. The plant is vigorous with glossy green foliage and performs best in cooler temperatures. Introduced in 1974.

Multicolored roses

Here's a dazzling collection of multicolored floribundas:

- 🌸 **'Betty Boop':** AARS 1999. Eye-catching ivory yellow flowers edged in bright red are semi-doubles with 6 to 12 petals and a moderately fruity fragrance. 'Betty' is free-blooming even without regular deadheading. Nicely shaped, rounded bush has glossy green leaves and is disease resistant.

- 🌸 **'Blastoff':** An explosion of color! Big clusters of ruffled, molten scarlet-orange blossoms, with 35 to 40 petals, seem to vibrate with the bright white reverse. Slightly fragrant flowers are long-lasting. The bush has deep green, disease-resistant foliage. Performs consistently in all climates. Introduced in 1995.

'Charisma': AARS 1978. Ever-changing hues of yellow, orange, and red combine in abundant blooms set against glossy, dark green leaves. At times, the lightly scented flowers (with 40-plus petals) totally obscure the compact, bushy plant. A little heat brings out the best color.

'Eyepaint': Buds open into lightly scented scarlet flowers of five to six petals with white centers and golden stamens. The shrub is tall, spreading, and dense with small, shiny, dark green leaves, and it flowers continuously. The disease-resistant and hardy-in-winter bush can be used as a hedge. Introduced in 1975.

'Judy Garland': As charming as its namesake, strongly perfumed blossoms with 30 to 35 petals blush from yellow to hot orange to scarlet. Blooms abundantly in clusters. Glossy green leaves adorn a rounded, bushy plant. Introduced in l978.

'Little Darling': A salmon-pink and yellow duo-tone rose (24 to 30 petals) with a hybrid tea shape and a spicy fragrance, this 'Darling' blooms abundantly in clusters in early to mid-season and reblooms well. It makes a long-lasting cut flower. The plant is bushy and spreading with glossy, leathery, dark green leaves and is disease resistant and hardy in winter. Introduced in 1956.

'Nicole': Abundant small sprays of large white, double blooms (30 to 35 petals) are strikingly edged with dark red. Tall, upright plant has deep green foliage. Introduced in 1985.

'Playboy': A dazzling red-orange flower stamped in the center with a large, golden eye full of orange stamens, and five to seven petals blooms almost continuously in clusters that are excellent for cutting flowers. This bushy, spreading shrub has glossy, disease-resistant foliage. Introduced in 1976.

'Pure Poetry': Yellow buds open into large flowers in a mixture of yellow, orange, and pink. The blooms are cup-shaped with over 40 ruffled petals and an old-garden-rose quality and light fragrance. Compact, vigorous bush has dark green, disease-resistant foliage. Introduced in 1995.

'Purple Tiger': Aptly named, this rose has a deep purple color with stripes and flecks of white and pink. The flowers are large (26 to 40 petals) and bloom in small clusters on shiny stems, and have a nice fragrance. Medium, bushy plant has glossy green leaves. Introduced in 1992.

'Redgold': AARS 1971. Each of the 25 to 30 petals is deep yellow with a bright scarlet edge. 'Redgold' produces an abundance of long-lasting, mildly scented flowers suitable for cutting, and it grows vigorously in all climates. Leaves on the upright, bushy plant are dark green with red new growth. It is hardy in winter and disease resistant.

'Regensberg': From a group of roses known as the "hand-painted" series, all of which have flowers that look like they've been splashed with different colors of paint, this one truly looks handcrafted. Bright white flowers with 20 to 25 petals are splashed with hot pink. At times, the low, compact plant can be completely covered with sweetly scented blossoms. Flower size increases in cool weather. Works well as a landscape plant or in a container. Introduced in 1979.

'Scentimental': AARS 1997. Shocking burgundy-red flowers have swirls of creamy white on the petals. Each bloom is different — some are splashed white, others are striped white, and still others are almost all white with red markings. Flowers have 25 to 30 petals, a strong, spicy fragrance, and a cup shape. The rounded plant has excellent disease resistance.

'Sorbet Bouquet': Warm pink with yellow reverse, this 'Bouquet' is a double with 25 to 30 petals and light fragrance. Upright plant has dark green leaves. Introduced 2000.

'Sweet Vivien': Pink, lightly scented flowers with soft yellow centers bloom in clusters on short stems and have 17 petals. The plant is bushy and compact with small, dark, glossy leaves. The large, pear-shaped hips are colorful in the fall. Introduced in 1961.

Chapter 11

Miniature Roses

• •

In This Chapter

▶ Understanding what a miniature rose is

▶ Exploring the origin of miniature roses

▶ Caring for miniature roses

▶ Landscaping with miniature roses

▶ Identifying miniature rose varieties

• •

*F*ew groups of plants, roses or otherwise, are as versatile and useful as miniature roses. Miniatures, as you can probably guess, are perfectly scaled, smaller versions of larger roses, with all the colors, forms, substance, and often, fragrance of full-sized roses. Like other types of roses, each variety of miniature rose has different characteristics, with plant size ranging between 6 inches and 4 feet or more and plant shapes that include bushy, compact, climbing, and cascading. But no matter what the shape or growth habit, a good miniature rose has flowers and leaves in perfect proportion, as shown in Figure 11-1.

Figure 11-1:
A miniature rose plant with flowers and leaves in perfect proportion.

Smaller definitely doesn't mean less attractive or less fun to grow. Happily, in most cases, smaller does mean easier to grow. Their smaller habit makes miniatures ideal for growing in containers, and they also make excellent landscape and bedding plants.

The flowers provide bright and constant spots of color throughout the growing season, and their flowers can be cut for mini-bouquets and arrangements. (See Figure 11-2 for a close-up of a miniature rose flower.) As well, the selection of varieties is awesome, with hundreds of new ones being introduced each year.

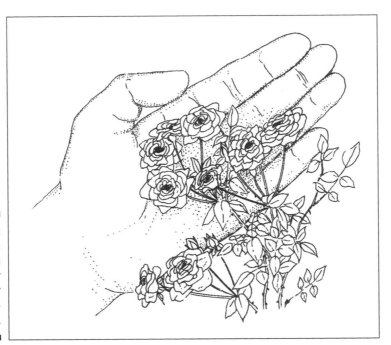

Figure 11-2:
A miniature flower looks quite similar to a flower on a full-sized plant.

From the Land of the Little People

Many stories about the origin of miniature roses exist, and it appears that miniatures have come and gone over many centuries at least. Genetically, miniature roses have been traced back to the miniature China rose, *Rosa chinensis minima,* but the forerunner of today's miniature roses was discovered in a window box in Switzerland in 1917. This variety, named 'Rouletii' (for Colonel Roulet, who owned the window box and the rose), was propagated and used to hybridize the first of the modern miniatures.

The very first miniature sold in the United States, 'Tom Thumb', was introduced in 1936. Since those days, hybridizers of miniroses have crossed miniature varieties with virtually every other type of rose, creating the huge diversity of color, form, and habit you find today.

Tiny but Tough: Protecting and Pruning

Miniature roses are actually pretty tough plants. They are almost always propagated and grown on their own roots, which gives them greater hardiness in cold weather than many other types of roses. Like most plants, however, they're not real thrilled with harsh winter winds and the nasty freeze-and-thaw cycles that some winters bring. Even though your miniature roses will most likely live and do fine the next season no matter what you do or don't do, if you live where temperatures regularly fall below 10°F (–12°C), they'll suffer less damage and thrive more readily if you mulch the base of the plant with leaves for winter protection. For more information about own-root roses, see Chapter 15.

Smaller plants mean smaller roots. Smaller roots don't grow very deep in the soil. Therefore, your minirose needs more frequent watering if Mother Nature doesn't comply and provide water in the form of rain. Also, smaller plants require smaller doses of fertilizer. A general rule for fertilizing miniatures is this: a third as much, twice as often.

As with full-sized roses, regularly removing faded flowers (called deadheading) is pretty much all the pruning you need to do during the growing season. There's no need for cold-climate gardeners to cut back minis in the fall, and in spring you need only prune away the dead parts.

If you have lots of minis to prune, a hedge trimmer — you know, that tool that looks like giant scissors — does a great job. Shear plants back about halfway, meaning that 12-inch-high plants should be some 6 inches tall after pruning.

However, many gardeners like to treat their miniatures with a little more respect, so if you want, you can prune them just like you would hybrid teas. The result will be fewer but bigger flowers. (Check out Chapter 19 for more information.)

One other thing: People may try to convince you that growing miniature roses indoors on a windowsill is easy. Don't buy it. Although a miniature may stay in bloom for a week or two inside, eventually the plant needs to go outside where light is sufficient and conditions are better for healthy growth. Many people do have success growing miniatures indoors, but they usually have a greenhouse or provide some type of supplemental lighting.

Small Spots of Bright Color: Landscaping with Minis

Miniatures are wonderful landscape plants. Because the plants are so small when you buy them, it seems as if they'll take forever to grow and put on a good show. But don't let that small size fool you. Miniature roses reach full size quickly, and they flower big-time all season long.

Miniatures make beautiful up-front plants. Use them to edge a flower border or walkway, or plant them at the base of taller-growing plants. And don't forget about containers. You'll be hard pressed to beat the appeal of a good-looking miniature rose growing in a handsome pot. You can find specifics about landscaping with miniatures in Chapter 5. For more on growing roses in containers, refer to Chapter 7.

The Lowdown on Miniature Varieties

Miniature roses seem to show up in a lot of places where you don't usually see rose plants for sale, like at supermarkets and florist shops. So you don't have to look far to find them. But if you want varieties that really have proven themselves in garden situations, you're better off buying from a local nursery or a mail-order catalog that specializes in roses.

Better yet, look at catalogs from companies like Nor'East Miniature Roses or Sequoia Nursery, which specialize in miniatures. You can find their addresses in Appendix C.

More new miniatures are released each year than just about any other type of rose, so you have many varieties to choose from. The following sections list some of our favorites — a nice mix of the new and the tried and true. Miniatures given the American Rose Society Award of Excellence have been judged outstanding in test gardens throughout the United States.

Red miniatures

Here are some of our favorite red miniatures. If we had to pick three to start with, we would choose 'Beauty Secret', 'Red Cascade', and 'Starina'.

'Acey Deucy': The fragrant, orange red flowers with 20 petals and a hybrid tea shape on a small, bushy plant with medium green, glossy leaves grows about 12 inches high. Introduced in 1982.

'Beauty Secret': American Rose Society Award of Excellence 1975. Elected to ARS Miniature Hall of Fame in 1999. Pointed, bright red buds open into very fragrant hybrid tea-type blooms with 24 to 30 petals medium red in color. The prolific and dependable plant is 10 to 18 inches tall with shiny, medium green leaves. Disease-resistant and winter-hardy, it grows well indoors under lights. Introduced in 1965.

'Black Jade': American Rose Society Award of Excellence 1985. Pointed, near-black buds (the stage at which the rose has its best color) open to chocolatey red blossoms on long stems. The blooms have 30 petals and a slight fragrance. The plant is an 18- to 24-inch bush with glossy, dark green leaves. Introduced in 1985.

'Centerpiece': American Rose Society Award of Excellence 1985. Long-lasting deep red, velvety blooms have 35 petals and a light fragrance. The small, compact plant reaches 12 to 16 inches high and is covered with deep green leaves. Introduced in 1984.

'Cherry Hi': Dark red double blooms with little fragrance are held generously above a compact plant. This fine landscape plant is free blooming even in hot climates. Introduced 1997.

'Debut': All-America Rose Selection (AARS) 1989. Radiant scarlet blooms blend from cream to yellow at the base. Older blossoms turn cherry red and white at the base. The fragrance-free flowers have 15 to 18 petals and grow singly. The plant is short and bushy, about 12 to 15 inches high, and has shiny, dark green foliage. Introduced in 1988.

'Jingle Bells': American Rose Society Award of Excellence 1995. The large, bright red blooms have a lighter reverse. The plant has a nice round habit, reaching about 20 inches high, with glossy, dark green leaves and good disease resistance. Introduced in 1995.

'Kathy': Soft red and fragrant, this hybrid tea-like blossom has 24 to 30 petals. The plant blooms abundantly and has a tendency to spread. Leathery, dark green leaves cover the vigorous, disease-resistant, winter-hardy plant which grows 8 to 10 inches tall. Introduced in 1970.

'Miss Flippins': Beautifully formed double blooms are bright red with pink reverse and make great cut flowers. The plant grows 24 to 30 inches high with glossy dark green foliage. Introduced in 1997.

'Old Glory': American Rose Society Award of Excellence 1988. Large, lightly fragrant, red blossoms of 23 to 25 petals grow alone or in small sprays. The plant is a vigorous grower, 16 to 20 inches high, with medium green, glossy leaves. Introduced in 1988.

'Red Cascade': American Rose Society Award of Excellence 1976. This climbing miniature, which can reach up to 5 feet high, is excellent for hanging baskets. Deep red, cup-shaped flowers with 35 petals bloom abundantly and have little or no fragrance. The plant has dark green, shiny leaves and is winter hardy and disease resistant, although it needs protection from mildew in some climates. Introduced in 1976.

- **'Starina':** The pointed buds of this hybrid tea-type flower blossom into a deep orange-red flower with 35 petals. Abundant, continuous blooms and a light fragrance make this consistent, easy-to-grow rose a crowd-pleaser. The plant is 12 to 18 inches tall, bushy, and dense with dark green, glossy leaves. It is disease resistant and winter hardy. Introduced in 1965. Elected to the ARS Miniature Rose Hall of Fame in 1999.

Pink miniatures

You have many pink miniatures to choose from. Our favorites include 'Baby Betsy McCall', 'Jeanne Lajoie', and 'Judy Fischer'.

- **'Angelica Renae':** American Rose Society Award of Excellence 1996. Free-blooming, medium pink blooms with a splash of orange at the base form a nice, rounded, 2-foot-high bush with dark green foliage. Introduced in 1996.

- **'Baby Betsy McCall':** The small, cup-shaped, light pink, fragrant flowers have 20 to 24 petals and bloom continuously on a 12- to 18-inch bush. Leathery, light green leaves adorn the winter-hardy, disease-resistant bush, which grows 12 to 18 inches high. Introduced in 1965.

- **'Cuddles':** American Rose Society Award of Excellence 1979. Deep coral-pink petals unfurl evenly into slightly fragrant, long-lasting blossoms with 55 to 60 petals. The 14- to 16-inch tall bush with glossy green leaves is easy to grow and produces abundant blooms. The plant is disease resistant and winter hardy. Introduced in 1978.

- **'Cupcake':** American Rose Society Award of Excellence 1983. This rose produces lots of pastel pink flowers and buds with 45 to 50 petals and a slight fragrance. The hybrid tea-shaped flower grows on a bush which is 12 to 18 inches tall with glossy green foliage and a neat, rounded appearance. The plant is disease resistant and winter hardy. Introduced in 1981.

- **'Jeanne Lajoie':** American Rose Society Award of Excellence 1977. A climbing miniature (pictured with the Pink Favorites) whose medium pink flowers grow in clusters nonstop throughout the season, the slightly fragrant blossoms have 35 to 40 petals. The vigorous bushes grow 4 to 8 feet tall and have abundant, small, and glossy foliage. The plant has good disease resistance and is winter hardy. Introduced in 1975.

- **'Judy Fischer':** American Rose Society Award of Excellence 1975. One of the best pink miniatures (see with the Pink Favorite in the Color Section), the rose pink flowers last for weeks and don't fade, even in hot weather. The hybrid tea-shaped flower carries 24 to 30 slightly fragrant petals. The easy-to-grow plant is very low and bushy, growing between 18 and 24 inches in height, with abundant, small, glossy green leaves. It is disease resistant and winter hardy. Introduced in 1968.

◉ **'Minnie Pearl':** Perfectly formed, double pink blooms have a touch of yellow at the base. Nicely shaped, slightly spreading bush grows 18 to 24 inches high and has bright green foliage. Introduced in 1982.

◉ **'Renny':** Wonderful pink flowers with 25 pointed petals have a moderate fragrance and a generous bloom. The bushy plant is thornless and grows 12 to 18 inches high. Introduced in 1989.

◉ **'Sweet Sunblaze':** This is one the new Sunblaze series (all have "Sunblaze" in the name) of roses, which are often described as shrubs. But they look like minis to us, so that's where we put them. The series is available in many colors but this one has clear pink, fully double (26 to 40 petals) flowers with showy yellow stamens and a slight fragrance. The bushy plant grows 15 to 18 inches high. Introduced in 1989.

Orange miniatures

Here are eight great orange miniatures. You can't miss with any of them.

◉ **'Dee Bennett':** American Rose Society Award of Excellence 1989. This delightful blended rose is washed with shades of orange and yellow. The nicely formed flowers are borne singly and in clusters; they have 25 petals and a light fruity fragrance. The plant is medium-sized with bushy growth and dark green, semi-glossy foliage. Introduced in 1988.

◉ **'Little Flame':** American Rose Society Award of Excellence 1999. The bright orange, double (25 petals) blooms fade to burnt orange and have a slight fragrance. The plant has a neat, mounded habit, 12 to 18 inches high with glossy green foliage. Introduced in 1998.

◉ **'Loving Touch':** American Rose Society Award of Excellence 1985. Creamy apricot blossoms with 20 to 25 petals are set against abundant medium green leaves and have a mild fragrance. The bush is 12 to 18 inches tall and rounded. Moderate temperatures produce the deepest colors. Introduced in 1993.

◉ **'Mary Marshall':** American Rose Society Award of Excellence 1975. Deep coral flowers (we show it with the Orange Favorites) with a yellow base blossom all season. Hybrid tea-type blooms have a slight fragrance. The bush grows 10 to 14 inches tall; the climbing form can reach 5 feet, and both forms have medium green, glossy leaves. The plant is winter hardy and disease resistant. Introduced in 1970.

◉ **'New Beginning':** AARS 1989. This bright orange-yellow flower has lots and lots of petals (40 to 50) but no fragrance. The compact plant has glossy green leaves and grows 16 to 20 inches high. Introduced in 1988.

◉ **'Orange Honey':** Bright orange yellow, double (23 to 25 petals) with a fruity fragrance, this rose is perfect for pots or hanging baskets. The bush is compact and spreading and grows 18 to 22 inches high. Introduced in 1979.

'**Playgold':** American Rose Society Award of Excellence 1998. Bright orange, single blooms with little fragrance take on shades of pink as they fade. The bushy plant grows 15 to 18 inches high and has excellent disease resistance. This is a great landscape plant. Introduced in 1998.

'**Sheri Anne':** American Rose Society Award of Excellence 1975. Profuse clusters of bright orange-red flowers bloom continuously on this upright bush, 22 to 30 inches high with glossy, dark green leaves. The blossoms have 15 to 18 petals and a light fragrance. Introduced in 1973.

Yellow miniatures

These are all excellent yellow miniatures, but 'Center Gold', 'Rise 'n' Shine', and 'Yellow Doll' always stand out in a crowd.

'**Behold':** Nicely formed, bright yellow flowers are produced in abundance. Vigorous, winter-hardy plant grows 16 to 20 inches high with medium green foliage. Introduced 1997.

'**Cal Poly':** American Rose Society Award of Excellence 1992. Blazing yellow, round blooms set against large, rich green leaves look like water lilies. The mildly scented flowers have 20 to 25 petals. The bush grows 14 to 18 inches and blooms best in warm summer climates. The plant is also available in a climbing form. Introduced in l991.

'**Center Gold':** American Rose Society Award of Excellence 1982. Deep yellow flowers occasionally shade toward white. You may find an all-white bloom among the yellow, or you may see flowers with yellow centers and white outside petals — 25 to 35 of them. The hybrid tea-type blossoms have little or no fragrance. Glossy, medium green leaves adorn the vigorous 14- to 18-inch plant, which is disease resistant and winter hardy. Introduced in l981.

'**Golden Halo':** American Rose Society Award of Excellence 1991. Bright yellow blooms sometimes have a touch of red. The flowers have a slight fragrance and 24 to 26 petals. Vigorous, bushy plant grows about 16 to 20 inches high with dark green leaves. Introduced in 1991.

'**Rise 'n' Shine':** American Rose Society Award of Excellence 1978. One of the finest yellow miniatures, 'Rise 'n' Shine' delivers abundant and continuous blooms of brilliant yellow flowers with 30 to 40 petals set against dark green foliage. The plant is bushy, compact, 16 to 20 inches high, disease resistant, and winter hardy. Introduced in 1977.

'**Sequoia Gold':** American Rose Society Award of Excellence 1987. Golden yellow blossoms with 20 petals bloom singly or in clusters and have a moderate, fruity fragrance. The bushy, spreading plant has glossy, medium green leaves. Introduced in 1986.

@ **'Little Tommy Tucker':** American Rose Society Award of Excellence 1999. Buttery yellow, double flowers with a slight fragrance. Free-blooming, bushy plant reaches 18 to 22 inches high and has excellent disease resistance. Introduced 1998.

@ **'Yellow Doll':** Free-blooming, the large, light yellow flowers have 24 to 30 petals and a slight fragrance. The 8- to 10-inch plant is low, compact, and rounded with leathery green leaves. It is disease resistant and winter hardy. It's pictured with the "Yellow Favorites" in the color section. Introduced in l962.

White miniatures

These are all top-notch white miniatures:

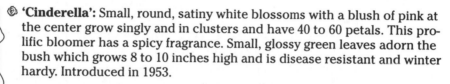

@ **'Cinderella':** Small, round, satiny white blossoms with a blush of pink at the center grow singly and in clusters and have 40 to 60 petals. This prolific bloomer has a spicy fragrance. Small, glossy green leaves adorn the bush which grows 8 to 10 inches high and is disease resistant and winter hardy. Introduced in 1953.

@ **'Fairhope':** White to light yellow blooms are perfectly formed and have only slight fragrance. The plant is tall, 24 to 36 inches high, with disease-resistant, dark green foliage. Introduced in 1989.

@ **'Figurine':** American Rose Society Award of Excellence 1992. The 18 to 25 petaled blooms are ivory, dipped in a pastel pink wash. Long, pointed buds and high-centered, hybrid tea-type flowers look almost like fine china. The roses, which have a moderate, sweet fragrance, bloom abundantly on long stems that are suitable for cutting. The plant grows 14 to 20 inches high with dark green foliage. Introduced in 1991.

@ **'Gourmet Popcorn':** Small, flat, bright white blooms explode all over this vigorous plant in cascading clusters. Extremely fragrant blooms have 15 to 20 petals. The easy-to-grow, bushy plant is usually 20 to 28 inches tall and is disease resistant and winter hardy. Introduced in 1986.

@ **'Little Eskimo':** The fluffy white, double blossoms (55 petals) have little fragrance. Vigorous, upright plant grows 20 to 30 inches high and produces lots of blooms. Introduced 1981.

@ **'Simplex':** Five white petals frame a large nucleus of fluffy, golden stamens. Lots of flowers bloom throughout the season on this vigorous, upright bush that produces pink blossoms in cool, cloudy weather. Light green, shiny leaves adorn the 15- to 18-inch tall bush which is disease resistant and winter hardy. Introduced in 1961.

⊛ **'Snow Bride':** American Rose Society Award of Excellence 1983. Formal, creamy white buds open to large, full blossoms with 20 to 25 petals and a mild scent. The rounded bush, 12 to 18 inches tall, has deep green leaves. This plant forms the best flowers in moderate climates. Introduced in 1982.

⊛ **'Starglo':** American Rose Society Award of Excellence 1975. Extremely fragrant, white blossoms have a classic hybrid tea shape and 35 petals. It blooms midseason and repeats blooming. The upright bush, 10 to 14 inches tall, can grow indoors in a pot over the winter. It is disease resistant and winter hardy. Introduced in 1973.

Lavender miniatures

Here are five of our favorite lavender-flowered miniature roses:

⊛ **'Incognito':** New England Rose Trials Award, 1996. Unusually colored flowers of dusty light mauve with a yellow reverse have a perfect exhibition form (see Chapter 2 for more about form). A vigorous grower, and always covered with flowers, the bush grows to 30 inches tall. Introduced in 1995.

⊛ **'Lavender Delight':** Showy, semi-double to double (10 to 20 petals) lavender flowers have little fragrance. The free-blooming plant grows upright to about 14 inches high. Introduced 1994.

⊛ **'Lavender Jewel':** The mauve color of the open, cup-shaped flowers with 12 to 20 petals stays true. The blooms have little fragrance, but the plant produces many blooms throughout the season. Dark green, glossy leaves adorn the bush, which grows 10 to 15 inches tall with long, spreading canes. It is also disease resistant and winter hardy. Introduced in 1978.

⊛ **'Scentsational':** The first of Nor'East Miniature Roses' series of fragrant miniatures (see Appendix C for Nor'East's address). Others include 'Seattle Scensation' (mauve pink) and 'Overnight Scentsation' (pink). The nicely fragrant flowers are pink, edged with mauve, and have a creamy pink reverse. This easy-to-grow rose makes a good cut flower. The bush has medium green foliage on a 24-to 30-inch plant. Introduced in 1996.

⊛ **'Sweet Chariot':** Ruffled, fluffy blossoms of 45 to 50 petals seem to burst forth in fragrant, cascading blooms. As the flower ages, the deep purple gives way to lavender, creating a two-toned effect. Small, deep green leaves grow on the 12- to 18-inch, bushy plant, which is highly disease resistant. Introduced in 1984.

⊛ **'Winsome':** American Rose Society Award of Excellence 1985. Big, pointed buds and large, shapely, magenta blooms with 35 to 40 petals appear freely all season on this vigorous, easy-to-grow bush. The 16- to 22-inch rounded plant with dark green leaves has little fragrance, but is disease resistant. See it with the "Lavender Favorites." Introduced in 1984.

Multicolored miniatures

These are all popular miniatures, but you have to love the award-winning 'Child's Play'. Otherwise, choose by your favorite color combination.

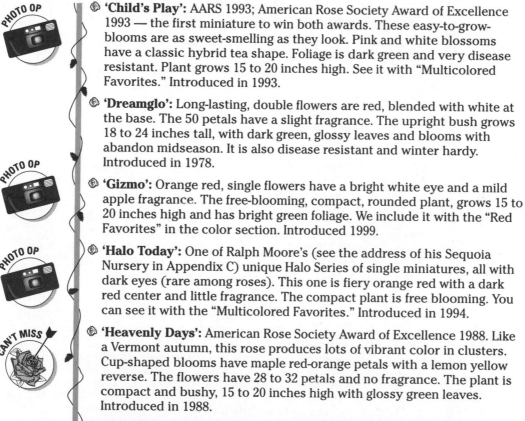

⊛ **'Child's Play':** AARS 1993; American Rose Society Award of Excellence 1993 — the first miniature to win both awards. These easy-to-grow-blooms are as sweet-smelling as they look. Pink and white blossoms have a classic hybrid tea shape. Foliage is dark green and very disease resistant. Plant grows 15 to 20 inches high. See it with "Multicolored Favorites." Introduced in 1993.

⊛ **'Dreamglo':** Long-lasting, double flowers are red, blended with white at the base. The 50 petals have a slight fragrance. The upright bush grows 18 to 24 inches tall, with dark green, glossy leaves and blooms with abandon midseason. It is also disease resistant and winter hardy. Introduced in 1978.

⊛ **'Gizmo':** Orange red, single flowers have a bright white eye and a mild apple fragrance. The free-blooming, compact, rounded plant, grows 15 to 20 inches high and has bright green foliage. We include it with the "Red Favorites" in the color section. Introduced 1999.

⊛ **'Halo Today':** One of Ralph Moore's (see the address of his Sequoia Nursery in Appendix C) unique Halo Series of single miniatures, all with dark eyes (rare among roses). This one is fiery orange red with a dark red center and little fragrance. The compact plant is free blooming. You can see it with the "Multicolored Favorites." Introduced in 1994.

⊛ **'Heavenly Days':** American Rose Society Award of Excellence 1988. Like a Vermont autumn, this rose produces lots of vibrant color in clusters. Cup-shaped blooms have maple red-orange petals with a lemon yellow reverse. The flowers have 28 to 32 petals and no fragrance. The plant is compact and bushy, 15 to 20 inches high with glossy green leaves. Introduced in 1988.

⊛ **'Holy Toledo':** American Rose Society Award of Excellence 1980. Deep apricot blossoms with yellow at the base burst into bloom throughout the season. Borne singly and in clusters, the flowers have 25 to 30 petals and a slight fragrance. The medium-to-tall, vigorous bush has glossy, forest green foliage. Introduced in 1978.

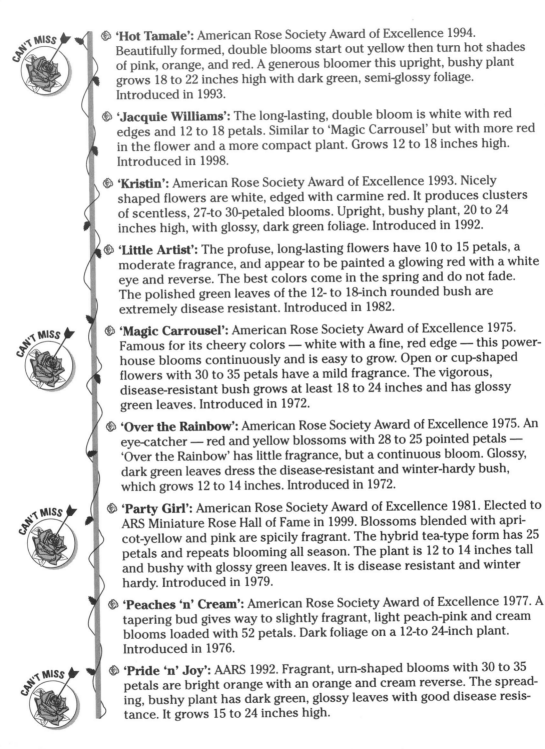

'Hot Tamale': American Rose Society Award of Excellence 1994. Beautifully formed, double blooms start out yellow then turn hot shades of pink, orange, and red. A generous bloomer this upright, bushy plant grows 18 to 22 inches high with dark green, semi-glossy foliage. Introduced in 1993.

'Jacquie Williams': The long-lasting, double bloom is white with red edges and 12 to 18 petals. Similar to 'Magic Carrousel' but with more red in the flower and a more compact plant. Grows 12 to 18 inches high. Introduced in 1998.

'Kristin': American Rose Society Award of Excellence 1993. Nicely shaped flowers are white, edged with carmine red. It produces clusters of scentless, 27-to 30-petaled blooms. Upright, bushy plant, 20 to 24 inches high, with glossy, dark green foliage. Introduced in 1992.

'Little Artist': The profuse, long-lasting flowers have 10 to 15 petals, a moderate fragrance, and appear to be painted a glowing red with a white eye and reverse. The best colors come in the spring and do not fade. The polished green leaves of the 12- to 18-inch rounded bush are extremely disease resistant. Introduced in 1982.

'Magic Carrousel': American Rose Society Award of Excellence 1975. Famous for its cheery colors — white with a fine, red edge — this powerhouse blooms continuously and is easy to grow. Open or cup-shaped flowers with 30 to 35 petals have a mild fragrance. The vigorous, disease-resistant bush grows at least 18 to 24 inches and has glossy green leaves. Introduced in 1972.

'Over the Rainbow': American Rose Society Award of Excellence 1975. An eye-catcher — red and yellow blossoms with 28 to 25 pointed petals — 'Over the Rainbow' has little fragrance, but a continuous bloom. Glossy, dark green leaves dress the disease-resistant and winter-hardy bush, which grows 12 to 14 inches. Introduced in 1972.

'Party Girl': American Rose Society Award of Excellence 1981. Elected to ARS Miniature Rose Hall of Fame in 1999. Blossoms blended with apricot-yellow and pink are spicily fragrant. The hybrid tea-type form has 25 petals and repeats blooming all season. The plant is 12 to 14 inches tall and bushy with glossy green leaves. It is disease resistant and winter hardy. Introduced in 1979.

'Peaches 'n' Cream': American Rose Society Award of Excellence 1977. A tapering bud gives way to slightly fragrant, light peach-pink and cream blooms loaded with 52 petals. Dark foliage on a 12-to 24-inch plant. Introduced in 1976.

'Pride 'n' Joy': AARS 1992. Fragrant, urn-shaped blooms with 30 to 35 petals are bright orange with an orange and cream reverse. The spreading, bushy plant has dark green, glossy leaves with good disease resistance. It grows 15 to 24 inches high.

CAN'T MISS

◎ **'Rainbow's End':** American Rose Society Award of Excellence 1986. Golden yellow blossoms blush prettily to their orange-red tips. Shapely, hybrid tea-type flowers have 30 to 35 petals, a mild fragrance, and abundant, repeat blooms. The plant is 12 to 18 inches tall with glossy green leaves, and is disease resistant and winter hardy. Also available in a climbing form. Introduced in 1984.

◎ **'Splish Splash':** Double blooms in ever-changing shades of yellow and pink put out a nice fragrance. Medium size bush makes a nice 18- to 24-inch hedge. Introduced in 1994.

◎ **'Tropical Twist':** American Rose Society Award of Excellence 1997. This slightly fragrant double bloom's 20 to 25 petals are tropical sunset shades of orange and pink. The 18- to 24-inch high plant has dark green, glossy leaves with good disease resistance. Introduced in 1997.

◎ **'Toy Clown':** American Rose Society Award of Excellence 1975. Beautiful hybrid tea-type blossoms are white with red or deep pink edges and 12 to 20 petals. Flowers have little or no fragrance. The free-blooming and attractive bush is 10 to 14 inches tall with smallish, leathery green leaves, and is disease resistant and winter hardy. Introduced in 1966.

Chapter 12

Climbing Roses

• •

• •

Climbing roses represent a diverse group of plants, producing long, supple canes that, in some varieties, can reach over 20 feet long. The plants are not true vines in that they don't cling to, climb on, or in any way attach themselves to an upright support. Left on their own, they tend to be large, sprawling shrubs.

But most climbing roses are not left on their own. You usually tie them in an upright fashion to some type of vertical support, such as a fence, arbor, trellis, or wall. But you don't just train them straight up to the sky. Grown like that, they would only bloom at the very tip-top of the canes — closer to the clouds than anywhere you'd be able to enjoy the flowers.

So that you can benefit from climbing roses, you develop more floriferous (love that word, which means blooms a lot) horizontal side shoots (see Chapter 19 for more information on pruning climbing roses). But we're getting ahead of ourselves.

As landscape plants, climbing roses present many opportunities. Following are some planting suggestions:

✔ Plant climbing roses in a narrow area, where there isn't room for much else (see Figure 12-1).

✔ Turn a blank wall into living art, with a trellis and a climbing rose plant.

✔ Cover up that ugly chain-link fence.

✔ Use a climbing rose to increase the shade from your arbor.

✔ Brighten an old wooden fence with a light-colored climber.

✔ Create a stunning garden entryway with a rose-covered arch.

✔ Make Victorian magic by training a red climber on a white picket fence.

✔ Use a climbing miniature for a vertical statement on lamp posts or porch support.

You can find more ideas on how to use climbing roses, including different types of supports and ways to attach climbing roses to them, in Chapter 5.

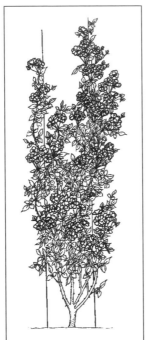

Figure 12-1:
You can train climbing roses to make a vertical statement in your garden.

So Many Climbers, So Little Time

A number of different types of climbers exists, including many shrubs and old garden roses that grow vigorously, and which you can train to grow upright. We describe some of those types in Chapters 13 and 14, respectively.

Most climbing roses, however, fall into one of the following categories — three for regular climbers and one category for miniatures.

✔ **Large-flowered climbers** are the most popular and widely used climbing roses. They produce clusters of flowers (see Figure 12-2) on stiff, arching canes that generally reach 8 to 15 feet. They bloom most heavily in spring but do produce flowers throughout the growing season. Large-flowered climbers are generally hardy to 15° to 20°F (–10° to –7°C) and need winter protection wherever temperatures regularly drop lower. They are, nonetheless, your best bet for a climbing rose if you live in an area with cold winters. (For more information about protecting these plants in winter, see Chapter 20.)

Figure 12-2: Some climbers produce clusters of flowers.

✔ **Climbing sports** result from unusually vigorous canes that grow from popular hybrid teas, grandifloras, shrubs, and floribundas. They produce the beautiful flowers of their shrubby parent but on a more sprawling plant. Climbing sports don't usually bloom as heavily as large-flowered climbers, but they do produce flowers with excellent size and character throughout the growing season. These plants are generally hardy to 10° to 20°F (–12° to –7°C) and need protection in regions with colder winters.

Climbing sports are generally named after their original variety. Favorites include 'Climbing First Prize' from the pink and silver hybrid tea, 'Climbing Iceberg' from the generous-blooming (or floriferous) white floribunda, 'Climbing Cécile Brünner' from the pink polyantha, and 'Climbing Queen Elizabeth' from the famous pink grandiflora. (You can find descriptions of these flowers in the chapters describing the class of roses from which the climber originates.) Some climbing sports, such as 'High Noon', described later in this chapter, are listed as climbing hybrid teas even though they don't have a popular hybrid tea version Why? Who knows.

✔ **Ramblers** are less popular than other types of climbing roses, primarily because they bloom only once a year, in spring. These plants are very vigorous and can grow up to 20 feet tall. They are hardy to about 10°F (or about –12°C).

✔ **Climbing miniatures** are a fourth type of popular climber. Some are sports of popular miniature varieties. Others were created by crossing miniatures with more vigorous roses. Favorites include 'Jeanne Lajoie' and 'Climbing Rise 'n' Shine'. (You can find descriptions of their flowers in Chapter 11.)

Climbers in Every Color of the Rainbow

Climbers are the high risers of the rose world. They can grow up and over whatever you can tie them to and produce flowers in all the rose colors, as proven by the following lists of climbers by color.

Red climbers

All these red varieties are large-flowered climbers. Don't overlook 'Altissimo' with its glorious single flowers. It's a stunner.

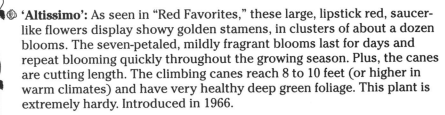

🌸 **'All Ablaze':** Fiery clusters of ruffled, bright red, double flowers (at least 35 petals) adorn this free-blooming plant, which has a light, spicy fragrance. The clean, green foliage is on canes that reach 8 to 12 feet. It is widely adapted (meaning it grows well in lots of different places) and disease resistant. Introduced in 2000.

🌸 **'Altissimo':** As seen in "Red Favorites," these large, lipstick red, saucer-like flowers display showy golden stamens, in clusters of about a dozen blooms. The seven-petaled, mildly fragrant blooms last for days and repeat blooming quickly throughout the growing season. Plus, the canes are cutting length. The climbing canes reach 8 to 10 feet (or higher in warm climates) and have very healthy deep green foliage. This plant is extremely hardy. Introduced in 1966.

🌸 **'American Beauty':** Beautiful, large, double, cupped, pinkish red flowers with a strong fragrance bloom just once a season. This vigorous plant grows 12 to 15 feet high and has deep green leaves. Introduced in 1909.

🌸 **'Don Juan':** Deep red flowers, with an intense fragrance and 35 petals, bloom profusely from midseason on. Dark green, glossy leaves cover the climbing canes, which reach 12 to 14 feet. 'Don Juan' makes an excellent trellis rose: It blooms repeatedly, is disease resistant, and warm nights bring out its best color. It is not, however, dependably winter hardy. Introduced in 1958.

- **'Dublin Bay':** Cupped blossoms with 25, true-red petals bloom profusely in midseason and follow up with a good repeat bloom later. Flowers open in cool or hot weather, on old wood or new, and are moderately fragrant. The bush is upright and vigorous with lots of dark green leaves. Climbing canes reach 8 to 14 feet and are disease resistant and winter hardy. Introduced in 1974.

- **'Dynamite':** These dark red, clustered flowers with 40 petals have a slight fragrance. The plant has dark green, glossy foliage and a spreading, vigorous growth. It's also disease resistant. Introduced in 1992.

- **'Improved Blaze':** This, the most popular climbing rose, is easy to grow and produces large, cup-shaped flowers of pure red in clusters all season long. The lightly scented roses have 20 to 25 petals and blossom on new wood and old. Climbing canes reach 12 to 14 feet and have medium green, shiny leaves. The plant is winter hardy and disease resistant. Introduced in 1932.

- **'Tempo':** These flowers are deep red and full, with 35 to 45 petals and a slight fragrance. The large foliage is a glossy dark green. The plant has good disease resistance and winter hardiness. Introduced in 1975.

Pink climbers

'America' is always a favorite from these pink climbers:

- **'America':** All-America Rose Selection (AARS) 1976. Large, well-formed, cup-shaped flowers of coral pink broadcast a spicy fragrance and have 40 to 45 petals. The plant is vigorous and bushy with bright green leaves, and its climbing canes reach 10 to 12 feet. Flowers bloom on old and new wood, and the plant is disease resistant and winter hardy.

- **'Dorothy Perkins':** This rambler bears fragrant, many-petaled, rose-pink flowers, which bloom only in spring. This very vigorous plant, with glossy, dark green leaves, can grow 10 to 20 feet high. Introduced in 1901.

- **'Dr. J. H. Nicolas':** The large, round, rose-pink flowers, with 45 to 50 petals, are heavily fragrant. Upright and slender with leathery, dark green leaves, the plant blooms profusely. Climbing canes reach 8 to 10 feet. It's disease resistant and winter hardy. Introduced in 1940.

- **'Clair Matin':** The large, semi-double (15 petals) medium pink flowers appear in rounded clusters and have a pleasant sweetbriar fragrance. The leaves are dark green and very disease resistant. The plant is winter hardy but somewhat shorter than many climbers, rarely reaching over 10 to 12 feet high. Introduced in 1960.

- **'Dream Weaver':** This easy-to-grow and -train rose produces slightly fragrant, coral-pink blooms in large clusters. The flowers are medium in size with 30 petals. The plant has glossy, dark green leaves, good hardiness and disease resistance. Introduced in 1996.

- ◉ **'New Dawn':** Large, pale pink flowers, with sweet perfume and glossy, dark green leaves, have 35 to 40 petals. This plant produces blooms continuously throughout the season on climbing canes that reach 18 to 20 feet and are very hardy. Introduced in 1930.

- ◉ **'Pearly Gates':** Lovely pastel pink, double flowers have 35 petals and strong spicy fragrance. Blooms over a long season. Canes climb 10 to 12 feet high and produce dark green leaves. Introduced in 1999.

- ◉ **'Rosarium Uetersen':** This rose produces fragrant, medium-sized, deep pink flowers with an incredible number of petals — well over 100. The plant enjoys vigorous growth and has dark green, glossy foliage. Introduced in 1977.

- ◉ **'William Baffin':** This vigorous, climbing shrub puts out unscented, deep pink flowers in clusters containing as many as 30 blossoms with 20 petals each. The bush has glossy green leaves and is winter hardy. Introduced in 1983.

Orange climbers

A rare color among climbers. Here are the best:

- ◉ **'Christine':** A mandarin-orange-colored sport of 'Altissimo'. Single flowers have 5 to 7 petals and excellent substance but little fragrance. Canes climb 10 to 12 feet high (higher in warm winter climates). Dark green foliage is disease resistant. Introduced in 1998.

- ◉ **'Rocketeer':** Climbing miniature. Small, coral-orange blooms have 15 to 20 petals and a slight fragrance. A vigorous-growing but manageable plant with dark green leaves, it's great in containers, and disease resistant. Introduced in 1992

- ◉ **'Westerland':** This reblooming climbing shrub, with beautiful apricot-orange blooms borne in large clusters, is a double with 18 to 25 petals and a strong fragrance. The plant climbs at least 10 to 12 feet high, taller in mild winter areas. Its glossy green foliage has excellent disease resistance, particularly against blackspot. Introduced in 1969.

Yellow climbers

Here are six great yellow climbers. One of them, 'King Tut', is a climbing miniature.

- ◉ **'Autumn Sunset':** This climbing shrub, with rich apricot gold flowers in large clusters, this is a double with 20 to 25 petals and a strong, fruity fragrance. This generous bloomer is widely used, but produces its richest color in climates with cooler summers. The plant climbs 8 to 12 feet and has glossy dark green leaves with excellent disease resistance and winter hardiness. Introduced in 1986.

- **'Golden Showers':** AARS 1957. Large-flowered climber. These large, fragrant, bright yellow, ruffled flowers, with 20 to 35 petals, resemble a star burst when in full bloom, and they bloom abundantly all season. Climbing canes reach 12 to 14 feet and have bright green leaves. Cool temperatures give the roses their best color and size.

- **'High Noon':** AARS 1948. Climbing hybrid tea. Large, light yellow, loosely cupped flowers, with 25 to 30 petals, have a spicy fragrance and bloom all season. Climbing canes have leathery, glossy, green leaves, and reach 10 to 12 feet. It's disease resistant and winter hardy.

- **'Royal Gold':** Large-flowered climber. Yellow buds blossom into lasting, golden flowers that don't fade. The flowers have 30 to 40 petals and a moderate-to-strong scent in a hybrid tea-type shape. Borne singly and in clusters on long, strong stems, these flowers are not as prolific as other climbers. The roses have glossy green leaves and make a good cut flower. Climbing canes reach 8 to 10 feet. Introduced in 1957.

White climbers

You have two good ones to choose from, both large-flowered climbers. You might also check out 'Sally Holmes' a vigorous shrub that can be grown as a climber (see Chapter 13 for more information) and 'Sombreuil', which is a vigorous old garden rose that also can be trained upright (see Chapter 14 for the description).

- **'Lace Cascade':** Fragrant, full, white flowers with 26 to 40 petals grow in small and large clusters amidst large, dark green leaves. Tall plants have a spreading growth and are disease resistant. Introduced in 1992.

- **'White Dawn':** Free-flowering and vigorous, this rose delivers loads of bright white, ruffled flowers, with 30 to 35 petals, and a sweet perfume. Climbing canes, with glossy green foliage, reach 12 to 14 feet. The plant is disease resistant. Introduced in 1949.

Lavender climbers

Few lavender large-flowered climbers exist, but you can get the 'Climbing Blue Girl,' a sport of the hybrid tea rose described in Chapter 8.

Multicolored climbers

Following are seven of our favorite multicolored climbers, of which 'Dortmund,' with its beautiful single blooms, always ranks on top. Newcomers 'Peaches 'n' Cream' and 'Fourth of July' are also excellent.

- **'Berries 'n' Cream':** Large-flowered climber. Showy clusters of double rebloomers marked and striped with rosy pink and cream have 25 to 30 petals and a nice apple scent. Grows 10 to 12 feet high (higher in mild winter climates) with few thorns. You get more cream color in mild summer climates. Introduced in 1997.

- **'Dortmund':** Climbing shrub. Nail-polish red blossoms, which have a small, white eye, bloom in clusters. The rose has five to eight petals and a moderate scent. Climbing canes, with lacquered, deep green leaves, reach 10 to 12 feet. The plant is highly disease resistant and winter hardy. Introduced in 1955.

- **'Fourth of July':** AARS 1999 (first one in 23 years). Large, open faced, semi-double blooms (12 to 15 petals), borne in clusters, are bright red, striped with white. The very generous bloom has a sweet apple fragrance. Exceptionally disease resistant and easy to grow, the plant reaches 10 to 14 feet in height and is widely adapted.

- **'Handel':** Large-flowered climber. Ruffled, pale pink or white blossoms edged with deep pink unfurl singly on cutting-length stems. The bush is covered, top to bottom, all season, with lightly scented blooms that have 20 to 25 petals. Climbing canes with dark, olive-green foliage reach 12 to 15 feet. Blooms improve as this hardy plant gets older. Introduced in 1965.

- **'Joseph's Coat':** Large-flowered climber. Kaleidoscopic colors — shades of red, pink, orange, and yellow — dance on the petals of this very popular rose, often in the same cluster. The lightly scented roses have 23 to 28 petals and vigorous, glossy, bright green foliage. Climbing canes reach 10 to 12 feet. The plant is somewhat tender and susceptible to mildew. Introduced in 1964.

- **'Piñata':** Large-flowered climber. One of the most colorful climbers, this very heavy bloomer has yellow flowers edged in vermilion that grow in clusters, sometimes with as many as 15 blooms each. The roses have 25 to 30 petals and a slight fragrance. Its foliage is lush, shiny, and green. Introduced in 1978.

- **'Shadow Dancer':** Large-flowered climber. These ruffled, double blooms (15 to 20 petals), in swirling shades of light and dark pink, have a mild fragrance. You get the deepest colors in climates with mild summers. The plants have glossy green foliage on 6- to 8-foot high canes, which grow larger in mild-winter climates. Introduced in 1998.

Caring for Climbers

Climbing roses need a little different care than most other roses, particularly when it comes to pruning, training, and winter protection. You can find more information about those subjects in Chapters 19 and 20.

Otherwise, watering, fertilizing, and controlling pests on climbers is similar to doing all those things to other types of roses. See Part IV of this book for the details.

'Paradise' Hybrid Tea

'Double Delight'; fragrant

© Saxon Holt

'Dainty Bess'

© Saxon Holt

'First Prize'

© Saxon Holt

'Opening Night'

© Saxon Holt

'Timeless'

© Saxon Holt

'Ingrid Bergman'

© Saxon Holt

'Fragrant Cloud'; fragrant

'Sunset Celebration'

'Just Joey'; fragrant

'Midas Touch'; fragrant

© Saxon Holt

'Brandy'

© Scott Millard

'Artistry'

© Saxon Holt

'Sutter's Gold'; fragrant © Saxon Holt

'Sheer Bliss'; fragrant © Saxon Holt

'John F. Kennedy' © Saxon Holt

'Diana, Princess of Wales' © Saxon Holt

Roses make outstanding flowering shrubs. As shown here, they combine well with other flowering shrubs, such as azaleas.

© Saxon Holt

Roses can add color to any border, or you can build your garden around roses.

© Saxon Holt

Grandifloras

'Queen Elizabeth'; fragrant

© Saxon Holt

'Crimson Bouquet'

© Saxon Holt

'Gold Medal'; fragrant

© Saxon Holt

'Tournament of Roses'

© Saxon Holt

'Escapade'

© Saxon Holt

'Betty Prior'

© Saxon Holt

'China Doll' Polyantha

© Saxon Holt

'**Sun Flare**' © Scott Millard

'**Eyepaint**' © Scott Millard

'**Brass Band**' © Scott Millard

'**Amber Queen**' © Saxon Holt

'Livin' Easy'

© Saxon Holt

'Singin' in the Rain'

© Saxon Holt

'Intrigue'; fragrant

© Saxon Holt

'Sexy Rexy'

© Saxon Holt

'Simplicity'

© Saxon Holt

'Class Act'

© Saxon Holt

'Impatient'

© Saxon Holt

'Purple Tiger'

© Saxon Holt

'Betty Boop'

© Saxon Holt

'Carefree Beauty'

© Saxon Holt

'Leonardo de Vinci' Romantica rose   © Saxon Holt

'Marie Louise' Damask rose; fragrant   © Saxon Holt

Autumn Damask *R. damascena bifera*;   © Saxon Holt
fragrant

Rosa soulieana Species rose   © Saxon Holt

'Blanc Double de Coubert'   © Saxon Holt
Hybrid Rugosa

'Black Jade' © Saxon Holt

'Kristin' © Saxon Holt

'Scentsational'; fragrant © Saxon Holt

'Rainbow's End'

© Saxon Holt

'Gourmet Popcorn'

© Saxon Holt

'Incognito'

© Saxon Holt

'William Baffin'

© Michael MacCaskey

'Joseph's Coat' climbing
and close up

© Saxon Holt

'Dortmund'   © Saxon Holt

'America'; fragrant   © Saxon Holt

'Fourth of July';
fragrant   © Saxon Holt

'Chrysler Imperial' Hybrid Tea

© Saxon Holt

'Sunsprite' Floribunda

© Saxon Holt

'Mister Lincoln' Hybrid Tea

© Saxon Holt

'Scentimental' Floribunda

© David Cavagnero

Set off by perennials and hedges, roses are the star attraction here.

© Saxon Holt

Combine various sizes and shapes of roses in borders to create walls of color.

© Saxon Holt

'Country Dancer' © Saxon Holt

'Bonica' © Saxon Holt

'Fair Bianca'; fragrant © Saxon Holt

'Graham Thomas'; fragrant © Saxon Holt

'Henry Hudson'; fragrant

© Scott Millard

'Morden Blush'

© Michael MacCaskey

'Flower Carpet' Shrub

© Saxon Holt

'Heritage'; fragrant © Saxon Holt

'Carefree Wonder' © Scott Millard

'Cherry Meillandecor' © Saxon Holt

'Belle Story' © Saxon Holt

'Knock Out' © Saxon Holt

Rust disease

© Michael S. Thompson

Blackspot disease

© Michael S. Thompson

Powdery mildew disease

© Michael S. Thompson

Beetles

© Michael S. Thompson

Aphids on rose buds

© Michael S. Thompson

© Saxon Holt

A climbing rose in early spring before (top) and after pruning

© Saxon Holt

© Saxon Holt

Contrasting an unpruned and pruned (right) Hybrid Tea

© Saxon Holt

'Europeana' Floribunda © Saxon Holt

'Altissimo' Climber © Saxon Holt

'Showbiz' Floribunda © Saxon Holt

'Olympiad' Hybrid Tea © Saxon Holt

'Gizmo' Miniature © Saxon Holt

'Yellow Doll' Miniature

© Saxon Holt

Yellow Lady Banks
Rosa banksiae lutea

© Saxon Holt

'Graceland' Hybrid Tea

© Saxon Holt

'Windrush' Shrub; fragrant

© Saxon Holt

'Fame!' Grandiflora © Saxon Holt

'Touch of Class'
Hybrid Tea © Saxon Holt

'First Light' Shrub © Saxon Holt

'Judy Fischer' Miniature © Saxon Holt

'Jeanne Lajoie' Climbing Miniature © Saxon Holt

'Baronne Prévost' Old Garden -
Hybrid Perpetual; fragrant © Saxon Holt

'Alba Meidiland' Shrub

© Saxon Holt

'Honor' Hybrid Tea

© Saxon Holt

'Iceberg' Floribunda

© Saxon Holt

'Mt. Hood' Hybrid Tea

© Saxon Holt

'Pascali' Hybrid Tea

© Saxon Holt

'Mary Marshall' Miniature © Saxon Holt

'All That Jazz' Shrub © Saxon Holt

'Medallion' Hybrid Tea; fragrant © Saxon Holt

'Sarabande' Floribunda © Saxon Holt

'Octoberfest' Grandiflora © Saxon Holt

'Stainless Steel'
Hybrid Tea
© Saxon Holt

'Moon Shadow'
Hybrid Tea; fragrant
© Saxon Holt

'Angel Face'
Floribunda; fragrant
© Saxon Holt

'Wise Portia' Shrub
© Saxon Holt

'Lavender Dream' Shrub
© Saxon Holt

'Winsome' Miniature
© Saxon Holt

'Tiffany' Hybrid Tea; fragrant   © Saxon Holt

'Regensberg' Floribunda; fragrant   © Saxon Holt

'Peace' Hybrid Tea   © Saxon Holt

'Child's Play' Miniature   © Saxon Holt

'Halo Today' Miniature   © Saxon Holt

The pink 'Dainty Bess' makes a charming addition to any garden. Climbing up the wall in the background is the old-fashioned Noisette 'Mme. Alfred Carrière'.

© Michael MacCaskey

Chapter 13

Shrub Roses

· ·

· ·

Shrub roses are a diverse group of plants that don't neatly fit into any of the other rose categories. Shrubs, especially the modern ones, are very popular because of their long season of bloom, pest and disease resistance, and versatility in the landscape.

A Shrub by Any Other Name . . .

When we say that shrubs are a diverse group of plants, we really mean it. Many of these rose plants are more different than they are alike. Some are neat, compact little plants that stay about 3 feet high. (See Figure 13-1.) Others are upright giants that you'd swear would reach the clouds if you didn't whack them back once in a while. Still others are low-growing, sprawling plants that can grow to 10 to 12 feet wide.

To further complicate things, many roses that really don't need to be called shrubs often are. This is true with some floribundas and climbers. And then some rose growers call their shrubs landscape roses. In fact, some mail order catalogs group shrubs by landscape use, such as shrubs for ground covers, tall shrubs for hedges, and so. It can be a bit confusing.

Oh well — no matter. Shrubs are great roses with great flowers, as shown in Figure 13-2. Their diversity translates into versatility in the landscape, and we get to that a bit later in this chapter.

Figure 13-1:
A compact
shrub rose.

Figure 13-2:
Shrub roses
produce
beautiful
flowers in
addition to
being versa-
tile in the
landscape.

Even though shrub roses are diverse, some that resulted from the same breeding programs have similarities, such as the following groups:

- **Hardy shrubs:** Several breeding programs have concentrated on creating hardy shrubs for cold climates. These shrubs include Buck hybrids, such as 'Prairie Princess' and 'Applejack', which were bred by Dr. Griffith J. Buck at Iowa State University, and the Morden and Explorer (which are made up of varieties named after famous explorers) shrub roses from Canada. Most of these hardy shrubs can withstand temperatures down to –15° to –25°F (–26° to –32°C) and lower and have excellent disease resistance.

- **Meidiland roses:** These roses originate in France, from the renowned Meilland hybridizers. Most are sprawling plants that are useful as ground covers or hedges. They are good repeat bloomers, have excellent disease resistance, and are generally hardy to about –10°F (–23°C).

- **David Austin English roses:** These shrubs are meant to combine the ever-blooming characteristic and disease-resistance of modern roses with the flower form and fragrance of old roses. They've been selected by the famous rose hybridizer, David Austin. The problem is that they don't always keep that promise. Although many are beautiful roses, some varieties do not rebloom and are prone to disease, especially black spot. Also, many Austin roses are very vigorous plants that get huge, especially in mild-winter climates. So choose carefully. Most varieties are hardy to about 0°F (–18°C).

- **Generosa roses:** These could be called a French version of David Austin's English roses. Developed by one of France's oldest nurseries, Roseraie Guillot, plants tend to be smaller than the Austins, have equal or stronger fragrance, and have good disease resistance (although black spot can be a problem where summers are hot and humid). Most varieties are hardy to about 0°F (–18°C).

- **Flower Carpet:** These roses are well-behaved, spreading plants that make especially good ground covers. They are very free-blooming, disease resistant, and easy to care for. Flower Carpet roses are generally hardy to –10°F (–23°C).

Taking It Easy

Most shrub roses are easy-to-grow roses that can get by on little care, other than regular watering and occasional fertilizer. You can find out more about watering and fertilizing in Chapters 17 and 18, respectively.

Shrub roses can get along fine without much pruning, but you still want to deadhead them (remove the faded flowers) to keep them blooming over the entire season. A light shearing in late winter or early spring (earlier in mild climates, later in cold climates) keeps them compact. Otherwise, prune to keep some of the large varieties in bounds. For more on pruning, see Chapter 19.

Many shrub roses are grown on their own roots (see Chapter 15 for more information) and are pretty hardy, if not extremely so. But you still want to mound soil over their base in cold winter climates to protect them from freezing and thawing and to ensure that not all the above-ground parts are killed if the temperature gets really cold.

Shrubs in the Landscape

Shrub roses really come into their own as landscape plants. If you're thinking about planting any flowering shrubs, think hard before you overlook shrub roses. Plants like 'Carefree Beauty', 'Carefree Delight', 'Knockout', and the 'Flower Carpet' roses are tough to top when it comes to amount of bloom and ease of care. And they're versatile in the landscape. You can use sprawling types as ground covers and upright ones as hedges, and the smaller ones are ideal for pots, perennial borders, and low hedges. Chapter 5 lists specific varieties of shrub roses for various landscape uses.

Shrub Roses by Color

The following sections list the best of the most widely available shrub roses. (Hybrid rugosa roses, described in Chapter 14, are very hardy, useful shrubs, too. So you may want to check that chapter, as well.)

Red shrubs

These useful shrub roses have red flowers:

- **'Champlain':** Small blooms with 30 petals are cherry red edged with a darker red and slightly fragrant. The repeat-blooming flowers grow abundantly on a very hardy, compact bush with dark green leaves that reaches about 3 feet high. Introduced in 1982.

- **'Cherry Meillandecor':** Sometimes called 'Cherry Meidiland', these single, red flowers with white centers have little fragrance but a long bloom season. Growing at least 3 to 4 feet high and 3 feet wide, the plant is useful as a hedge. It is also disease resistant and hardy. Introduced in 1995.

- **'Flower Carpet Red':** Large clusters of deep red, ruffled blossoms with 25 to 30 petals and bright yellow stamens have little fragrance but generously bloom on a compact plant that grows about 2 to 3 feet high and 3 to 4 feet wide with deep green, disease-resistant foliage. Introduced in 2000.

'John Cabot': Bright red, medium-sized flowers with 40 petals are borne in fragrant clusters on a vigorous, arching shrub with yellowish green arching foliage. Very hardy. Introduced in 1978.

'John Franklin': Medium red, fragrant flowers with 25 petals bloom in clusters. The bushy, upright plant reaches 3 to 4 feet high, has round foliage and excellent disease resistance, and is very hardy. Introduced in 1980.

'Knock Out': AARS 2000: This top-notch landscape rose produces non-stop deep cherry-red flowers with 5 to 7 petals and a light fragrance. The compact, bushy plant has lustrous, deep green foliage and is exceptionally resistant to black spot.

'La Sevilliana': A profuse-blooming Meidiland rose that covers itself with fiery red, double blooms all season and red hips into winter. The upright, broad bush (5 feet tall and 4 feet wide) has bright, bronze foliage and makes an excellent traffic barrier or hedge, but is not hardy below −10°F (−23°C). Introduced in 1978.

'L. D. Braithwaite': David Austin English rose. Burgundy red, fully double blooms are cupped and open at the center. This rose is always in bloom during the growing season. The vigorous-growing and slightly spreading plant can reach 5 to 6 feet high and 6 to 7 feet wide. Introduced in 1987.

'Prospero': David Austin English rose. Dark red to purple flowers with more than 40 petals are large, flat, and very fragrant. Foliage is dark green on an upright plant, which grows 4 to 5 feet high. 'Prospero' is an excellent in mild-winter climates. Introduced in 1982.

'Prairie Fire': Pointed buds open into bright red flowers with a white base. Fragrant flowers with eight to ten wavy, heavily textured petals are almost always in bloom in enormous clusters — 35 to 50 blooms — on long stems. The bush is vigorous and tall (about 6 feet high) with dark, glossy foliage. Very hardy and disease resistant. Introduced in 1960.

'Red Meidiland': Rich, red blooms with white centers and five petals almost hide the bright foliage on this graceful bush. The flowers have no fragrance but start blooming in late spring and repeat blooming all season. Orange-red seed hips (rose fruits that form after the flowers) remain in the fall. The vigorous bush has a mounded shape and is winter hardy. It grows 1 to 2 feet high, 5 to 6 feet wide and works well as a ground cover. Introduced in 1989.

'Red Rascal': Cup-shaped flowers with 35 petals bloom in small clusters. The slightly fragrant flowers are good repeat bloomers. Foliage is small, light green and glossy, and resists mildew. The bushy plant makes a nice hedge, 3 to 4 feet high. Introduced in 1986.

‘**Red Ribbons**’: New England Rose Trials Award 1996. A vigorous, excellent ground cover with dark red, semi-double flowers that appear in huge quantities. ‘Red Ribbons’ is a good bloomer and grows well in difficult spots. The plant grows 2½ feet tall and about 4 feet wide, has good disease resistance, and is very winter hardy. Introduced in 1990.

‘**Scarlet Meidiland**’: Slightly fragrant, bright, cherry red blooms of small, ruffled flowers (15 to 20 petals) grow in huge clusters on a fast-spreading bush that makes an excellent groundcover. The plant can spread up to 6 feet in the season after planting and attain a height of 3 to 4 feet. It has glossy, disease-resistant leaves and is winter hardy. Introduced in 1987.

‘**Tradescant**’: David Austin English rose. This many-petaled deep crimson rose has an intense, sweet fragrance and is an excellent landscape rose. The compact plant reaches only 2½ to 3 feet high in cold climates, twice as high in warmer areas. Introduced in 1993.

Pink shrubs

So many pink shrubs to choose from: You can’t miss with any variety with ‘Carefree’ in the name or ‘Bonica’.

‘**Ambridge Rose**’: David Austin English rose. Apricot pink, double (up to 100 petals) blossoms have a strong fragrance. The plant is bushy and medium sized, about 3 to 4 feet high. Introduced in 1990.

‘**Baby Blanket**’: A tough ground cover with light pink, double flowers, ‘Baby Blanket’ has good repeat bloom. The shrub grows about 2 to 3 feet high and spreads about 5 feet wide, and is disease resistant. Introduced in 1991.

‘**Bibi Maizoon**’: David Austin English rose. Lovely rose-pink, double blooms are round and cabbage-like in the bud and cup-shaped when fully open. The pleasantly fragrant compact plant reaches at least 4 feet high and equally wide, with long, arching canes. Introduced in 1989.

‘**Bonica**’: AARS 1987. The first shrub to win the AARS award, this Meilland rose (sometimes sold as ‘Bonica Meidiland’) has small, ruffled, warm pink blossoms with 35 petals that open in clusters all summer. Fragrant and very free-blooming, the plant produces long, arching canes that reach about 4 feet high with glossy, deep green foliage. Beautiful as a hedge or planted in groups, ‘Bonica’ is highly disease resistant and winter hardy.

‘**Carefree Beauty**’: All that the name implies, this rose practically laughs at adversity. Large, pink, mildly fragrant flowers with 18 to 24 petals blanket the bushy, full plant all season. The plant’s bright, apple-green foliage is disease resistant and winter hardy. It grows about 6 feet high. Introduced in 1977.

◉ **'Carefree Delight':** AARS 1996. Slightly fragrant pink flowers with five petals and a bright white eye open each day of the growing season and disappear after blooming — no need to deadhead. The bush grows in a spreading mound, 2 to 3 feet high, and is winter hardy and disease resistant. 'Carefree Delight' is a consistent performer in all climates. Introduced in 1996.

◉ **'Cymbaline':** David Austin English rose. Light pink blooms with a strong fragrance have 35 petals. This is a slightly spreading plant 4 to 5 feet high with medium green leaves. Introduced in 1982.

◉ **'David Thompson':** Large and very fragrant red blossoms with bright yellow stamens have 25 petals. The plant grows upright, but is fairly rounded in appearance. Growing about 3 feet high and equally wide, this rose is disease resistant and very hardy. Introduced in 1979.

◉ **'Dove':** David Austin English rose. This low-growing plant has pink buds resembling those of a hybrid tea that open to rosette tea-like white blooms with a blush center. It has a light tea fragrance and, with somewhat glossy foliage, is considered to have above-average disease resistance. Introduced in 1984.

◉ **'English Sachet':** Light pink blooms have an old-fashioned, cupped and quartered form with 40 to 50 petals and a strong, sweet fragrance. The plant has medium green foliage and grows about 5 feet high. Introduced in 2000.

◉ **'First Light':** AARS 1998. The very free-flowering, light pink, single blossoms with dark red stamens have a mild, spicy fragrance. The compact shrub, reaching 2 to 4 feet high, has bright green foliage and excellent disease resistance.

◉ **'Flower Girl':** This light pink and cream semi-double with 8 to 15 petals has a mild apple scent. Generous repeat blooms grow in huge, drooping clusters. This medium size, 2 to 3 feet high, slightly spreading plant has good disease resistance. Introduced in 2000.

◉ **'Fuchsia Meidiland':** One of the first roses to bloom in the spring, this plant continues to bloom until frost. Covered with small, semi-double blooms of a startling fuchsia pink, the canes spread to a width of 4 feet, but the height is only 1½ to 2 feet, making the shrub an ideal ground cover or mass planting. Covered with shiny, bronzy green foliage, this rose is extremely disease resistant. Introduced in 1991.

◉ **'Gartendirektor Otto Linne':** Deep pink, slightly drooping flowers with 25 to 35 petals bloom in clusters, providing a nice contrast to the glossy, apple-green leaves. This repeat bloomer has a moderate fragrance. The upright, bushy, and spreading plant is winter hardy and disease resistant and can climb in mild climates. Introduced in 1934.

'Gertrude Jekyll': David Austin English rose. Bright pink blooms gently trail to pale pink edges. Fully double flowers provide strong perfume, though poor repeat bloom. The very vigorous plant can easily reach over 10 feet high in mild-winter climates. Introduced in 1986.

'Heritage': David Austin English rose. Clear, shell pink flowers with a cupped form have 40 or more petals and are extremely fragrant. This vigorous upright, bushy shrub with small, dark, glossy leaves, blooms recurrently throughout the season, and reaching at least 5 feet in height. Introduced in 1985.

'Lady of the Dawn': Large, light pink, semi-double flowers have 10 to 15 ruffled petals and a slight fragrance. The upright bush reaches at least 4 feet with big, dark green, leathery leaves and arching canes. Introduced in 1984.

'Lilian Austin': David Austin English rose. Named in honor of the hybridizer's mother, this rose produces cup-shaped, salmon-pink blooms with 33 petals in profuse clusters early in the season with reliable repeat blooms. The spreading, arching shrub has dark, glossy leaves. The plant needs winter protection where winter temperatures drop below −10°F (−23°C). Introduced in 1973.

'Mary Rose': David Austin English rose. This shrub produces abundant cup-shaped, rose-pink flowers with a gentle fragrance and good rebloom. Vigorous and wide, the bush can work as a hedge. Introduced in 1983.

'Mix'n'Match': Lovely soft pink blossoms are borne in large clusters. A semi-double with 10 to 15 petals. 'Mix 'n' Match' has a mild fragrance. The plant is slightly spreading with deep green, disease-resistant foliage. Introduced 2000.

'Morden Centennial': Developed at the Morden Research Station in Manitoba, Canada, this rose is really winter tolerant. Rarely out of bloom, the plant is dressed in clusters of clear pink, lightly perfumed blossoms with 50 petals and dark red hips. The bush is vigorous and bushy with dark green foliage. It is rugged and disease resistant and hardy to −40°F (−40°C). Introduced in 1980.

'Pink Flower Carpet': Deep pink flowers with a lighter reverse grow in large sprays. The cup-shaped flowers have 15 petals and a light fragrance. The low, spreading bush has small, dark green, glossy foliage that is disease resistant, a vigorous grower, and winter hardy. Introduced in 1991. 'Appleblossom Flower Carpet' has a lighter pink bloom.

'Pink Meidiland': The single, deep pink blossoms with big, white eyes bloom dependably and freely. The five petals have no fragrance. The plant is bushy and clean-looking, reaching 2 to 4 feet high, and is disease resistant and winter hardy. Introduced in 1985.

'Prairie Dawn': Bright pink, double flowers give you a good repeat bloom. The compact, very hardy plant with excellent disease resistance reaches about 5 feet high. Introduced in 1959.

'Prairie Joy': Medium pink flowers with 30 to 40 petals and a light fragrance are borne singly and in sprays. The tall, bushy plant with sparse foliage is a repeat bloomer and very hardy and disease resistant. Introduced in 1990.

'Prairie Princess': This princess blooms profusely with clusters of large, pastel pink, semi-double flowers in late spring. It rests a while and then blooms again, and repeats this blooming pattern all summer. This lightly perfumed rose makes an excellent cut flower. The upright, vigorous bush has dark, leathery leaves, is highly disease resistant and very hardy. Introduced in 1972.

'Queen Margrethe': Large flowers with over 50 petals of pure pink exude a delightful fragrance and is always in bloom. The compact, 2 to 3 feet high, round bush with bright, glossy foliage is disease resistant. Introduced in 1991.

'Royal Bonica': This Meidiland rose is always in bloom, producing clusters of small, long-lasting, rosy-pink double blossoms with a light fragrance. Easy to care for, 'Royal Bonica' is winter hardy and disease resistant. It grows about 5 feet high and equally wide, making it a good hedge candidate. Introduced in 1994.

'Sharifa Asma': David Austin English rose. Elegant, cup-shaped, many-petaled blossoms form a perfect rosette of delicate blush pink with a strong fragrance. It repeats blooming. The compact bush reaches about 3 feet high. Introduced in 1989.

'Sparrieshoop': A beautiful and popular rose, the fragrant blooms with five to seven petals open into a saucer shape, showing golden stamens. It blooms in clusters in spring and fall. The upright, tall, very vigorous bush with green, leathery leaves grows about 6 to 8 feet high and makes a fine hedge. It is also disease resistant and winter hardy. Introduced in 1953.

'Watermelon Ice': Large clusters of pink to lavender-pink blooms have 15 petals and a slight fragrance. The care-free, ever-blooming shrub grows about 18 inches high and twice as wide and has good hardiness and disease resistance. It is often grown as a ground cover. Introduced in 1996.

Orange shrubs

You have five to choose from, and all are great, especially the one with the musical name:

- ❁ **'Abraham Darby':** David Austin English rose. Large, fully double (50 to 100 petals) blooms come on like gangbusters all summer long. Delicate apricot tones and a rich fragrance create a delicious effect on the bush or in a vase. Tall to 6 feet high, moderately bushy, and vigorous, the plant is ideal for training its long, arching canes on a fence. The foliage is a shiny green, and the winter-hardy plant is noted for having long, red prickles. Introduced in 1985.

- ❁ **'Alchymist':** The yellow blooms are shaded with orange or red. Large flowers have many petals and a nice fragrance. The vigorous, upright plant grows to about 6 feet high and has deep green leaves tinged bronze. It blooms only in spring. Introduced in 1956.

- ❁ **'All That Jazz':** AARS 1992. Luminous, poppy-orange flowers with five to ten petals and a light scent are highly visible against the dark, super-glossy leaves. The bush is upright and tall and almost impervious to disease and winter weather. You can see it in "Orange Favorites."

- ❁ **'Perdita':** David Austin English rose. Blushing, billowy apricot blooms grow in small clusters among glossy green leaves. The continual blooms have at least 40 petals. The bushy, medium-sized plant is about 3 feet high. 'Perdita' won the Harry Edland Medal for fragrance from the English Royal National Rose Society in 1984, but some gardeners have been disappointed, unable to detect a scent. Introduced in 1983.

- ❁ **'Tamora':** David Austin English rose. Small clusters of medium-sized, apricot-yellow, cup-shaped blossoms have more than 40 petals and are very fragrant. Small, dark green leaves adorn the medium-sized, bushy shrub. Introduced in 1983.

Yellow shrubs

Here are the best shrubs with yellow flowers:

- ❁ **'Baby Love':** The bright yellow, single flowers (5 petals) have a light licorice scent. This very free-flowering plant is exceptionally disease resistant, especially to black spot. Glossy dark green foliage decorates the medium-sized, 3 to 5 feet high, upright plant. Introduced 1992.

- ❁ **'English Garden':** David Austin English rose. The double (50 to 100 petals), yellow blooms with a pleasing apricot-yellow center, tightly packed petals, and intense fragrance flowers profusely and is a repeat bloomer. The upright, bushy plant with pale green leaves grows at least 3 feet high. Introduced in 1990.

🌹 **'Golden Celebration':** David Austin English rose. Large coppery yellow, very double blooms with distinctive curved and wavy petals have a sweet, honey-like fragrance. Dark green foliage adorns a 4- to 5-foot shrub. Introduced in 1992.

🌹 **'Golden Wings':** American Rose Society Gold Medal 1958. 'Golden Wings' blooms early and remains in flower longer than most roses. Clusters of five-petaled, slightly fragrant, light yellow blossoms open into a saucer shape, showing bright gold stamens. The leaves on this upright, vigorous bush are dull and light green, and prone to black spot. The 4- to 6-foot bush is winter hardy. Introduced in 1956.

🌹 **'Graham Thomas':** David Austin English rose. The large, cupped, deep yellow, double (50 to 100 petals) blooms are richly fragrant. The first bloom in late spring is abundant. Subsequent blooms tend to be fewer in number and sit on top of tall stems that can reach over 8 feet in climates with a long season. Ruthless pruning helps to keep the flowers lower. Disease resistance varies, but the bush is winter hardy. Introduced in 1983.

🌹 **'Sunny June':** Daffodil-yellow, single-petaled blooms blanket this shrub all season long. The lightly scented flowers have five to seven petals. The hardy, vigorous bush can stand alone or be trained to a trellis, and climbs upwards of 8 feet high in milder climates. 'Sunny June' produces her best flowers in cool temperatures. Introduced in 1952.

🌹 **'Windrush':** David Austin English rose. Light yellow, semi-double blossoms with golden stamens grow abundantly on a strong, bushy plant. The flowers are large and very fragrant. One of the earliest to bloom in the spring, this repeat bloomer has medium-sized, light green foliage. The shrub grows vigorously to at least 5 feet high and is equally wide. Introduced in 1984.

White shrubs

Here's an extremely diverse and useful group of white-flowering shrub roses:

🌹 **'Alba Meidiland':** The large clusters of pure white flowers (shown among "White Favorites") loaded with over 40 lightly scented, ruffled petals blooms profusely throughout the summer. The old petals drop off completely, making deadheading unnecessary. The dark, glossy foliage makes a vivid contrast against the white flowers. The low, spreading bush, 2 to 3 feet high and twice as wide, is an excellent ground cover and requires no pruning. It is disease resistant and winter hardy. Introduced in the United States in 1987.

PHOTO OP

🌸 **'Fair Bianca':** David Austin English rose. Combining the extremely fragrant perfume of an antique rose with the repeat bloom of a modern rose, the large, cupped, fully double blooms of pure white, satiny petals open into a saucer shape. The foliage on this bushy, upright plant is shiny and bright green; new growth is reddish. One of the better English roses for a small garden, the shrub rarely exceeds 3 feet high and remains about as wide. This rose is an excellent addition to any garden viewed at dusk. Introduced in 1982.

🌸 **'Nevada':** White, with five petals sometimes tinged pink or splashed with red on the backsides, the big, big flowers are up to 5 inches across. 'Nevada' blooms abundantly in spring and fall, but has little fragrance. The upright, arching, bushy plant reaches at least 6 to 8 feet high. Leaves are small and gray-green and prone to black spot, but it is winter hardy. Introduced in 1927.

🌸 **'Pearl Meidiland':** Small, double flowers begin as soft pink blooms and then fade to a pearly white. They grow profusely and continuously in large clusters. Abundant dark green, glossy foliage covers the low, spreading plant which grows about 2 to 3 feet high and twice as wide. This excellent ground cover is disease resistant and winter hardy. Introduced in 1989.

🌸 **'Pillow Fight':** Huge clusters of small, white, double (about 35 petals) blooms have a strong, sweet fragrance. A seedling of 'Gourmet Popcorn', 'Pillow Fight' has bigger flowers. The bush has glossy, deep green foliage and grows about 2 to 4 feet high. Introduced in 2000.

🌸 **'Sally Holmes':** The lightly fragrant clusters of large, single (5 petals) white blooms have a touch of apricot in the bud. The vigorous, spreading plant has glossy green leaves. Treat it as a climber in mild-winter areas — its canes can grow over 15 feet long. Introduced in 1976.

🌸 **'Sea Foam':** This care-free, low-spreading shrub produces lightly scented, double, creamy white flowers abundantly and continuously. The plant is disease resistant, vigorous, and covered with small, shiny, dark leaves. It makes a good ground cover when given plenty of room, and you can also use it as a climber or a huge hedge. Introduced in 1964.

🌸 **'Snow Shower':** Small blossoms with 40 or more petals bloom in small, fragrance-free clusters. The diminutive, glossy, dark green leaves help give 'Snow Shower' the appearance of a sprawling miniature. The low and spreading plant barely reaches a foot high which makes it an excellent ground cover. It is also beautiful in hanging baskets and pots. Introduced in 1993.

🌸 **'White Flower Carpet':** A white-flowering form of 'Flower Carpet', this free-blooming plant gets by on a minimum of care. Double flowers have a light, sweet fragrance. It reaches about 2 feet high and is equally wide and is hardy and disease resistant, making for a good ground cover or container plant. Introduced in 1996.

❀ **'White Meidiland':** Heavily petaled (more than 40), snow-white blossoms grow in abundant clusters on arching, spreading canes. This repeat bloomer is lightly fragrant with lots of glossy, rich green foliage. The plant grows about a foot high and 5 feet wide and can be used as a ground cover. It is disease resistant and winter hardy, though it performs best in mild climates. Introduced in 1987.

Lavender shrubs

Shakespeare must have loved lavender roses. Why else would so many of his characters congregate here? You can see 'Lavender Dream' and 'Wise Portia' under "Lavender Favorites" in the color section.

❀ **'Lavender Dream':** Dainty, lilac-pink flowers with no fragrance are produced continuously in clusters on smooth, thornless stems with small, shiny leaves. The plant is mounded and bushy, and its arching canes reach more than 5 feet long and spread even wider. It has excellent disease resistance. Introduced in 1985.

❀ **'Othello':** David Austin English rose. Large, cupped, fully double blooms begin as crimson and then fade to purple. This repeat bloomer is extremely fragrant. The strong plant grows upright to at least 6 to 8 feet high with stiff canes covered with dark green leaves. Introduced in 1986.

❀ **'The Prince':** David Austin English rose. Velvety, rich, royal purple flowers have a heady perfume. Fully double blooms have a cupped, rosette form. The compact plant reaches about 2 to 3 feet high and is a good choice for smaller gardens. Introduced in 1990.

❀ **'Wise Portia':** David Austin English rose. Heavy-textured blooms with 40 petals display lovely shades of purple and mauve with golden centers. This repeat, abundant bloomer emits a rich fragrance. The bushy plant is about 4 feet high with dark, glossy leaves. Introduced in 1982.

Multicolored shrubs

Color preference should guide your choices among this kaleidoscope of shrub roses, but 'Carefree Wonder' is one fine plant.

❀ **'Carefree Wonder':** AARS 1991. This rose is amazingly care-free with superb disease resistance and hardiness. The large flowers are bright pink with a white eye and a creamy reverse. They practically cover the plant all season long. Lightly scented, they have 25 to 30 petals. The 4- to 6-foot bush has abundant, bright green leaves and grows in an upright, mounding fashion, and performs well everywhere. Introduced in 1990.

❀ **'Evelyn':** David Austin English rose. Full flowers (over 40 petals) with an apricot-pink color open into a rosette form. The roses appear in small clusters and are very fragrant. The plant is upright and bushy, at least 3 to 5 feet high, with glossy green leaves. Introduced in 1991.

❀ **'Kaleidoscope':** AARS 1999. Unusual shades of tan, lavender, and pink adorn this medium-size, double (25 to 30 petals) with a lightly sweet fragrance. The medium sized, upright plant grows 3 to 4 feet high and has deep, glossy green foliage.

❀ **'Oranges & Lemons':** The yellow blossoms are splashed with orange stripes so distinct that it seems as if someone painted them on. Moderately fragrant flowers have 30 to 35 petals. New foliage is mahogany red and ages to a deep green. The plant is a vigorous grower with tall, arching canes shaped like a fountain. You can train it to climb in milder climates, and it produces more blooms in cool weather. Introduced in 1992.

❀ **'Pat Austin':** David Austin English rose. The two tone copper, double bloom — bright copper on the inside of the petals, yellowish orange on the outside — emits a sweet, old-fashioned fragrance. The compact plant grows 3 to 5 feet high. Introduced 1995.

❀ **'Ralph's Creeper':** Dark orange-red flowers with a bright yellow eye and a yellow or white reverse grow in open clusters on a low, spreading bush. The blooms have 15 to 18 petals and a moderate scent. The bush grows about 30 inches high and 5 feet wide and has small, dark green foliage. Introduced in 1987.

❀ **'Rockin' Robin':** Lively blend of pink-, red-, and white-striped flowers with 45 to 50 ruffled petals. A mild, apple fragrance accompanies this free-blooming, mounding, 2 to 4 feet high plant with glossy green foliage. It has good disease resistance. Introduced in 1997.

Chapter 14

Antique Roses

● ●

● ●

*I*n the other chapters in this part of the book, we describe mostly modern roses — roses that originated in the 20th century. But those roses make up really only a fraction of all roses. The rose family is not unlike your family: You represent only one generation, which was preceded by many others. Your family tree stretches back for centuries, and so does that of the modern rose.

Roses that preceded modern varieties are the *species roses* and *old garden roses*. Both groups are sometimes referred to as *antique roses*. These roses are an incredibly diverse group of plants, with great variety in plant *habit* (the size and shape), flower form, and fragrance. Some have historical importance; others were useful to hybridizers as breeding stock to create modern rose varieties. Still others, such as the *rugosas,* are still used in breeding today to create new and better hybrids.

Species and old garden roses have always been popular. Some of the many reasons for this popularity include:

✔ The rugged toughness of many of the plants

✔ The singular beauty of their flowers

✔ The intensity of their fragrance

✔ A certain wildness that sets them apart from the more well-behaved, modern roses

Making a difference

To make the distinction between species roses and old garden roses clear (or at least somewhat more so): A species rose is a rose just as nature made it. You can still find many species roses growing naturally in various parts of the world. Each species rose has a specific botanical name, for example, *Rosa rugosa.* If you cross a species rose with itself, the roses that grow from the seed are identical, or nearly so, to the parents and to each other. Variants do occur; flower color may be a little different, or the plant may have a slightly different habit. If the variation is positive, someone (a nursery or rose lover) may propagate it and give it a variety name. For more information on variety names and propagation, see the Introduction and Chapter 22, respectively.

Exactly what makes an old garden rose an old garden rose is fairly precise. Any class of roses known to be in existence in 1867 is an old garden rose. So, many species roses are also old garden roses.

Old garden roses are most often descended from a mixed background of natural or created hybrids, and when you plant their seeds, the resulting plants are different from each other and from the parents, although there may be some family resemblance.

If that isn't confusing enough, we also throw in some classic shrubs here. Roses like hybrid rugosas and hybrid musks could also be listed in Chapter 13 on shrubs, but because they are so closely related to their parent species, we include them here. Besides, you usually find these roses sold by the same sources that sell species and old garden roses (see Appendix C for sources).

With these qualities come some drawbacks, however. For example, some species and old garden roses are very vigorous plants that literally can take over a small garden. Others are shy bloomers. In fact, many bloom only once a season. And some are extremely prone to disease.

So, you have to choose your species and old garden roses with care, especially if you're just getting into roses. And that's what this chapter is all about — selecting old roses that give you that wonderful antique quality without turning into garden monsters.

Old Families of Rosedom

Many old garden roses are a historical botanist's nightmare, with mixed origins and seemingly untraceable heritages. For the rest of us, their backgrounds and parentage can be downright dumbfounding. Suffice it to say that early rose growers and plant collectors loved to collect species in the wild and create new roses by crossing everything they could get their hands on. The results brought about the lovely modern roses you grow today.

The following sections list the main types of old garden roses. We describe our favorite varieties of each type, grouped by flower color. To be honest, some of the varieties may be considered modern roses by some (it's that classic shrub thing again). But, you know what, who cares? The difference of opinion is just another indication of how confusing this whole thing can be. If you really want to get to the bottom of antique roses, a degree in paleontological botany at Harvard is a good start.

Alba roses

These roses are thought to be hybrids between *Rosa damascena* or *Rosa gallica* and a white-flowering form of the dog rose, *Rosa canina.* Though once popular in Europe, few varieties are widely available today. Flowers generally range from white to pink, and are very fragrant, blooming primarily in spring. Plants grow upright to about 6 feet and are generally very hardy.

Pink

The color looks delicate, but the plant is very tough.

- **'Königin von Dänemark':** Clear pink flowers, with up to 200 petals, have a deeper pink center that resembles a button. This extremely weather-tolerant rose has an intense perfume and flowers once annually. The highly disease-resistant and hardy upright bush forms a mounded shrub 4 to 5 feet tall with blue-green foliage and large scarlet hips. Introduced in 1826.

White

Tall and imposing, 'Mme. Plantier' graces any garden with fragrance and beauty.

- **'Mme. Plantier':** Not for a small garden, 'Mme. Plantier' is a large, dense, arching bush that you can train as a climber. She sends out clusters of extremely fragrant, pompon-like blooms with over 200 petals once, early in the summer. The plant grows 6 to 8 feet tall with smooth, long, medium green leaves, and is disease resistant and winter hardy. Introduced in 1835.

Multicolored

This very shrubby plant gives your garden a wonderful aroma in the spring.

- **'Félicité Parmentier':** Ivory buds, tinged green, open into fluffy, very double, pink-and-cream flowers of exceptional fragrance. The flowers arrive in abundance in the spring on a compact, 4-foot-tall and equally wide bush with gray-green leaves. Disease-resistant but occasionally susceptible to mildew, this plant grows well in a variety of climates and is winter hardy. Introduced in 1834.

Bourbon roses

Bourbons originated on the island known as L'Ile de Bourbon (now Reunion Island) in the Indian Ocean. They are generally vigorous plants with a compact, shrubby, or slightly climbing habit. Bourbons are useful as hedges. The blooms are pink to red, cupped, and nicely fragrant. The plants are hardy to about 5°F (–15°C) without protection. Unfortunately, they are very susceptible to black spot.

Pink

Pretty in pink, and fragrant to boot, these roses make scents in any garden:

- **'Mme. Ernest Calvat':** Light pink petals twirl and swirl, creating a petticoat effect. The flowers are double, large, cupped, and intensely fragrant and bloom lavishly in late spring and again in autumn. The upright, bushy plant grows 5 to 7 feet tall and has dark, glossy leaves, which are susceptible to black spot. It is likely to be damaged by temperatures below –10°F (–23°C). Introduced in 1888.

- **'Mme. Isaac Pereire':** The parent of 'Mme. Ernest Calvat,' these flowers are large, double, cupped, and intensely fragrant. It blooms lavishly in late spring and again in autumn. The upright, bushy plant grows 5 to 7 feet tall and has dark, glossy leaves, which are susceptible to black spot. The bush is likely to suffer winter injury when temperatures dip below –10°F (–23°C). Introduced in 1880.

- **'La Reine Victoria':** Cupped, double, intensely fragrant flowers are rosy pink, shading to a deep pink on the outer petals. Flowers abundantly early to mid-summer and then again in the fall. The blooms last a long time whether on the plant or cut. The plant is upright and slender, 4 to 6 feet tall, with soft, dull-green leaves. It tolerates heat well and is disease resistant and winter hardy. Introduced in 1872.

- **'Louise Odier':** Deep pink, cupped flowers are very full and fragrant with 35 to 45 petals. It blooms from spring to fall and keeps well as a cut flower. The bush is slender, and 4 to 6 feet tall with light green foliage that is winter hardy. Introduced in 1851.

- **'Souvenir de la Malmaison':** Immense, wonderfully fragrant blooms start out cupped and then open flat. The flowers are the palest of pinks — a cream blush — with rose shading at the center and 65 to 75 petals. It repeats blooming steadily throughout the season. The bush is compact, 2½ feet tall and wide, with large, leathery leaves. The climbing form reaches 8 to 12 feet tall. This plant does not like wet weather and is hardy to –10°F (–23°C) and moderately disease resistant. This extremely popular rose is one difficult to establish in a garden. Introduced in 1843.

- **'Zéphirine Drouhin':** You can safely plant this rose along walkways because it is almost thornless. It is also very fragrant and produces peppermint-pink, loosely cupped blossoms with 20 to 24 petals all season. The plant is a climber, and grows up to 8 to 12 feet. It has medium green, glossy leaves and is shade-tolerant and winter hardy. It is subject to black spot and mildew. Introduced in 1868.

White

For the illusion of snowballs in summer, plant 'Boule de Neige'.

- **'Boule de Neige':** The name means "snowball" in French; that's what these flowers look like when they're in full bloom. Made up of about 100 petals, the outer petals curl inward, giving the flower a big ball effect. The bush of this fragrant repeat bloomer is 4 to 5 feet tall, upright, and slender with dark, leathery leaves. It is also disease resistant and winter hardy. Introduced in 1867.

Multicolored

Make room in your garden for this large, colorful rose bush:

- **'Honorine de Brabant':** Pale lilac blossoms striped in crimson and violet grow abundantly in spring and autumn on a large, bushy plant. The flowers are richly fragrant, full, and double. The bush grows to 6 feet tall and is covered with medium green foliage. The plant is disease resistant and winter hardy. Date of origin not known, probably mid-19th century.

Centifolia (Cabbage roses)

The true cabbage rose (see Figure 14-1) is *Rosa centifolia,* whose flowers have very thin, overlapping petals, making each one look somewhat like a small head of cabbage. But there is actually a group of roses called *centifolias* which have similar flowers. (In fact, any rose with a flower that looks like a cabbage could be called a cabbage rose, but shouldn't be. Or should it? Help! Get us out of this!) The flowers have a spicy fragrance. The plants bloom once in spring in pink to purple shades. Plant habit varies from shrublike to spreading. Most are hardy to –15°F (–26°C) without protection.

Pink

Tall and fragrant, either of the following can tickle your fancy.

Figure 14-1:
A cabbage
rose.

- **'Fantin-Latour':** Loads of petals (maybe 200) range from pale to deep pink. One profuse, annual flowering produces blooms with an intense fragrance. The upright, vigorous bush is 5 to 6 feet tall with smooth, light green leaves. It is disease resistant and winter hardy. Introduced around 1850.

- **'Tour de Malakoff':** Double flowers with about 55 petals are intensely fragrant. They begin as pink but age to mauve and bloom only once in a season. The plant is vigorous, sprawling, and 6 to 7 feet tall, disease resistant, and winter hardy. Introduced in 1856.

China roses

China roses, descendants of *R. chinensis*, contributed many of their good characteristics, including repeat bloom, disease resistance, and a compact habit, to various modern roses. The variety 'Minima', with its dainty leaves and small flowers, is the forerunner of modern miniature roses. Chinas are excellent in pots, and as edgings. However, they lack hardiness and are tough to grow without winter protection if you live where temperatures drop below −15°F (−26°C).

Red

This low-growing bush produces highly scented roses.

- **'Archduke Charles':** Intensely fragrant blossoms appear all season on this low bush with sparse, red-green, glossy leaves. As is typical of Chinas, the petal color intensifies with age. Rosy pink, double blooms with 35 to 40 petals become deep, marbled red. The plant is vigorous and bushy, growing 2 to 3 feet tall, and is disease resistant but not winter hardy. Introduced in 1840.

Pink

Choose either of these for repeat blooming throughout the season:

- **'Hermosa':** Rarely out of bloom, producing clear pink, double flowers with 35 petals in clusters from spring until frost. As the flowers age, they take on darker tones of crimson. The shrub is compact, growing 2 to 3 feet tall with small blue-green leaves. It is moderately disease resistant and hardy to −10°F (−23°C). Introduced before 1837.

- **'Parsons' Pink China':** Also called 'Old Blush,' this plant is one of the China roses that contributed its repeat-blooming characteristics to modern roses. The fragrance-free, cupped, pink flowers have 24 to 30 petals and bloom continuously in loose clusters. You can plant them in masses or in containers. The bushes are 3 to 5 feet tall with pointed, glossy leaves and are moderately disease resistant; winter hardy to −10°F (−23°C) with winter protection. Introduced in 1752.

Lavender

This relatively small bush produces large, scented flowers all season.

- **'Eugène de Beauharnais':** Bears large, wonderfully fragrant, purple, double flowers all season. The 3-foot-tall plant is bushy and very disease resistant. Not winter hardy below 10°F (−12°C) without protection. Introduced in 1838.

Damask roses

These roses date all the way back to early Greek civilization. Their clustered flowers are intensely fragrant and come in shades of white, pink, and red. The plants are very hardy and don't need winter protection until temperatures drop below −20°F (−29°C). They have thorny stems and usually bloom only once a year.

Pink

Ranging from pale pink to almost lavender, these damask roses offer variety in color and habit.

- ✪ **'Autumn Damask':** Medium pink, double flowers with a rich fragrance bloom in clusters in the spring and then again in autumn. The plant is compact enough to be grown in a container — 3 to 5 feet tall and 2 to 4 feet wide. The foliage is dull green and rough, and the plant is winter hardy. Also known as the 'Rose of Castile', 'Four Seasons Rose', and 'Quatra Saisons'. Introduced prior to 1819.

- ✪ **'Celsiana':** Pale pink, semi-double flowers have 12 to 15 crinkled petals and a nice fragrance. Foliage is gray-green on a vigorous, upright plant that reaches about 4 to 5 feet. Introduced prior to 1750.

- ✪ **'Ispahan':** Also known as 'Pompon des Princes', these bright pink, double flowers have an intense fragrance and bloom over a long period. The plant has small green leaves and grows about 4 feet high and equally wide. It can be trained as a climber. Introduced prior to 1830.

- ✪ **'Marie Louise':** A lovely mauve-pink rose that the Empress Josephine grew at Malmaison. The flowers are large, very double, with many petals and an intense fragrance. 'Marie Louise' blooms only once a year, in spring. The plant is full-foliaged, reaching about 4 feet high. Introduced prior to 1813.

White

'Hardy' is her name, hardy is her game:

- ✪ **'Mme. Hardy':** 'Mme. Hardy' is a study in style. Elegant, tight buds open to lush, snow-white flowers with an eye-catching green point in the center (called a *pip*). The blooms occur in clusters, with the center blossoms opening first. The flowers have probably 200 petals and are richly fragrant. The plant is sturdy and vigorous, covered with ample gray-green leaves. Growing 5 feet tall, this rose is disease resistant and winter hardy. Introduced in 1832.

Multicolored

Red and white, or white and red — you choose:

- ✪ **'Léda':** Soft, fragrant flowers with 200 petals are white, edged in red, and bloom once in the summer. The bush is low, 2 to 3 feet tall, and grows in a spreading, trailing fashion. The bush can be trained upright as a climber (see Chapter 5 for more information), is disease resistant, and winter hardy. Introduced before 1827.

- ✪ **'York and Lancaster':** For history buffs, this rose is an interesting one — named after rival families in 15th-century England. The emblem of York was the white rose (White Rose of York), the emblem of Lancaster, the red rose. The battles between York and Lancaster for the English throne came to be known as the Wars of the Roses.

The war seems to be still going on in this rosebush — the white and pink petals battle for dominance. Some flowers may be half pink and half white, and others are almost all one color or the other. The fragrant blossoms have 24 to 30 petals formed in a loose cup shape. They bloom once in the summer on a 3- to 4-foot-tall bush with rough, gray-green leaves. Not a vigorous plant; it's rather a slow grower, but it is disease resistant and winter hardy. Thought to have originated in 1551.

Gallica roses

Various forms of *Rosa gallica* have been grown for centuries, and some have interesting histories (see the description of *Rosa gallica officinalis* later in this chapter). The red, pink, or purple flowers are intensely fragrant, have showy yellow stamens, and are followed by bright red hips. The foliage turns red in the fall. Plants are stiffly upright but have a neat, shrub-like habit. They are very hardy to at least –20°F (–29°C).

Red

History and beauty combine in this useful flower.

⊛ *Rosa gallica officinalis:* This flower is the "Red Rose of Lancaster," used as the badge of the Lancasters during the Wars of the Roses in England. The plant has been in cultivation since before 1300. Also known as the Apothecary's Rose, it is used in fine potpourris, preserves, syrups, and medicinal powders.

The intensely fragrant flowers are light crimson with 12 to 18 petals and bloom once, in late spring. The bush grows 3 to 4 feet tall with green, rough foliage and has a tendency to sport. (See "Moss roses" for a definition of *sport*.) They are disease resistant and winter hardy.

Pink

Fit for a queen, the 'Empress' graces any garden.

⊛ **'Empress Josephine':** The Empress Josephine's gardener grew this rose in her palace gardens and named the flower after her. Luminous pink, with deeper pink tones toward the center, the ruffled blooms have a papery quality and 24 to 30 petals. This slightly fragrant flower blooms once per year. The upright, compact bush is 3 to 4 feet tall with narrow, gray-green leaves. It's winter hardy and disease resistant. Introduced prior to 1824.

Lavender

'Charles' may not give you consistent color from bush to bush, but he does provide consistent beauty.

⚜ **'Charles de Mills':** 'Charles de Mills' has been known to flower in many variations of purple and red: maroon, crimson, grape, wine, and violet. The fully opened, fragrant blossoms have about 200 swirling petals and a flat-topped appearance because the petals are so evenly spaced. Only one bloom occurs, midseason, on the upright, vigorous bush, which is 4 to 5 feet tall and 5 feet wide with rough green leaves. It is disease resistant and winter hardy. Origin date is unknown, probably 19th century.

Multicolored

You can't miss with these striped, fragrant flowers.

⚜ **'Camaieux':** In spring this plant produces rose-pink-and-white-striped blossoms with 65 petals on its compact, rounded bush. Wonderfully fragrant, the flowers are cupped and camellia-like. The bush grows 3 feet tall and wide and is easy to grow, although it is prone to mildew in warm, humid regions. It is winter hardy and was introduced in 1830.

Hybrid musks

Another group with a confusing background, most hybrid musks can be traced to the musk rose, *Rosa moschata*. The flowers have that strong, musky fragrance that most people call old rose fragrance. Most hybrid musks are vigorous, spreading plants that are best treated as climbers, but some are more like shrubs. They can be considered modern roses (don't set us off again) and bloom most heavily in spring and fall. Most varieties bloom in shades of pink, and many produce bright orange hips. Hybrid musks tolerate more shade than many other roses and need winter protection where temperatures drop below –15°F (–26°C).

Pink

For a spot that gets only filtered light, take your pick of these pinks:

⚜ **'Ballerina':** Perpetually blooming clusters are covered with masses of small, fragrant, pale pink flowers with white centers and five petals. Some say the compact, arching bush with thick foliage achieves the effect of a ballerina's skirt. The plant gets tiny orange-red hips in the fall, and tolerates filtered light. It grows 4 to 5 feet wide and about as tall, and you can train it as a low climber. It is hardy to –10°F (–23°C) and is prone to mildew. Introduced in 1937.

‘**Felicia**’: Large clusters of very fragrant, pink, double flowers grow repeatedly on long, arching canes. ‘Felicia’ tolerates filtered light well. The plant is 5 feet tall with glossy green foliage and is hardy to –10°F (–23°C). Introduced in 1928.

Multicolored

This wide bush gives you clusters of flowers throughout the season.

‘**Nymphenburg**’: A most beautiful and fragrant rose, salmon-colored flowers, shaded yellow at the base, are borne in clusters all summer. The blooms have 18 to 24 petals, and the bush has large, glossy leaves and grows 4 to 7 feet tall and 6 feet wide. It is vigorous and disease resistant. Introduced in 1954.

Hybrid perpetuals

The heritage of these roses is pretty confusing. Hybrid perpetuals were popular in the 19th century, prior to the development of the hybrid tea. The fragrant flowers come in shades of pink, purple, red, and sometimes white. They're great in bouquets. They bloom best in spring, but you often get some flowers throughout the summer — hence the name perpetuals. Plants are vigorous with arching canes and need protection where winter temperatures drop below –20°F (–29°C).

Red

For a truly red red rose, choose one of these:

‘**Henry Nevard**’: A rugged, hardy bush that produces loads of dark red, aromatic flowers with 30 petals all season. Reaching 4 to 5 feet tall, the bush has dark, glossy leaves. It is winter hardy and disease resistant. Introduced in 1924.

‘**Hugh Dickson**’: Fragrant, deep crimson, double blossoms with 38 petals are always in bloom until hard frost on this easy-to-grow bush. The plant reaches 5 to 6 feet tall and is disease resistant. Introduced in 1905.

‘**Linda Campbell**’: Large clusters of deep red, semi-double flowers with contrasting yellow stamens and 25 petals are borne on arching stems 6 to 8 feet tall. It's a good repeat bloomer that grows best in heat and has lovely, textured gray-green foliage. It can develop mildew in coastal conditions. Introduced in 1990.

Pink

All are pink, all are fragrant — take your pick:

- ❀ **'Baroness Rothschild':** Cupped, fragrant blossoms with pale pink outside petals (40 of them), offset by deep pink inside petals, bloom profusely in spring and then again in autumn. Usually produces one flower per stem with lots of foliage surrounding the blossom, and makes long-lasting bouquets of cut flowers. The upright, bushy plant grows 4 to 6 feet tall and has light green leaves. Introduced in 1868.

- ❀ **'Baronne Prévost':** Candy-pink blooms with a silvery reverse flower continually until frost. It has a classic old-rose shape — big, flat, open flowers with many tightly packed petals (about 100 of them) — and a rich perfume. Tall, erect plant is 4 to 6 feet tall and bushy, winter hardy, and disease resistant. Introduced in 1842.

- ❀ **'Heinrich Münch':** Soft, pink blooms, with 50 petals, measure up to 7 inches across and are exceptionally fragrant. Occasionally repeat blooms. The 4- to 5-foot-tall bush is very vigorous. Introduced in 1911.

- ❀ **'Paul Neyron':** Tightly packed with deep pink petals (65 to 75 of them), this fragrant rose blossoms lavishly in late spring and then again in autumn. The bush has glossy green leaves, grows to 5 or 6 feet, and is winter hardy but prone to mildew. Introduced in 1869.

White

Warm summer nights bring out the best in this missus.

- ❀ **'Frau Karl Druschki':** Very large, full flowers of pure white bloom in early summer and again in the fall. The slightly fragrant blooms, which have 30 to 35 petals, open best with warm summer nights. The plant grows 5 to 7 feet tall, has dark olive-green leaves, and is disease resistant and winter hardy. Introduced in 1901.

Multicolored

Pink and white stripes adorn this ever-blooming plant:

- ❀ **'Vick's Caprice':** This reliable, repeat-blooming rose with cup-shaped, large, double, pink-and-white-striped flowers is pleasantly fragrant. The bush grows 4 feet tall and less wide, and is not reliably disease resistant. Introduced in 1891.

Moss roses

In their true form, moss roses (see Figure 14-2) are naturally occurring mutations — called sports (*sports* are shoots that mutate naturally and produce a different rose, so that the same bush may have one or more variations) — of *Rosa centifolia* and damask roses. They get their name from the small hairs on their stems and the bottoms of their flowers. (However, now almost any rose that has mossy hairs is called a moss rose.) The flowers are double, come in shades of white, pink, and red, and are very fragrant. Early moss roses bloom only in spring, but newer hybrids are good repeat bloomers; hardiness varies.

Figure 14-2:
A moss
rose.

Pink

Tougher than they look, both these bushes are hardy and disease resistant.

❀ **'Alfred de Dalmas':** Also known as 'Mousseline' because the petals resemble a delicate French muslin. Light blush pink, cupped blooms with 55 to 65 petals fade to white. Blooms repeatedly in clusters, and has a strong perfume. Compact, spreading bush is 2 to 3 feet tall with a sparse, brownish moss on stems.

❀ **'Maréchal Davoust':** Deep pink flowers, with a lighter pink reverse, have 100 petals and are wonderfully fragrant. The plant blooms once in early summer. The upright, vigorous bush is 5 feet tall and bears some sparse moss. Introduced in 1853.

Noisette roses

These roses are historically important because they contributed orange and yellow shades to many modern climbing roses. You're usually better off treating these plants as climbers, and supporting them with a trellis or fence. They are not hardy plants and, if you don't protect them, they suffer damage in temperatures below freezing. Flowers are fragrant and come in shades of white, cream, yellow, orange, and sometimes red.

Red

This bush may spread its dark red flowers throughout your garden:

- **'Fellenberg':** Bright crimson flowers with 35 petals in a cupped form. The bush grows vigorously and tends to spread. Grows 3 to 5 feet high. Introduced prior to 1835.

Yellow

Dramatic color in both the rose and its foliage make this a stand-out:

- **'Alister Stella Gray':** The buds are dark orange-yellow, the color of egg yolks, and open to honey yellow, fading to cream. Richly perfumed and almost perpetually in bloom, the flowers show well against lush green foliage. Grows 7 to 12 feet tall. Can be trained as a climber. When grown as a bush, the plant forms a mound about 5 feet tall and 5 feet wide. Disease resistant. Not winter hardy below 10°F (–12°C). Introduced in 1894.

White

Intensely fragrant, both of these whites do better in warmer climates:

- **'Jeanne d'Arc':** Dainty-looking yet vigorous, with an intense fragrance, 'Jeanne d'Arc' displays countless white, semi-double blossoms in clusters, with an especially fine bloom in the fall. Red hips often appear along with the flowers. The plant grows 5 to 8 feet tall and needs a warm climate, so it doesn't grow in areas where it gets colder than 10°F (–12°C). Introduced in 1848.

- **'Mme. Alfred Carrière':** One of the most fragrant roses. The gardenia-shaped blossoms — pearly pink aging to cream — have 35 petals and are borne continuously in clusters. The 10- to 15-foot-tall bush is vigorous, upright, and arching. An excellent climber, or pillar rose, it is also disease resistant and hardy to –10°F (–23°C) with winter protection. Introduced in 1879.

Portland roses

These roses have a mixed heritage with traces of China, damask, and gallica roses in their background. Although few are grown today, they were once loved for their repeat blooming and their very fragrant, multipetaled flowers, usually in shades of pink. The original plant from France was named *Rosa portlandica,* hence the name. You may be able to find one of the following varieties if you look hard.

Red

This royal red beauty is worth a search:

 'Rose du Roi': One hundred rich, velvet-red petals make for a regal flower. Add the intense fragrance and continuous bloom, and you have a prince of rosedom. The bush is compact and upright with glossy green leaves, and is disease resistant and winter hardy. Introduced in 1815.

Pink

Whether you call it "he" or "she," this rose is a stunner:

'Jacques Cartier': Also known as 'Marchesa Boccella', this richly fragrant rose blooms continuously, producing clear pink flowers with hundreds of petals resembling powder puffs. The compact, upright plant, 2 to 4 feet tall, has closely spaced, light green leaves and is winter hardy. Introduced in 1842.

Rugosa roses

Rugosas (derived from *Rosa rugosa*) and their many hybrids are tough, extremely useful shrub roses valued for their spicy scent, attractive crinkled foliage, disease resistance (a good thing too, since many rugosas don't take well to chemical sprays), and hardiness (they are among the hardiest roses, able to withstand temperatures down to –35°F [–37°C] with little protection). Actually, some of the newer hybrids can be, and often are, included in the category of modern shrub roses, but to us they're classic shrubs. They are compact plants, 4 to 8 feet high, which bloom in spring and fall in shades of white, pink, red, purple, and yellow. Many varieties produce colorful hips. (See Figure 14-3.)

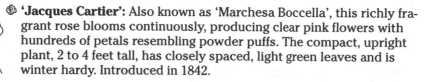

Figure 14-3:
A rugosa
rose.

Red

A couple of fine reds:

- ✿ **'F. J. Grootendorst':** Small, red, semi-double flowers, resembling carnations, grow continuously on mounded shrubs that are 4 to 5 feet tall and wide. The blooms have a slight fragrance and 25 petals. The foliage is bright green and crinkled. Disease resistant, they may develop some black spot by the end of the season. They are winter hardy. Introduced in 1918.

- ✿ **'Linda Campbell':** Large clusters of deep red, semi-double flowers with contrasting yellow stamens and 25 petals are borne on arching stems 6 to 8 feet tall. It's a good repeat bloomer that grows best in heat and has lovely, textured gray-green foliage. It can develop mildew in coastal conditions. Introduced in 1990.

Pink roses

You can choose how much scent you want among these fragrant pinks.

- ✿ **'Belle Poitevine':** Lilac-pink, semi-double flowers with pleated petals bloom continuously on a 4- to 6-foot shrub. This extremely fragrant flower with lush, dark, textured leaves gets large, red hips in fall. It's winter hardy and disease resistant and does not need pruning. Introduced in 1894.

- ' **Pink Grootendorst':** This small, lightly scented, rose-pink flower blooms continuously. Its 25 petals are lightly toothed, or serrated, resembling carnations. Mounded shrubs grow 4 to 5 feet tall and wide and are disease resistant and winter hardy. The foliage is bright green and crinkled. Introduced in 1923.

- **'Sarah Van Fleet':** These extremely fragrant pink blossoms, with 18 to 24 petals and showy yellow stamens, bloom repeatedly all summer. The 6 to 8 foot bush is upright and vigorous with dark green, leathery, patterned leaves and makes an excellent hedge. It is disease resistant and winter hardy. Introduced in 1926.

- **'Thérèse Bugnet':** Produces abundant large, rose-red, double blossoms that are outstandingly fragrant and have 35 to 40 petals. This repeat bloomer is round and shrubby and covered with quilted gray-blue-green leaves. Exceedingly disease-resistant and winter hardy, this rose is recommended for all climates. Introduced in 1950.

Yellow

This gem of a rose is fragrant, reblooming, requires no deadheading, plus it has a nice, mellow color.

- **'Topaz Jewel':** The first reblooming yellow rugosa rose. The frilly, light yellow blossoms, which have 25 petals, emerge all season in scented clusters on the arching, dense bush. Old flowers drop off cleanly. The 5-foot-tall and 7-foot-wide bush has is disease resistant and winter hardy. Introduced in 1987.

White

These white roses are all repeat bloomers and very hardy.

- **'Blanc Double de Coubert':** Ruffled, snow-white, intensely fragrant blossoms, with 18 to 24 petals, appear early in the season and repeat their performance later. Spent blooms tend to hang on, looking a little like dirty white socks. The bush is upright and vigorous and grows 4 to 6 feet tall with light green, leathery leaves. It is disease resistant and very winter hardy. Introduced in 1892.

- **'Henry Hudson':** Large white flowers with showy yellow stamens are very fragrant. This repeat bloomer has 25 petals and the plant has a low, bushy growth pattern. It's very hardy and disease resistant. Introduced in 1976. You can see it pictured with our favorite white roses.

- **'Sir Thomas Lipton':** Double, cupped, white blooms grow abundantly and repeatedly throughout the season on a vigorous, bushy plant. Leathery, dark green foliage adorns a very hardy bush that grows 6 to 8 feet tall. Introduced in 1900.

Lavender

The flowers are more purple than lavender, and the bush's leaves turn bronze in autumn.

◉ **'Hansa':** This tall, arching shrub produces plentiful, intensely fragrant, purple-red blooms in late spring, with good repeat blooms. The flowers have 35 to 45 petals in a loose, cupped form. Large red hips appear in late summer, adding to the interest this plant provides in a garden. The shrub grows 6 to 7 feet tall and wide and is covered with green, wrinkled leaves that turn bronze in the fall. It is disease resistant and winter hardy. Introduced in 1905.

Scotch roses

Scotch roses (sometimes referred to as *hybrid spinosissimas*) are attractive shrubs with white, pink, or yellow, mostly single, blooms. Many varieties have handsome, finely cut, or crinkled foliage and colorful hips. These plants require winter protection in areas that get colder than –15°F (–26°C).

Pink

Both of these roses are notable for their pink-plus blooms:

◉ **'Frühlingsmorgen':** Pink, saucer-shaped blossoms with amber centers reveal startling maroon stamens. A fragrant and profuse bloom in late spring of flowers with five to seven petals is not repeated. The 5- to 7-foot bush is upright, arching, and vigorous with soft, dark green leaves. It is disease resistant and winter hardy. Introduced in 1942.

◉ **'Stanwell Perpetual':** Light pink, fading to white flowers bloom singly on very short stems and have 45 to 55 petals. Fragrant flowers bloom repeatedly after the plant is well established in the garden. The bush is attractive, vigorous, and spreading, with small, blue-green leaves. It grows 3- to 5- feet tall and is disease resistant and winter hardy. Introduced in 1838.

Yellow

Catch the gorgeous show this plant puts on in the spring:

◉ **'Frühlingsgold':** In full bloom, 'Frühlingsgold' puts on quite a show, covering the plant with large, fragrant, saucer-shaped flowers of pale yellow with a lemon glow at the center. The blooms, which have five petals, show themselves only once — in late spring. The bush is upright, arching, and vigorous with soft green leaves. It's disease resistant and winter hardy. Introduced in 1937.

Species roses

Various species of rose (a *species* is a plant that, when crossed with itself, produces seedlings that are identical to the parent and to each other) are native throughout most of the northern hemisphere and don't fall into the neat rose classes described here. They are a diverse group of plants that have contributed many valuable characteristics to modern roses through natural and planned selection.

Pink

Light pink flowers grace the tall bushes of these roses:

- ✿ *Rosa eglanteria:* Light pink blooms with five petals show off bright yellow stamens in one annual blooming. Both the flowers and leaves are scented — the flowers have a true rose fragrance, the leaves smell of sweetbriar (hence the common name, sweetbriar rose). Clusters of bright red hips appear in fall. The upright, vigorous bush, with copious, glossy green foliage, reaches 8 to 10 feet. It is disease resistant and winter hardy. In cultivation before 1551.

- ✿ *Rosa roxburghii:* Also known as the chestnut rose because the hips resemble chestnuts. Light pink, paper-like blossoms appear early in the season in cool locations and continuously in warmer climates. Outer petals open to reveal a mass of 45 to 55 shorter, central petals. The bush is upright but irregularly shaped, reaching 7 to 9 feet tall. Leaves are long and narrow and regularly spaced, like a ladder. It is disease resistant but not winter hardy. Introduced prior 1841

Orange

Fragrant and old, this rose has a distinctive coppery color:

- ✿ *Rosa foetida bicolor:* Austrian copper rose. Orange-red, simple blossoms with five petals bloom early in the season, giving off a heavy fragrance. The upright plant is irregularly shaped and has rather sparse, dull green leaves. It's prone to black spot and not reliably winter hardy. In cultivation prior to 1542.

Yellow

For sheer size, you can't beat these yellows:

- ✿ *Rosa banksiae lutea:* Also known as a Lady Banks' rose. Large clusters of small, double, yellow, fragrant flowers cover the sprawling, thornless bush in late spring. You can see it pictured with our yellow favorites in the color section. The plant is vigorous and can spread over 20 feet, taking over a yard. It has small, light green leaves and stays evergreen in mild climates.

It's disease resistant, but not winter hardy below 15°F (–9°C), and can be used to climb on sturdy supports such as trellises or as a mounding ground cover. In cultivation since 1796.

Several forms of Banksias exist. 'White Lady Banks' holds several records for size. The largest Lady Banks was planted in 1855 by a homesick bride upon her arrival at a mining camp in Tombstone, Arizona. The bush is growing to this day and covers an 8,000-square-foot arbor.

- *Rosa bracteata* **'Mermaid':** Huge, 5-inch, light yellow, single flowers bloom all season on a vigorous, climbing plant that can reach 30 feet or higher. The saucer-like, single blooms are fragrant. Its leaves are a glossy, deep green and remain evergreen in mild climates. It is disease resistant and hardy to –10°F (–23°C). Introduced in 1918.

- *Rosa harisonii:* Also known as 'Harison's Yellow', this is a tough, hardy, disease-resistant, and drought-tolerant shrub. Deep yellow, semi-double flowers are fragrant and bloom in spring. Rich green, fernlike foliage covers the spreading plant, which can grow to 6 feet. Can grow in poor conditions, including shade, and is fairly hardy. In cultivation since 1830.

- *Rosa hugonis:* Also know as 'Father Hugo Rose,' this plant produces sprays of pale yellow, single flowers with five petals in spring. The blooms, which have little or no fragrance, are borne on arching stems reaching 6 to 8 feet, covered with fern-like, deep-green leaves. It is disease resistant and extremely hardy. Introduced prior to 1830.

White

Have a semi-shady spot calling out for a tall, cool rose? Try this:

- **Rosa soulieana:** This plant bears small, single, white flowers in clusters. The blooms have orange-red hips and little fragrance. The vigorous, arching shrub grows to 10 feet high and can tolerate partial shade. Introduced in 1896.

Tea roses

The original tea rose was a cross between a China rose and *Rosa gigantea*. Remnants of its free-blooming character and shapely flower buds can be found in many modern hybrid teas. (See Figure 14-4.) Fragrant flowers come in shades of creamy white, pink, and yellow. The bushy plants are best adapted to milder climates, where winter temperatures stay mostly above 15°F (–9°C), because they lack hardiness. They do have good disease resistance, however. The first tea roses came from China on ships owned by the East India Trading Company, which carried mostly tea. That alone may be the origin of their name but it may have also been that the long trip actually made the rose smell like tea. By themselves, these roses do not smell like tea.

Figure 14-4:
A tea rose.

Pink

Choose one of these fragrant pinks to match your climate:

- **'Catherine Mermet':** The buds are unusually elongated, and the big, light pink, double flowers have a stiff-fabric quality. The rose blooms on long, drooping stems, which make gorgeous bouquets with a strong perfume. Flowers repeatedly and grows 3 to 4 feet high. Thrives in summer heat. Introduced in 1869.

- **'Duchesse de Brabant':** Very fragrant, pearly pink, cupped flowers with 45 petals grow lavishly on a 3- to 5-foot plant with apple-green, wavy leaves. This flower is one of the first to bloom in the spring and one of the last to quit in fall. Disease-resistant but not reliably winter-hardy, it does well in humid areas and performs best in mild climates, needing little care. Introduced in 1857.

Yellow

Both of these have touches of apricot, but the total effect is vastly different for each:

- ✿ **'Lady Hillingdon':** When the flowers first open, they are a deep apricot, but they fade to cream with lots of sun exposure. Blooms all season, producing masses of cup-shaped, fragrant blossoms with 18 to 24 petals. The leaves are bronze-green, and new foliage is dark plum-purple. The bush form is slow-growing but healthy. The climbing form is more vigorous. Hardy to 10°F (–12°C). Bush grows 4 to 6 feet high and 3 to 4 feet wide; the climber reaches 15 feet. Introduced in 1910.

- ✿ **'Rosette Delizy':** The vigorous, compact plant bears spice-scented blossoms of cadmium yellow edged with deep pink and an apricot reverse. This repeat bloomer has 55 to 65 petals. The plant grows 3 to 5 feet tall and has dark green, glossy leaves. Extremely disease resistant but not winter hardy. Introduced in 1922.

White

Be prepared for many flowers with many petals if you add 'Sombreuil' to your garden.

- ✿ **'Sombreuil':** Incredibly full flowers, with about 100 petals, cover this climbing tea throughout the summer. Fragrant blossoms are creamy white and open flat, displaying their many petals on an upright, vigorous bush with leathery green leaves. The 10-foot-tall or higher bush is disease resistant and hardy to 10°F (–12°C). Introduced in 1850.

Antiques in the Garden

The size and habit of species and old garden roses dictate how you can use them in the landscape. Vigorous types, like Portland roses, can be trained to a fence or arbor like a climbing rose, or left to sprawl over a slope as a ground cover. Shrubbier rose types, like the rugosas, make excellent hedges, or you can mix them in with perennial borders. (See *Perennials For Dummies*, by Marcia Tatroe and the National Gardening Association, also published by IDG Books Worldwide, Inc., for more information about creating perennial borders.) Even though many bloom only once, in the spring, old roses often make up for it by producing colorful hips that last long into winter. Others, like the rugosas and some of the Scotch roses, have attractive foliage that looks good throughout the growing season.

Most antique roses have very interesting flowers. In fact, in many parts of this book, we describe modern roses, such as the David Austin English roses, as having "old rose character." The phrase is not very precise, but it usually means that the flower is flat-topped, rounded, and rather cup-shaped, with many petals. That's quite a bit different from the high, pointed, urn-shaped buds and swirling petals of the classic hybrid tea, to which roses are usually compared.

If you like cut flowers, antique roses are tops. Although most don't have the strong, straight stems of modern hybrid teas, their beautiful flower form makes for a unique bouquet. And, oh, the fragrance! It's not always there, but when it is, it can be overpowering.

Just remember one thing about many species and old garden roses: They usually grow on their own roots; therefore, they often spread like crazy, forming dense thickets. Make sure that you plant these roses where they have plenty of room to grow. If you have any questions about where best to plant, contact the folks at one of the mail-order catalogs that specialize in species and old garden roses. You can find their addresses and phone numbers in Appendix C.

Caring for antiques

Many species and old garden roses need less care than modern roses do. In fact, many seem to thrive on neglect. However, where summers are dry, regular watering is necessary to keep the plants healthy. And almost anywhere, applying fertilizer regularly keeps the plants growing vigorously.

Prune your plants to keep them within bounds and remove dead branches. But, other than that, less pruning is probably better than more. Roses that bloom just once in spring should be pruned after they bloom, if at all. If you prune in winter or late spring, prior to blooming, you remove branches that would otherwise produce flowers. You can prune repeat bloomers in winter to early spring as with other types of roses.

For more information about caring for species and old garden roses, refer to Part IV of this book.

You can't find a good antique just anywhere

Few nurseries and garden centers carry a wide selection of species and old garden roses. For the best selection, you have to order plants from one of the catalogs that specializes in antique roses. Several catalogs are listed in Appendix C, including the Antique Rose Emporium, Vintage Gardens, and Heirloom Old Garden Roses. Even if you don't buy anything, these catalogs make for fun reading.

Old roses meet new technology

Yesterday's Rose, at www.countrylane. com, has pages dedicated to a variety of old, and old-fashioned, garden roses. Though the comments reflect its Washington State (USDA Zone 8) location, the site helps you to hunt down specific roses and offers links to other rose sites.

Via the I Can Garden site, James Bowick lists Canadian sources for Old Roses and Heritage Roses at www.IcanGarden.com/roses/rs1.htm.

The Texas Rose Rustlers site is dedicated to antique roses and includes a great deal of useful information. Reach them at www.texas-rose-rustlers.com.

Part IV
Growing Healthy Roses

The 5th Wave   By Rich Tennant

What I like about this routine, Stacey, is the way Marcos maintains the health of the rose by drooling a liquid rooting hormone from his mouth onto the flower's cut end.

In this part . . .

We get down and dirty in this part, working with roots, soil, planting, pruning, watering, feeding, and bugs. There's no way you come out of these chapters with clean fingernails. But as messy as it may get, this stuff is important. You need to know what to do and what not to do when planting and caring for roses. Read this part slowly and carefully; you may get dirty, but you'll come out smelling like a rose.

Chapter 15

Shopping for Roses

● ●

In This Chapter
▶ Telling the difference between rootstock and own-root roses
▶ Going bareroot or picking potted

● ●

So this rose deal sounds pretty good to you. Maybe you want to get a couple of plants and give it a try. Good decision, but where are you going to get the perfect plants? These days you can buy roses almost anywhere, from supermarkets to drugstores, not to mention the usual places like nurseries and garden centers. You can also shop in the convenience of your own home through mail-order catalogs. (You can find a list in Appendix C.)

But before you rush out waving your credit card, you need a little background information on how roses are grown and sold. You need to take a look at the roots of the whole system, because without good roots, you don't get good roses.

Whose Roots Are These, Anyway?

To really understand how a rose plant gets its start, you need to read Chapters 1 and 22, but basically, most rose plants have two parts: the top part that produces the nice flowers, called the *scion*, and the bottom of the plant that produces the roots, called the *rootstock* (see Figure 15-1). These parts are joined at the *bud union*. During winter, if you slip a small bud from the scion variety, say a 'Mister Lincoln' rose, into the bark of a rootstock, in a few months, the two fuse together and become one plant.

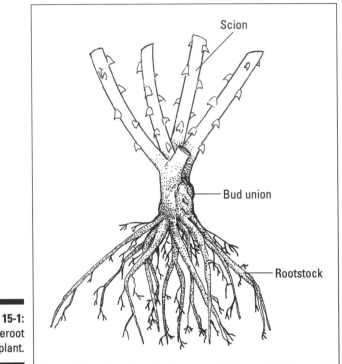

Figure 15-1:
A bareroot
rose plant.

We know why growers want the top of the plant to be 'Mister Lincoln' — it's a great rose. But why do they need the roots of another rose? A rootstock can provide a number of advantages that wouldn't exist if a 'Mister Lincoln' were grown on its own roots, including the following:

- Greater vigor than its own roots can provide

- Resistance to certain soil-borne insects and diseases

- Adaptation to certain soil types

Commercial rose growers choose which rootstock to use (they may have 10 or 15 to choose from), but they don't label them on the plant you buy. That's all you really need to know about rootstocks, except for one other thing: The rootstock roses always live within the plant and may sprout again, except you won't know what variety they are.

Some commercial rose growers propagate rose varieties on their own roots (especially shrub and old garden roses), calling them *own-root roses*. These roses are grown as rooted cuttings and take less time to grow to salable size. Own-root roses can be an advantage in some areas, particularly where winters are very cold. Here's why: Suppose that the weather gets really cold — so cold that the temperature kills the top of your rose plant. The roots, insulated by the soil, live to resprout in the spring. But, if the rose was budded on a rootstock, the new sprouts may come from the rootstock, and you have no idea what variety that is. So instead of the 'Mister Lincoln' roses you had last summer, you get who-knows-what. If, on the other hand, the rose was grown on its own roots, you still have the rose you want.

The way an own-root rose sprouts *true to type* (meaning that it produces the type of flower you expect it to) is also an advantage when you grow shrub or landscape roses that need to be sheared. Pruning often causes the plants to sprout at the base, and if they're on their own roots — you guessed it — the sprouts are the type of rose you want.

Own-root modern shrubs are offered in the same venues as budded roses (the ones with rootstocks). Unless you inspect it very carefully, you don't know whether a plant is own-root or budded. It really doesn't matter, as long as the plant thrives for you.

Own-root roses have a potential downside, especially when you're dealing with a very vigorous shrub or old garden roses. On their own roots, these plants often spread by root *suckers* — sprouts that come from the roots, as shown in Figure 15-2 — and spread is the key word. These sprouts can literally take over a garden. Rootstock roses usually don't produce root suckers, therefore, the plants are easier to manage.

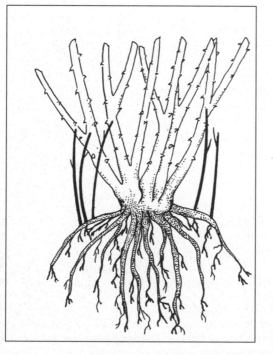

Figure 15-2: A downside to own-root roses is that root suckers can spread all over your garden.

How Doth the Rose Plant Grow?

How your roses come to you dictates how you plant them, so knowing what you're getting into before you buy is important. You can buy roses in three ways: bareroot, potted, or in packages. How you get them depends on where you buy them.

- Some nurseries offer *bareroot roses* (dormant roses with no soil on their roots) early in the season.
- Many garden centers offer potted rosebushes grown in containers.

Commercial growers plant and grow roses in huge rose fields for two years. Most of these large fields are in Arizona, Texas, or California. If you visit Wasco, California, just north of Bakersfield in California's San Joaquin Valley, you can see thousands of acres of rose plants — literally millions of plants. Make your visit in September when the plants are in full bloom, and you'll see and smell one of the most staggering and colorful displays of flowers imaginable.

What are roots without soil? Bare!

Come late fall to winter, when all the roses growing in the commercial fields are going *dormant* (resting) and losing their leaves, the growers prune them and dig them out of the ground, leaving all the soil in the ground, and none on the roses' roots. These roses are called — surprise — *bareroot roses.* Removing all the soil from the roots doesn't hurt the plant. As long as the rose plant is dormant and the roots are kept moist, the plant is in great shape. Plus, without soil, the plant weighs next to nothing — perfect for shipping.

The bareroot roses are then either bundled or packaged individually in plastic, usually with moist sawdust packed around the roots in both cases. Next, the roses are shipped off to retail nurseries all over the world, although they can be put in boxes and shipped directly to gardeners. (Not all the roses are shipped at the same time. In mild-winter climates, bareroot roses are shipped as early as December. In colder climates, the plants are stored until early spring and then shipped.)

Upon arrival, the folks at the retail nurseries unpack the bundled bareroot roses and display them for sale, often in large bins with their roots packed in — you got it — moist sawdust. Actually, the packing can be any lightweight organic matter that holds moisture, including peat moss and wood shavings.

When roses get potted

In many cold-winter and some mild-winter climates, bareroot roses are planted in pots immediately upon arrival. Bareroot roses are fine as long as the weather is cold and the plants are dormant, but if spring warms up and the plants start growing, you have to plant them — and fast. So, in late winter or early spring, that's exactly what most retail nurseries do if they haven't planted them already. Any remaining bareroot plants are potted and sold the rest of the year with their roots growing in black plastic containers filled with soil. You can transfer them to more attractive pots on your own. (See Figure 15-3.)

Some roses, particularly miniatures and old roses, aren't barerooted. Instead, they spend their entire lives in containers. The vast majority of miniature roses are propagated and grown on their own roots in greenhouses and offered for sale in leaf or even in bloom. They usually come in 2 ½-inch or 4-inch pots, ready for transplanting into a garden or into containers for outdoor or indoor culture. A huge variety of miniature roses are sold this way. Larger mail-order rose companies may send you field-grown bareroot miniatures that arrive looking more like big roses than minis. Treat them the same way you do other bareroot roses.

Figure 15-3:
The roots of container roses grow in potting soil. Plant them any time of year.

For the most part, roses go from bareroot to you, or they go from bareroot to pot to you. Some nurseries pot the roses before others, but the process is basically the same. A few wholesale growers even take bareroot roses, plant them in peat pots, and enclose them in plastic or cardboard for shipping. A *peat pot* is a lightweight pot made of pressed peat. You can plant the rose, pot and all, and the peat pot eventually breaks down, allowing the roots to grow out into the surrounding soil. However, the breakdown process takes too long for us. We remove the rose from the peat pot and plant it like any other container plant.

Choosing Bareroot or Potted

Okay, so you can purchase roses two ways: bareroot or potted. How do you make the choice? Read on for a discussion of when each works best.

Buying the best of the bareroot

Buying bareroot has its advantages. In general, these roses are less expensive than those sold in containers. (Obviously, the pot and the soil add to the cost of a container plant.) Bareroot roses are also easier to handle, especially if you buy several plants. So, if you're going to plant a lot of roses, you're better off buying bareroot roses during the dormant season.

Bareroot roses are available during winter and early spring. You can buy them at retail nurseries or garden centers, or, for greater variety, you can purchase from one of the mail-order catalogs listed in Appendix C.

Most mail-order nurseries send you top-quality bareroot plants, and the plants arrive in good condition. If they don't, you're entitled to a replacement. But when you shop in a nursery or garden center, examine the plants closely before you buy. Not that stores are trying to rip you off, but you want to be able to tell what's really a bargain and what isn't. You also need to be able to recognize a plant that's been hanging around too long or has been neglected. Small, shriveled stems and dried roots are sure signs of neglect.

The American Association of Nurserymen set the standards for grading roses. The grades — #1, #1½, and #2 — are based on the size and number of *canes* (branches) on the plant. More and thicker canes means a higher grade.

- ✔ A #1 is the highest-grade rose and represents a more vigorous, sturdy plant that should grow faster and make more blooms the first year after planting.

- ✔ The #1½ and #2 are usually the roses you find on sale at discount prices.

Although you often find good deals among the #1½ and #2 roses, if you want to get off to the best start, we think that you should pay a little extra for a #1. Most roses have the grade listed on the package.

Other things to look for when buying bareroot roses include:

✔ Make sure that the packaging and the roots haven't dried out — a sure sign of trouble ahead.

✔ If you can examine the roots (they may be securely wrapped in plastic and not easy to get at) choose a plant that has a moist, well-developed root system. Avoid those with dry, broken, or mushy roots.

✔ Look for plants with thick, dark green canes — the more the better. Avoid plants that look dry, brownish, or shriveled.

Picking perfect potted roses

Buying roses in containers has its advantages — the main one being that you can get them almost anytime. But you can also buy growing, even blooming plants. These babies are ready to go in the ground immediately and give you instant beauty. Wahoo!

Now, truth be told, in some climates, such as hot-summer areas of the American Southwest, you really shouldn't plant when it's blazing hot. The heat is just too tough on a newly planted rose. (You can find out more about when to plant in Chapter 16.) But if your climate is right, potted plants can give you a great-looking rose garden instantly.

When buying potted roses, keep these points in mind:

✔ The optimal time to buy potted roses is as early in the season as possible, when new growth is minimal.

✔ If you do buy potted roses later in the season, choose plants with healthy, deep green foliage that is free of insects and disease. Vigorous new growth — deep red in many varieties — is a good sign.

✔ In cold-winter climates, don't buy roses way late in the season, even if they're really, really cheap. The plants will go into shock, perhaps irrevocably, when you transplant them into your garden. And they won't have enough time to get established in the garden before winter comes. It's better to buy an expensive rose in the spring that will live than a cheap one in the fall that will die.

✔ Check the soil in the top of the pot. A pot full of twisting, circling roots can be a sign that the plant has been in the pot too long. Skip this plant — it probably won't grow well in the ground.

✔ Flower buds are a good sign. They mean that the plant has been well kept. Choose plants with buds over those that have just finished blooming.

When you understand how to buy roses — bareroot or potted; budded or on their own roots — you're well-rooted in the knowledge you need as you start to think about planting!

Now You've Bought 'Em, What Do You Do with Them?

So you plant your roses as soon as you get them, right? That may seem like good advice, but it's not always practical. What if your bareroot roses arrive in the dead of winter and the ground is frozen solid? Or what if it rains for 40 days and nights? Then what are you going to do?

Storing bareroot roses

Unless you're lucky and the weather is perfect and the ground is soft, you'll probably have to store bareroot roses for some time before you can plant them, particularly if you purchase them through the mail. The key is to keep the plants cool so that they don't start growing and the roots moist so that they don't dry out.

You should inspect bareroot roses, whether purchased through the mail or at a nursery, as soon as they arrive or you get them home. As long as plenty of moist packing is around the roots, rose plants can be stored in a cool (not freezing) place like a garage or basement for a week to ten days (even longer if you have some empty refrigerator space). Keep the top of the plastic wraps open, the roots moist, and don't store the roses in direct sunlight. If you have to store the plants longer, however, completely unpacking them and heeling them in is best.

Heeling in is a way to store bareroot roses by packing their roots in moist (not soggy) soil until planting time. Where and how you heel in your roses depends on how many roses you have and on the soil conditions outdoors.

✔ If you have just a few roses, place them in a bucket or box and pack the roots and top third of the plant with moist sawdust, compost, peat moss, or soil. Store the whole thing in a cool (35° to 40°F or 1° to 4°C) place and check the packing often to make sure that it's moist. Unpack the roses at planting time, being very careful not to do too much harm to the tiny root hairs that may have grown along the main roots.

✔ If you have to store a lot of roses and can work the ground outdoors, dig a shallow trench (about a foot deep), as shown in Figure 15-4, slightly slanted on one side, in a shady area of the garden (like the north side of the house). Lay the roses on a 45-degree angle and pack the roots and the bottom third of the plant with moist soil or compost. Check the packing often to make sure that it's moist. Add water if necessary. Gently remove the roses from the trench at planting time.

Figure 15-4:
If you can't plant bareroot roses immediately when you get them, lay them in a shallow trench and cover their roots with organic matter to heel them in.

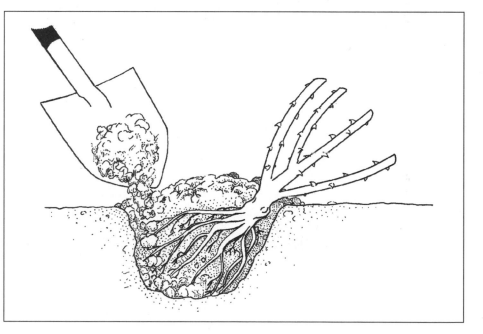

Don't keep roses heeled in much past the earliest planting time in your area, because the plants start to develop fragile new roots and fragile new top growth, both of which can be damaged when you start handling the plants.

Storing potted roses

Potted roses are easier to store until planting time. Just keep the soil moist so that the plants don't dry out. If you store growing roses for more than a week or two, you may want to fertilize them with a diluted liquid fertilizer, following the label instructions.

Of course, you may want to grow your roses in pots or other containers. In this case, you can rest assured that you'll need a bigger pot than the one in which you bought your rose. See Chapter 7 for more information about growing roses in containers.

Once you understand all about buying roses, with bare roots or with roots in soil, budded or on their own roots, you're well rooted in the knowledge you need as you start to think about planting!

Chapter 16

Planting Roses

• •

In This Chapter

▶ Understanding soil types

▶ Improving drainage

▶ Using organic matter to improve soils

▶ Checking and adjusting soil pH

▶ Planting your roses, whether bareroot, potted, or miniature

• •

You're probably ready to get those roses in the ground so that they start growing and, better yet, start blooming! But wait just a minute. First, we need to discuss some timing issues. Also, planting means dealing with dirt — actually, soil in gardeners' parlance. Because that soil will be your rose's home for its entire life, you need to know some things about it before you go rushing outside with your shovel.

The way you plant your roses is the most important step in growing roses. Because they may be living in the place you plant them for many years, you really have only one chance to start them off right. You should pay special attention to soil chemistry, the rose hole, and drainage. If you just skim any chapter in this book, don't let it be this one!

Getting in Touch with Your Inner Soil

We think that any gardener worth his or her salt should have an intimate relationship with soil. You need to grab it, squeeze it, smell it — you need to love it so much that you know everything about it: the good, the bad, and the ugly. Why? Because healthy soil means healthy roots, healthy roots mean healthy plants, and healthy plants mean fabulous flowers.

Provided that drainage is good, roses grow well in most soils. But if you wait until after you plant to find out that your soil has problems, you'll find those problems difficult or impossible to correct.

Basically, soil is a combination of mineral particles and organic matter (the remnants of living things such as leaves, animal waste, and so on). The size of the particles and the amount of organic matter determine soil texture. And your soil's texture determines not only how you plant but also how often you have to water and fertilize.

The ideal soil — and you probably don't have it — is well aerated; space for air in a soil is absolutely necessary for healthy root growth. The ideal soil also retains some moisture and nutrients and drains well (water passes through it freely). Poorly drained soil often becomes water-logged, suffocating roots and killing the plants that try to grow in it.

Although many in-betweens exist, you can conveniently break soils into three types:

- **Clay soils** are made mostly of small mineral particles that cling tightly together. They hang on to water, are slow to dry out, and are poorly aerated.

- **Loamy soils** are a happy mixture of large and small mineral particles, and they usually contain an abundance of organic matter. They are well aerated and drain properly, while still being able to hold water and nutrients.

- **Sandy soils** are made mostly of large mineral particles. Water moves through these soils quickly and, as it does, takes nutrients with it. Sandy soils are well aerated and quick to dry out; they often lack some nutrients that plants need.

You can get a pretty good idea of what kind of soil you have by grabbing a moist handful and squeezing. When you let go, sandy soil falls apart and doesn't hold together in a ball. Clay soil oozes out between your fingers as you squeeze and stays in a slippery wad when you let go. A loamy soil usually holds together after squeezing, but it falls apart easily if you poke it with your finger.

You can also get some idea about your soil by watching what happens when it rains:

- Water passes through clay soils slowly, so rainfall quickly puddles up and drains away slowly. As clay soils dry, they often crack and become hard-crusted.

- Loamy soils maintain just the right amount of moisture — not so little that your plant dries out quickly, and not so much that the roots are swimming.

- Water passes quickly through sandy soils, leaving the soil barely moist.

The quality and texture of the soil just a few inches down may be completely different from the topsoil, however.

Checking below the topsoil — how does your garden drain?

Even though you may have good loam on the surface, something completely different may be 6 to 12 inches (or farther) below. If a big rock or *hardpan* (a compacted or impenetrable layer of soil) lurks beneath the surface, it may prevent water from properly draining away from the root area. And that's trouble.

Check your soil drainage by digging a 12- to 18-inch hole where you want to plant. Fill the hole with water, let it drain, and then fill it again. If the hole takes longer than two hours to drain after the second filling, you have a problem.

You may be able to break through a thin hardpan that's near the bottom of the hole, but you'll probably get a sore back from doing so. If you' recently won the lottery, call a landscape contractor; he or she may be able to install drainage pipes to carry excess water away.

When we encounter bad drainage, we either plant somewhere else or plant in containers or raised beds (see Chapter 7). In areas such as the southeastern United States, where abundant summer rainfall, clay soils, and hardpan make gardeners' lives difficult, planting in containers or raised beds may be the only way to grow roses.

Adding the big O

The big O is *organic matter* — stuff that is or once was alive, such as leaf mold, shredded bark, compost, peat moss, manure, and the like. You can incorporate organic matter into your soil when you plant — it helps to loosen and aerate clay soils, and improves the water- and nutrient-holding capacity of sandy soils. (You can also use organic matter as a mulch to protect your roses at ground level.) If you don't have some organic matter lying around, you can buy one of several different kinds available from your local nursery or garden center.

If you're planting a large area with a lot of roses, you can incorporate organic matter into the whole area with a shovel or rototiller. Just lay down 2 to 3 inches of the stuff and turn it in to a depth of at least 6 to 8 inches.

If you're planting just a few roses, mix in the organic matter with the *backfill soil* — the soil you take out of the hole while you're digging it — and use this mixture to fill in the hole after you plant. If you combine this backfill soil with about 25 percent volume (or more) organic matter, your roses should get off to a better start.

If you have good loamy soil and no problems with excess clay or sand, you don't have to add any organic material; we always add as much as we can, no matter what the soil looks like. It can never hurt, and it always helps.

Checking your soil pH: A little acid helps a lot

The chemistry of your soil is the single most important element in successful rose culture. Before you even think about immersing those rose roots in your garden, you have to check the soil's pH.

Soil pH is a measurement of the soil's acidity or alkalinity, measured in a range from 1 to 14. A pH of 7 is neutral. Soils with a pH below 7 are acidic and become more acidic the lower the number goes. Soils with a pH above 7 are alkaline and become more alkaline as the number goes up.

Roses prefer a slightly acidic soil pH. Ideal soil pH for most roses is between 6 and 6.5 but they grow pretty well in range from 5.6 to 7.2. If soils are overly acidic (as is most often the case) or too alkaline (as it naturally is in some areas), adjusting the pH with one of several soil amendments is vital. A soil pH that is too high or too low interferes with or prevents the chemical reactions that make nutrients available to plants.

Your local nursery or cooperative extension office can give you a general idea of what your soil pH is or perform a soil test using a sample of your garden soil. You can adjust acidic soils by adding dolomitic limestone. Correct alkaline soils by adding soil sulfur. Again, a local professional is the best source of how much and what to add.

You can also test your soil's pH with inexpensive testing tapes or with more expensive testing monitors that you can get via mail-order (see Appendix C) or from nurseries and garden centers.

If you have fairly acidic soil, it's a good idea to avoid using acidifying mulches like pine needles. If you have alkaline soil, acidic mulches and soil additives slowly lower the pH, but it may take years to get it in the right range.

It's a good idea to check soil pH every few years, especially if you have trouble keeping your roses green and healthy. For more information, see Chapter 17.

Returning Roots to Their Rightful Home

This section presents the basic procedure for planting bareroot roses. The key idea to remember? Don't plant a $10 (or more!) rosebush in a 50-cent hole. Whether you're planting several roses in a new bed or just one in the middle of nowhere, dig a proper hole.

Digging a proper hole

Dig a hole at least 2 feet deep and 2 feet wide. Put the backfill into a wheelbarrow where you can mix it with fertilizers or amendments. This is, after all, the best time to adjust soil pH or add nutrients that are in short supply.

Preparing your bareroot roses for planting

Before planting bareroot roses, we prefer to soak the roots in a bucket of muddy water overnight. The water moistens the roots and the mud lightly coats them to slow drying out during planting.

We also know rose growers who dip their new roses in a soil polymer slurry instead of muddy water. *Soil polymers* are powdery materials that turn to a gelatinous substance when mixed with water. Usually they're added to soil to increase its water-holding capacity, but when roots are dipped in a slurry, the coating keeps extra moisture right where it's needed. Ask your local nursery person about soil polymers.

On a few occasions, we receive bareroot roses that look really dried out. The buds are all shriveled and shrunken looking, and the poor plants need special treatment. So we *sweat* them. Here's how:

1. **Soak the entire plant in water for 24 hours.**

2. **Enclose the whole thing in a clear plastic bag and keep it at room temperature (but out of sunlight) for 24 hours.**

   Boy, that plumps everything up!

Planting bareroot roses

To plant bareroot roses, follow these steps:

1. **Prune all the canes to about half their length and cut off any broken or mushy roots.**

Most bareroot roses have 10- to 16-inch canes to start with, so shorten them to between 5 and 8 inches. This shortening reduces the stress on the canes and roots while the new roots become established.

2. **Prune an inch or so off the roots to stimulate new growth.**

3. **Add a small amount of backfill to the hole and form it into a cone of soil. Fit the bareroot neatly over this cone (see Figure 16-1).**

   Planting at the proper depth is very important:

   - **In mild-winter climates:** Position rootstock plants so that the bud union (the swollen part of the main stem where the rootstock joins the scion variety; see Chapter 15 for more information) is at the same level or just above the level of the surface soil.

   - **In cold-winter climates:** Plant so that the bud union is 3 to 4 inches below the soil surface.

     Some rose growers prefer to plant deeper, covering the bud union with several inches of soil. Doing so should protect the bud union from cold, and it may also allow the top part of the plant to develop roots of its own, which, in turn, enables the plant to support itself if the rootstock is damaged. See Chapter 15 for more about bud unions and rootstock.

   - **For own-root roses:** Plant so that the point where the roots join the branches is just below the soil surface. See Chapter 15 for more about own-root roses.

   If, after planting, the rose settles in too deeply, grab the main stem near the bud union and gently pull upward. When you let go, the plant should settle slightly higher. If the plant settles too deep (or too high), it's best to pull it out and start over again.

4. **After planting, create a soil basin around the plant and add lots and lots of water to the filled hole (see Figure 16-2).**

   Adding water to the filled hole settles the soil and eliminates air pockets. After the water drains away, the soil and rose may settle lower than you want. If so, add more backfill and water again.

5. **After you water the rose, mound the soil over the top of the plant so all but the last few inches of the cane tops are covered, as shown in Figure 16-3.**

   Mounding the soil helps keep the plant from drying out before the roots have time to develop. When you see new growth, carefully remove the soil from around the canes.

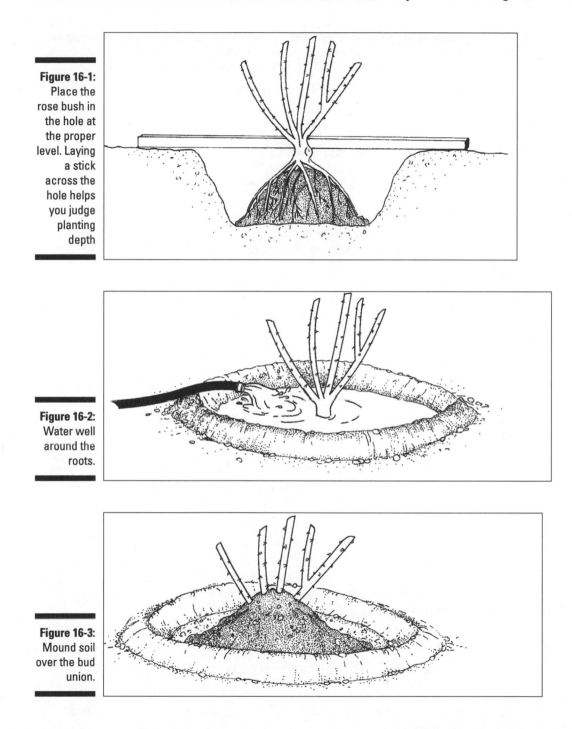

Figure 16-1:
Place the rose bush in the hole at the proper level. Laying a stick across the hole helps you judge planting depth

Figure 16-2:
Water well around the roots.

Figure 16-3:
Mound soil over the bud union.

Covering a newly planted rose with a brown paper bag (like you get from the supermarket) can also provide protection. Place the bag over the rose, cut a few holes in the top for air circulation, and seal the bottom with soil. We've also seen people protect new roses with Styrofoam caps usually used for winter protection.

Planting potted roses

Here are some tips for planting roses that come in containers:

✔ Water plants thoroughly the day before planting.

✔ Dig a hole and add soil amendments to the backfill just as for a bareroot rose (see the previous section, "Digging a proper hole"), but leave the bottom of the hole flat.

✔ Place your new rose into the hole, pot and all, so that you can estimate proper planting depth. Again, the bud union should be at or slightly above the soil surface in mild-winter areas, or up to several inches below the soil in cold-winter areas.

✔ Remove the container. Because you want to disturb growing roots as little as possible during planting:

- If your container rose is in a wood fiber pot, use a heavy knife to cut the bottom off the pot before placing the plant in the hole. When you have the plant in just the right position, slit the pot from top to bottom and remove it.

- If your rose is in a metal or heavy plastic container, remove the rootball from the pot. If the roots form a solid, circling mass, gently loosen or cut them, or the rose will be slow to adapt to the new soil. If the roots are really tight, make three or four vertical cuts along the sides of the rootball with a knife. Don't go any deeper than an inch. The roots will eventually branch at the cuts and grow out into the surrounding soil.

✔ If you're planting in hot weather, don't let the new plant dry out. Until the roots grow into the surrounding soil, you have to treat the plant like it is still in a pot. That means you may have to water every few days, if not more.

✔ If you're planting in winter, mound soil over the canes as previously mentioned for bareroot roses.

✔ Water all newly planted roses every three days — more often if the weather is hot.

See Figures 16-4 and 16-5 for the basic procedures for planting container-grown roses.

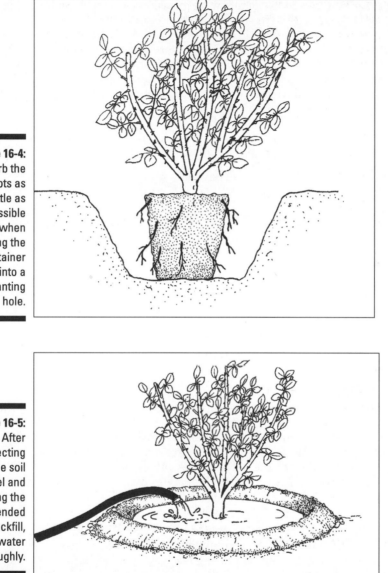

Figure 16-4:
Disturb the roots as little as possible when setting the container rose into a planting hole.

Figure 16-5:
After correcting the soil level and adding the amended backfill, water thoroughly.

Planting miniature roses

Miniature roses are usually sold in 2½-inch or 4-inch pots, whether you buy them at a local retail nursery or by mail order. They should have fully developed root systems. In fact, they may be *rootbound* (running out of room for new root growth) and more than ready to be transplanted.

Remember that these little plants were grown in a comfy greenhouse, so they may need time to adjust to natural, outdoor conditions. This adjusting process is called *hardening off*. Help potted plants adjust to your weather conditions by gradually moving them to more extreme temperatures and sunlight. From the porch to outside in partial sun and finally to full sun over a week's time should do the trick. You may want to transplant the mini into a larger pot before you harden-off. This encourages the roots to grow sooner. Chapter 7 gives instructions on transplanting into pots.

In cold climates, potted miniatures can be planted from the time the forsythias bloom in early spring well into mid-summer. In warm climates, they can be planted just about anytime.

Digging a smaller hole

Digging a hole for a potted mini is somewhat easier than digging a hole for a big rose. You can dig the hole with a trowel, although removing a couple of spadefuls of soil ensures that the roots have a generous area in which they can spread.

In any case, prepare the hole much as you would for a big rose (see "Digging a proper hole" earlier in this chapter). Because your plant is smaller, the hole should be smaller — about 1 foot wide and 1 foot deep. Add smaller amounts of the same soil amendments you use for big roses. Make a small cone of soil in the bottom of the hole.

Putting the plant in the ground

Your mini rose should come out of its pot quite easily. Notice how all those roots have grown round and round inside the pot? To encourage the roots to spread out and grow into the new soil in your rose bed (or container), insert both of your thumbs into the bottom of the rootball and tear apart the bottom third, then place the entire torn rootball over the cone in the bottom of the hole. Next, backfill and water exactly as described in "Planting your bareroot rose," earlier in this chapter.

Remember that miniature roses always have shallower root systems than big roses and, therefore, need more frequent watering.

Chapter 17

Watering and Mulching Roses

• •

In This Chapter

▶ Watering rules

▶ Knowing how often to water and how much water to apply

▶ Understanding sprinklers, drip irrigation, and other watering systems

▶ Mulching

• •

Getting your roses in the ground is just the beginning of the cycle of care that results in gorgeous blooms for faithful gardeners. Watering and mulching are critical to your success. Like anything else, however, what sounds relatively simple can raise a lot of questions.

How often should you water your roses? How much water should you apply? How should you apply the water? Should you use a hose? A sprinkler? Or do you just let Mother Nature take care of it all with summer rainfall? What about mulch? How much and how often? Can you do without it?

Questions about water are often hard to answer even for the most experienced rosarian. The reason is that, like any other plant, a rose's water needs depend on a number of factors, many of which are determined by conditions that may be unique to your own garden. And what does that mean? It means that the only person who really can know the answers to tough watering questions is you.

Okay, now that we've put pressure on you, relax. Watering is really a matter of common sense and careful observation. You may even find watering to be one of the more enjoyable gardening chores. This chapter gives you tips that make setting up a watering schedule and applying the right amount of water painless and easy. You also see the role of mulch in keeping your roses moist and disease-free.

The Basic Watering Rules

First, you need to accept the fact that, just like people, roses need water to be healthy and bloom beautifully. No water? No rose bush. Just a dried-up dead stick poking through parched soil. Here are some general guidelines for determining water needs:

- ✔ Roses need more water more often in hot weather than in cool weather.

- ✔ Even if it rains often, that rain may not be enough water to keep your roses healthy.

- ✔ Roses growing in sandy soil need more frequent watering than roses growing in clay soils. (See Chapter 16 for more information about the different types of soils.)

Once you accept that your roses need a steady slurp or two of water, tattoo these rules on your arm:

- ✔ When you water, water deeply so that you wet the entire root zone. Don't just sprinkle lightly! That does little good.

- ✔ If you really want to know whether your roses need water, get down and dig in the dirt. That's the only way to know for sure. If the top 2 to 3 inches of soil are dry, you need to water.

- ✔ To reduce disease problems, water the soil, not the leaves. Roses can benefit from overhead watering once in a while, especially in dry summer climates where black spot is not usually a problem; however, make sure that you water early enough (in the morning on a sunny day is ideal) so that the foliage can dry before nightfall.

- ✔ Mulch! Mulch! Mulch! Doing so conserves water. You can find out how to mulch later in this chapter.

Now we're getting somewhere. In the following sections, we get down to the nitty-gritty and answer the tough questions about how often and how much your roses need water.

How often to water

Naturally, if you live in Phoenix, Arizona, where even the lizards need an occasional drink, you need to water more frequently than you do if you live in rainy old Seattle.

"Yeah, sure," you say. "And if the soil is sandy, I have to water more frequently than if the soil is mucky clay. My tattoo tells me that. But exactly how often should I water?"

The old guideline is that a mature, full-sized rosebush uses about an inch or two of water a week. Therefore, if you got an inch or two of rain last week, no problem. If you didn't, you need to water. But watering is usually not that simple. In fact, it is never that simple and that rule is stupid. Forget we mentioned it. Soil type and weather play too great a role in how much water a rose needs to make generalizations.

As we mentioned, clay soil holds more water, so you need to add water less often or you flood your plant; sandy soil holds little water, so you need to water more often. Likewise, if the weather is blistering hot and dry, common sense suggests that more water is necessary; if the weather has been cool, perhaps your roses can go well beyond a week between drinks.

Keep in mind that, theoretically, you can't overwater a rose. Of course, if there's no sun and it rains steadily for ten days, your roses won't be thrilled. But if drainage is good, the extra water usually won't hurt them, either. However, in some parts of the southeastern United States, where clay soils and heavy rain are a fact of life, drainage is a problem and roses can suffer in overly wet soils. There you often have to create good drainage by planting in raised beds. You can find out more about how to do that in Chapter 7.

Start with a watering schedule: Water once every five or six days, for example. If you live in a hot, dry climate, make it every two or three days. Watch the plant carefully and check the soil often, especially when you get to the end of the period. If the soil is bone dry about 2 to 3 inches below the surface at the end of your test period, it's time to water. If the soil is still moist, wait a few days and check again. If the rose's foliage ever starts to look dull or droopy, you've definitely waited too long. Get those babies some water now and water more frequently.

Over time, you'll get to know your soil and how quickly it dries out, no matter whether the weather is warm or cool, rainy, or dry.

How much water to apply

Water deeply so that the entire root zone gets wet — for roses, that means to a depth of at least 18 inches. How far a given amount of water can penetrate into the soil depends on the soil type. For example, if you applied an inch of water evenly over dry sandy soil, it would go down about 12 inches. In a clay soil, it would reach only about 4 to 5 inches. In a loam soil, an inch of water would go down about 6 to 10 inches. If your soil is already lightly moist (you should never let it go bone dry), water will penetrate further.

Chapter 16 gives you some general guidelines on determining what type of soil you have. But what you really want to know is how long you need to water to wet your particular soil to the proper depth. To find that out, you need to play in the mud a bit.

We consider different types of irrigation systems and how fast they apply water later in this chapter. But for now, assume that your watering system, even if it's just a hose, is in place. Run your system for ten minutes or fill up your *water basin* (the 3- to 6-inch-high circle of soil you make around your rose when you plant it) once. Let the water soak in and then probe the soil with a stiff rod or stick.

The rod or stick should move smoothly through wet soil and then be hard to push when it reaches dry soil. Digging with a spade at a test spot away from your roses also lets you see exactly how deep the water has gone. From there, calculating how long to water is easy. For example, if the soil is wet to a depth of 6 inches after ten minutes of watering, you need to water for a total of 30 minutes to get the water down 18 inches.

You may want to water a little longer than it takes to get the water down 18 inches, just to make sure that you're doing a good job and watering your roses thoroughly. But don't overdo it. If you water too long, the water will penetrate far below the roots and be wasted.

What are some tools of the watering trade?

Two tools can help you fine-tune your watering schedule. The first is a *soil probe* — an approximately 3-foot long hollow metal tube about an inch in diameter that removes a small core of soil from the ground. By examining the soil core, you can tell how deeply you're watering or how dry the soil is.

The second useful tool is a *rain gauge*. It can tell you exactly how much rain has fallen, and you can adjust your watering schedule accordingly.

You can purchase soil probes and rain gauges through the irrigation supply stores listed in your local Yellow Pages. Or you can order through the mail from companies such as The Urban Farmer or Gardener's Supply Company, whose addresses and telephone numbers are listed in Appendix C.

How should you water? Just count the ways

You can use a number of methods to water roses. The key is to apply the water only over the soil where the roots are — and not so fast that it runs down the gutter toward the next town.

Building a basin

One simple way to water is to build a 3- to 6-inch-high basin of soil around the plant and fill it using a handheld hose. Just make sure that the basin is wide enough to hold the amount of water your rose needs. The basin should be at least 18 inches wide for new plants, and at least 36 inches wide for really big roses. And don't forget, you may have to fill the basin twice to get the water deep enough.

Using sprinklers

Many types of sprinklers are available, including ones that attach to the end of hoses (see Figure 17-1) and ones connected to underground pipes (see Figure 17-2). You can get sprinklers that cover large areas or small, that water fast or slow, that apply a spray or a even a slow gurgle (called a *bubbler*).You can hook sprinklers to timers or controllers to prevent overwatering. They can even water while you're on vacation.

Using drip irrigation

Drip irrigation (see Figure 17-3) is a particularly useful watering system for areas that are dry in summer, for areas where water shortages are common, or for busy gardeners who don't have time to water as often as they should. In fact, drip irrigation is a great way to water just about anywhere. Most drip irrigation systems are built around ⅜- to 1-inch black tubing and specifically designed emitters. The emitters drip or spray water slowly — no faster than the soil can absorb it — and only wet the root area. Less wet ground means fewer weeds.

Figure 17-1: If you have just a few roses and a long hose, a hose-end sprinkler is a convenient way to water roses.

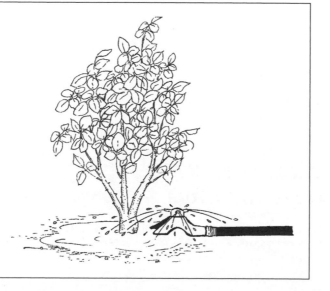

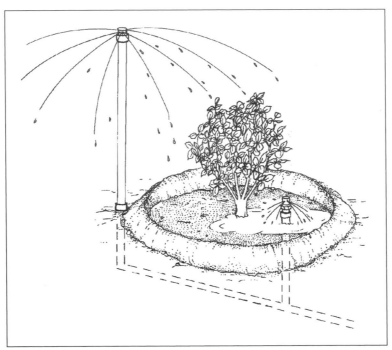

Figure 17-2:
An under-
ground
watering
system
delivers
water over-
head or
right at the
roots.

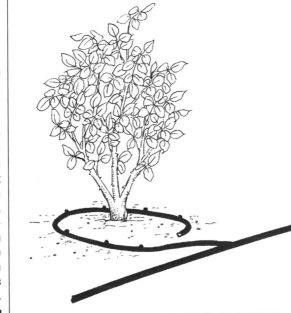

Figure 17-3:
Watering
roses with
a drip
irrigation
system is
convenient
if you have
many roses,
and it is effi-
cient if you
live where
water is a
precious
resource.

Most hardware stores and nurseries carry a variety of sprinklers and watering devices. In most areas, you can also find drip systems. A salesperson can usually help you with design and installation. Or you can write or call mail-order companies that specialize in irrigation equipment, such as Gardener's Supply Company and The Urban Farmer. The addresses and telephone numbers for both companies are listed in Appendix C.

Watering to minimize disease

You have to think about one last thing before you decide how you're going to water. Many rose diseases, including black spot, rust, and downy mildew, thrive on wet foliage. If you live in areas where such diseases are problems (see Chapter 4 for more information about where these diseases are most troublesome), you may want to water in a way that keeps the leaves dry. Drip systems or bubbler-type sprinkler heads apply water at the base of the plant and do a good job of keeping the leaves from getting wet.

To complicate matters, some diseases, such as powdery mildew, spread more rapidly on dry foliage. And insect pests, like mites, thrive on dirty, dusty leaves (you can find out more about rose insects and diseases in Chapter 21). In both cases, drenching the entire plant cleans the foliage of disease spores and dust, reducing pest problems. Remember, if you're going to water with overhead sprinklers, be sure to do it early in the morning on a sunny day so that the leaves have a chance to dry before nightfall. And whether or not you water overhead, keeping debris and dead leaves out of the garden really pays off.

Mulch for Success

Mulch is any material, organic or not, that you place over the surface of the soil. Mulches really are a waterer's best friend. By reducing soil temperatures and evaporation, and by smothering greedy weeds (the seeds won't germinate if they're covered by several inches of mulch) that compete with roses for moisture, mulches not only conserve water but also even out rapid changes in soil moisture that can spell disaster in hot weather.

The best time to apply mulch is in early spring, about the same time you remove winter protection (see Chapter 20 for more information). Or in areas with warmer winters, apply mulch just before your roses start to leaf out and before weeds start to sprout. But keep in mind, you can apply mulch anytime, and you usually need to replenish it every two to three months.

Organic mulches

Organic mulches include grass clippings, compost (naturally decomposed organic matter), wood chips, leaf mold (partially decomposed leaves), pine needles, shredded bark, nut shells, cotton gin waste, straw, hay, grain and fruit by-products, composted manure, mushroom compost, peat moss, sawdust, and even newspaper. Specific types may be easier or harder to find, depending where you live.

We recommend organic mulch for roses because, as the mulch breaks down, it adds organic matter to the soil, improving its texture and sometimes adding nutrients. It also makes your garden look better by giving the ground a cleaner, more orderly appearance.

Many organic mulches break down fairly rapidly, so they need to be replenished often. For effective mulching, apply a good, thick layer (at least 3 to 4 inches) of mulch in spring before the weeds start to grow. Spread it evenly under the roses, over an area slightly wider than the diameter of the plant. Or spread it over the entire rose bed. Mulching is that easy!

Check the mulch every three months or so, adding a fresh layer whenever the first one starts to deteriorate. Figure 17-4 shows a properly mulched rosebush.

Figure 17-4:
Use a layer
of organic
mulch to
improve root
growth.

Composted manures make particularly good mulches, looking neat while adding nutrients to the soil as they break down. Just make sure that the manure is fully composted (it's sometimes hard to tell if you buy by the bag) and that you don't add too much. Fresh manures contain salts that damage the plant and make its leaves look as if they've been burned by a blow torch. Basically, uncomposted manure is too much of a good thing. (Too much of just about any fertilizer, manure included, supplies excess nutrients, usually nitrogen.) Think of salt in your soup: A little is good, but too much makes it inedible.

On the other hand, former U.S. President Harry Truman credited his ability to spread "manure" for the health and vigor of his roses!

Different types of manure — that is, from different animals like horses, cows, or chickens — have varying amounts of nitrogen. Horse manure is generally safest and chicken manure the most dangerous. We like to mix manure 50/50 with some other organic mulch, particularly good garden compost. That way, you won't burn your roses, but they still get some nitrogen.

You can buy bags of composted manure in most nurseries and garden centers. You can also buy it in bulk from farms or dairies. However, if you buy in bulk, make sure that the manure is well composted before you put it on your roses. We like to let fresh manure sit around for a year before we use it.

Using organic mulches has some downsides, so think about the materials you use and what they may do to your garden:

- Bark mulches, such as pine, are quite acidic. So if you use them, you need to keep a close eye on soil pH and correct it accordingly. (See Chapter 16 for more information about soil pH.)

- If you intend to use grass clippings, make sure that no herbicides (weed killers) have been used on your lawn, the residue of which can damage or kill your roses. Grass clippings decay quickly and must be replenished often. But that's okay; grass clippings are usually pretty abundant. But if the grass goes to seed before you cut it, you could end up with grass growing in your rose beds, which not only looks bad, but the grass will rob your roses of water and nutrients.

- Some organic mulches — such as fresh sawdust — need extra nitrogen to break down properly, so you may have to add supplemental nitrogen to your roses to make up for it. (We discuss fertilizers in Chapter 18.)

- Peat moss can get hard and crusty when exposed to weather. Water may not penetrate it, so the water runs off instead of soaking through to the roots. It's best to avoid peat, or to mix it with something else, like compost.

- Some lightweight mulches, like straw and cocoa hulls, can blow around in the wind, making a mess and leaving your roses unmulched. So you may want to avoid them if you live in a windy area.

You can purchase organic mulches like shredded bark, compost, and leaf mold in bags, or sometimes in bulk, from nurseries and garden centers. Grass clippings, compost, and, if you have a chipper, wood chips come free from your garden.

Inorganic mulches

Inorganic mulches include plastic, gravel, stone, and sand. We usually prefer organic mulches because they improve the soil and look better. However, if you live in a cool-summer climate, a layer of gravel or rock beneath a rose can reflect heat and light up onto the plant. The extra heat may improve the quality of bloom for varieties that normally prefer warmer climates, and it may also cause water to evaporate off the foliage more quickly, reducing disease problems.

Generally, though, inorganic mulches, particularly plastic, are hard to handle, especially on roses, where you need continual access to the soil for fertilizing, watering, and so on. So unless you need to heat up your garden, or like the look of plastic, steer clear of these mulches.

There's one exception. Landscape fabrics are water-permeable, plastic or woven materials sold in rolls in most nurseries and garden centers. You lay them over the planting area, cut x-shaped holes in the fabric, and plant the roses through it. Landscape fabrics do a good job suppressing weeds, but water and nutrients pass right through. Add a thin layer of organic mulch on top and they even look good.

Chapter 18

Fertilizing Roses

● ●

In This Chapter

▶ Knowing the nutrients your roses need most

▶ Testing your soil

▶ Following specific fertilizer programs

▶ Timing your fertilizing

● ●

*M*ost roses need frequent applications of fertilizer to keep them growing vigorously and blooming repeatedly. If that's all you want to know about the mind-boggling world of fertilizers, that's fine. Go to your local nursery, buy a bag or box of fertilizer labeled "Rose Food," and follow the directions on the package. You'll get perfectly fine roses.

If, however, you want to go for perfectly spectacular roses, we can tell you about that, too. You see, compared to most other plants, roses have to be considered "heavy feeders," meaning they like lots of nitrogen (more on that in a bit). In fact, many rose experts regularly apply quite a bit more than the amount recommended on the labels of rose foods. So in this chapter, we spell out the theory of fertilizing, and then we give you a few options.

The Whats and Whys of Fertilizing

For some people, plant nutrition is a complicated science that they spend their whole lives studying. But it doesn't have to be that complicated. We're just talking nutrition here — how and what to feed roses so that they grow their best. The following sections give you a primer of rose nutrition.

But before we launch into all the whys and wherefores, keep in mind that no fertilizer on earth will help your roses if the pH of your soil is too high or too low. When the pH is off, important nutrients already in the soil are unavailable to plants.

As we explain in Chapter 16, roses prefer a slightly acidic soil with a pH between 6 and 6.5, but they grow pretty well in a range of 5.6 to 7.2. When the pH is right, your roses' roots can interact with the bacteria and enzymes in the soil and get full benefit of natural nutrients and those you add.

Fertilizers come in three basic forms:

- **Granular:** You spread over the soil at the base of the plant and water it in.

- **Water soluble:** Dissolve either the powdered or liquid variety in water to feed the soil or foliage.

- **Timed-release:** Either spread this fertilizer on the soil or mix it with the soil for a constant release of nutrients over a long period of time.

Note: Roses growing in containers need special care — see Chapter 7.

It doesn't really matter which type of fertilizer you use, as long as you apply it often enough. Most rose growers prefer the granular form because it's easy to use and doesn't need mixing. Water soluble fertilizers get to roots quickly and are easy to use on container plants, but they usually have to be applied more often. Timed-release fertilizers are convenient, but alone they often do not supply enough nutrients to keep roses growing well over a long time. They usually have to be supplemented with granular fertilizers.

When you buy a package of fertilizer , you see three numbers together on the package, such as 5-9-6 (see Figure 18-1). These numbers show the percentages of major nutrients present in the formula in this order: nitrogen (N), phosphorus (P), and potassium (K). Fertilizers also include directions on the label. The following sections explain the major and minor nutrients your rose plants may need.

Figure 18-1:
Fertilizer
labels
provide
valuable
information.

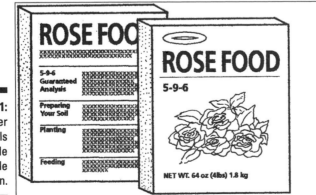

Nitrogen: The number one need

Plants actually require 16 different elements for healthy growth, but most of these elements are already in your soil (or in the air!) and don't need to be added regularly. Nitrogen, however, is what fuels the growth of a rosebush and you must add it to the soil regularly — the nitrogen already present in the air and soil is not enough. This element stimulates dark green, healthy foliage growth; because a plant's energy to make flowers is manufactured in its leaves, healthy leaves mean more flowers.

Most rose foods have several times more nitrogen than phosphorous and potassium. Why? Because that's the element roses need the most. However, don't worry about the numbers too much. Just don't buy one of those "bloom" foods that has no nitrogen at all. Trust us, it won't make your roses bloom more.

Phosphorus and potassium: Part of the macronutrient trio

Along with nitrogen, phosphorus and potassium are called *macronutrients* because they are needed in larger supplies than other nutrients. However, some soils contain enough phosphorus and potassium for healthy rose growth; adding more to them does little good. Besides, phosphorus doesn't move easily through the soil like nitrogen and potassium — it gets "tied up" (you don't want to know the reasons why) and has to stay put. If your soil is short on phosphorus, add some directly to the planting hole when you put in your roses so that it gets where it needs to go.

Only a soil test can tell you for sure whether your soil needs either of these nutrients. But if you use a complete fertilizer — one with a lot of nitrogen and a little phosphorous and potassium (remember, the three numbers on the fertilizer package tell you the percentages of each) — on a regular basis, you should be okay.

Iron: An alkaline addition

In areas where the soil is on the alkaline side, a rose plant may need applications of fertilizers containing iron. You know your roses need iron when their leaves turn yellow with green veins.

Iron is called a *micronutrient,* meaning that the plant needs it only in small quantities. Zinc and manganese are other micronutrients that problem soils may need. And if nitrogen isn't greening-up your roses, it's a good idea to apply not only iron but also zinc and manganese. The fastest way to correct these deficiencies is to apply a liquid fertilizer containing *chelated* micronutrients (forget about all the terminology — it just means that they work better) to both the foliage and the soil. That's right, just spray the fertilizer over the whole plant. But look for cautions on the fertilizer label.

Most manufacturers recommend that you not spray plants when they need water or when the temperature is above 85°F (29°C).

Magnesium: A rose enhancer

Many experienced rose growers swear by magnesium applications. And who are we to argue? *Magnesium sulphate* — called Epsom salts in drugstores — is the form that's usually applied. This chemical can help intensify flower color and increase production of new flowering canes. Apply ¼ to ½ cup per plant once or twice a year and water it in. But this procedure only does any good if your soil is deficient in magnesium.

Finding a Fertilizing Program Just for You

Fertilizing is kind of a personal thing. Of course, you want to keep your plants healthy, but how you do so really depends on the type of gardener you are or want to be. So in this section we describe a few successful fertilizer programs we've seen. Take your pick.

Lazy and cheap formula

Fertilizers that contain all three major nutrients — nitrogen, phosphorus, and potassium — are called *complete fertilizers.* They are the types of fertilizers usually packaged as "rose foods." Although necessary for healthy growth, phosphorus and potassium often already exist in sufficient amounts in the soil and don't need to be replaced regularly. If this is the case with your soil, you can use a fertilizer, such as ammonium sulfate or urea, that contains only nitrogen. You can purchase these fertilizers at dramatically cheaper prices than complete fertilizers. You can also usually find bargain bags of *high nitrogen – low phosphorus and potassium* fertilizers in most nurseries.

If you have doubts, have the soil tested

If you have problems keeping your roses green and growing, have your soil tested or show a sample of the foliage to a local nursery worker or cooperative extension agent (a university specialist assigned to your county to help you — look in the phone book under your county offices).

In many states, your cooperative extension agency can perform a soil test for you. If it can't,

the employees should be able to recommend a private lab that can. A soil test tells you exactly what's wrong with your soil, and then your nursery can help you correct the problem. Costs vary from area to area and depend on how detailed the test is. If you can't understand your soil test results, consult your cooperative extension agent.

Ammonium sulfate, an acidifying fertilizer that gradually lowers soil pH, works well on alkaline soils but has a negative effect on acidic soils — it makes them even more acidic. One rose grower we know saves money and time by jaunting through the garden giving each rose one handful of ammonium sulfate (he wears gloves) every six weeks. He spreads the fertilizer evenly under each plant (shown being done with a can in Figure 18-2) and then waters thoroughly to dissolve the granules and wash the nutrients into the soil. Simple, cheap, and his roses look great.

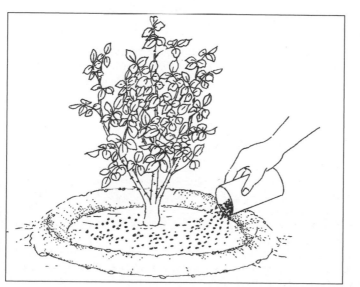

Figure 18-2: Spreading fertilizer at the base of a rose plant.

Just plain lazy formula

There are several brands of timed-release fertilizers you apply once or twice a year, which provide enough nutrients for an entire season. But you pay more for the convenience.

Follow the label instructions carefully and watch your roses closely. If they slow down and stop blooming, the fertilizer may have run out early. Most rose growers who use time-released fertilizers supplement their use with one or two applications of a regular fertilizer in spring and late summer, just to make sure that the plants have enough nitrogen.

Tree-hugger's formula

Many gardeners prefer to use organic fertilizers — ones that occur naturally — over chemical-based fertilizers. And their reasons for doing this are good ones. Organic fertilizers, such as fish emulsion, composted manures (fresh manures can burn plant foliage), and blood meal (dried animal blood, which is high in nitrogen), contribute organic matter to the earth and are better for all those weird micro-organisms that populate the soil. They are also slow acting, so there is very little chance of overdoing things and burning your roses.

The downside of organic fertilizers is that the nutrient content is usually low and cannot always be predicted precisely. The nutrients also take time to change into forms that the plant can use, so you don't get that immediate blast of nitrogen like you do from other fertilizers. Using organic fertilizers takes some trial and error before you get the right results.

One successful formula we've seen mixes equal amounts of alfalfa meal and cottonseed meal. Spread ten cups of the formula at the base of each plant every ten weeks and then cover them with a thick mulch of compost. Try it; your worms will love it.

If you have trouble finding a good selection of organic fertilizers, see the list of mail-order catalogs in Appendix C.

Water and spray, water and spray, oh, how I love to water and spray

You can't argue with the fact that half the fun of gardening is actually spending time in the garden. One friend of ours applies liquid fertilizers (make sure the label says the fertilizer can be applied to the foliage and follow instructions carefully) through a hose-end sprayer, as shown in Figure 18-3. (You may also want to try a siphon feeder — a little deal that goes on to the end of your hose and connects to a bucket of diluted fertilizer with a little tube. Ask your nursery worker.)

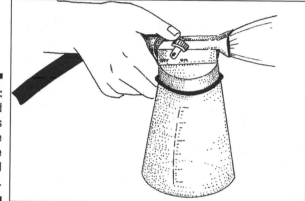

Figure 18-3: A hose-end sprayer lets you fertilize both the leaves and the soil.

Anyway, our friend applies the fertilizer to the leaves, called *foliar feeding*, and the soil, so she gets both the immediate effects of foliar feeding and the long-term benefits of soil application. (Believe us, applying fertilizers to the leaves works if the label says that doing so is okay — try it! Roots aren't the only part of the plant that can absorb nutrients; leaves can do so, too. And they do it fast — much faster than roots do.) Our friend follows this routine at least every two weeks, but sometimes she mixes the fertilizer at half strength and applies it weekly.

If only we had the time. . . .

Gung-ho fertilizing for gung-ho rose growers

Rose society members, especially those who show their roses at local and national rose shows, are pretty finicky about how they care for their plants. But you can't argue with their results, which are large, perfect flowers and wonderful foliage. One trophy winner (and former president of the American Rose Society) we know has a particularly high-powered fertilizer program.

About a week after his plants leaf out in spring, he applies a water-soluble 20-20-20 fertilizer, diluting 2 tablespoons of fertilizer in 2 gallons of water and giving each plant the whole 2 gallons. A week later, he puts ½ cup of Epsom salts (magnesium sulfate) around each bush. The third week, he applies fish emulsion at the same dilution as he applied the 20-20-20 fertilizer two weeks earlier. During week four, he applies a liquid fertilizer (16-4-2), which includes chelated micronutrients, at 1 tablespoon per gallon, 2 gallons per bush. In week five, he starts all over again.

Whew, a lot of work — but, he says, twice the blooms and bigger flowers. Better yet, you can now buy a simplified version of the fertilizer program, packaged as one product called Magnum Grow. If you can't find it in local nurseries, you can buy it through the mail from Primary Products. Their address can be found in Appendix C.

Feed Often, but Don't Overdo It

To keep roses blooming again and again, you should fertilize them about every four to six weeks, although the type of fertilizer you use may alter this rule a bit. (Refer to the basic fertilizer programs discussed previously in this chapter.) However, if you go overboard and apply too much or too often, you can burn a plant — the edges or the entire leaf turn brown and scorched looking. Always follow label instructions when determining how much fertilizer to use.

Roses that bloom only once in spring, like many of the old garden roses, don't need to be fertilized as often as repeat bloomers. Fertilizing once in early spring may be enough. But, if your plants aren't green and healthy-looking or aren't blooming up to your expectations, increase the number of applications.

Here are some general fertilizing guidelines:

- **Water before and after fertilizing:** A plant stressed from lack of water is more likely to be burned by nitrogen fertilizers, so make sure that the soil around the plant is wet before you add fertilizer. Watering after fertilizing helps to move nutrients into the root zone.

- **Start fertilizing in early spring:** Make your first application about four to six weeks before growth begins in spring or, in areas where winters are cold, about the time you take off your winter protection. Continue through summer until about six weeks before the average date of your first frost. (Employees at your nursery can tell you exactly when that date is.) Later fertilization may encourage growth that will be damaged by frosts and can result in roses that are not fully "cold resistant." (For more information about rose hardiness, see Chapter 4.)

- **Stop fertilizing in late summer or fall:** For most cold-winter climates, you stop fertilizing sometime in late August or September. In mild-winter areas, you can quit as late as October.

There, now you have all the nutrient know-how you need to keep your roses healthy, green, and free-blooming.

Chapter 19

A-Pruning You Must Go

- -

In This Chapter

▶ Understanding why roses need pruning

▶ Knowing when to prune

▶ Selecting tools for pruning

▶ Determining the right way to prune each type of rose

▶ Cleaning up after pruning

- -

*I*f you think that pruning roses is complicated, think again. Although pruning trees and other types of plants may be met with lots of head-scratching, you won't believe how simple and straightforward pruning roses is. And you won't believe the big-time results you get from performing a little lopping at the right time.

Feel better? Good. Because if you want to grow roses, you're going to have to prune them. Roses are tough plants, and even if you make every pruning mistake in the book, your roses will be better off than if you hadn't pruned them at all.

What is pruning, anyway? Obviously, it means cutting something or other. But what? When? And most of all, why? The answers are in this chapter, starting with the all-important *why*.

The Kindest Cut for Healthy Roses

Roses need to be pruned for several reasons. Most of the reasons have to do with keeping the plant healthy, and a couple of them have to do with keeping the plant pretty. And some of them have to do with keeping the plant from getting out of bounds, like the eggplant that ate Chicago.

When you prune, you cut the *canes* (think upright branches) of a rosebush. You may cut the canes near the top of the plant, you may cut them at the base of the plant, or you may cut them somewhere in the middle. You can cut 'em in all kinds of different places, depending on the result you're trying to achieve.

Here's the skinny on why you really do want to prune your roses:

- ✔ **To improve flowering:** Proper pruning results in more or bigger blooms. Especially with hybrid teas grown for cut flowers, good pruning practices give you huge flowers atop long, strong stems. What's sexier than that? In general, the further back you cut a rose, the fewer but bigger flowers you'll get. And they'll be on longer, stronger stems (better for cutting). Prune less, and you get smaller flowers but more of them.

- ✔ **To keep plants healthy:** Pruning removes diseased or damaged parts of the plant. It also keeps the plant more open in the center, increasing air circulation and reducing pest problems. (For more on controlling pests, see Chapter 21.)

- ✔ **To keep plants in bounds:** Without pruning, many rose plants get huge. Some of these monsters can take over an entire yard! Part of this problem may be that you chose the wrong varieties or planted in the wrong spot. In any case, it's a common problem. Pruning keeps them where they're supposed to be. Pruning also keeps the flowers at eye level, where you can enjoy them up close.

- ✔ **To direct growth:** More than just keeping the rose in bounds, pruning can direct growth (and flowers) to a spot you pick. The best example of directing growth is pruning a climbing rose to grow on a trellis or an arbor.

Pruning isn't something you do just for the sake of doing it. You prune to remove parts of a plant that you don't want to leave room for growth and circulation in the parts of the plant that you do want. So, whenever you take a pruner to a rose cane, ask yourself why. If you don't stop to question your pruning, you may not get the effect you want.

When to prune: On a cool, crisp, late winter day . . .

Whenever we're asked when is the best time to prune roses, we always answer, "Whenever the weather's right and you have the time." And that's the truth. There's no exact day, or even exact week, for pruning roses. You should do it yearly, and during the proper season for pruning, but don't get stressed out about hitting some made-up rose-pruning national holiday.

Just before growth begins in late winter or early spring — exact timing depends upon your climate — is the best season for big pruning. And if you do a good job then, you shouldn't have much to do throughout the rest of the season beyond _deadheading_ (cutting off spent roses, as explained later in this chapter) and cutting great roses. If you wait too long to do your heavy pruning — say after the plant's new growth is really in full swing — removing all that foliage will weaken the plant, delay blooming, and just make you and your roses unhappy.

Where winter temperatures predictably reach 10°F (–12°C) and lower, you want to wait until after the coldest weather has passed and any winter damage to the plant has already occurred. That's usually about a month before the average date of the last spring frost — March or April for most people — and coincides nicely with when you remove your winter protection. Your local nursery or cooperative extension office can give you exact frost dates for your area.

In climates where winters are cold or pretty cold (15°F or –9°C and lower), avoid pruning in fall. Any pruning after the first frost but before really cold weather sets in usually signals the plant to grow. New canes or shoots are very tender and will be killed by cold weather. Only if really long canes would whip around in winter's wind and damage the plant — or anyone walking by — should you cut anything off a rose plant in late fall.

If you live where winters are mild and temperatures rarely dip below 15°F (–9°C), you have to do your pruning earlier because plants start growing earlier. January or February is usually the best time.

In areas with very mild winters, rose plants never really go completely dormant or drop all their leaves. So you have to prune with some foliage still on the plant — late December to February are usual times. In such cases, pick off as many of the leaves as possible, but be careful not to damage the bark, which may lead to disease. Removing leaves helps force the plant into dormancy (even roses need a rest now and then) and removes any disease organisms that may be waiting out the winter on the foliage (see Chapter 21 for more on diseases).

Tools of the pruning trade

Before you can start pruning your roses, you need the proper equipment. Quality, well-maintained pruning tools make pruning a lot easier. They're also better for your roses, giving you nice clean cuts instead crushed stems and torn branches. If you're serious about roses, be serious about your pruning tools. Don't buy the bargain-basement equipment — you'll have to go back for a better set. And after you purchase your tools, take care of them. Store them indoors (not out in the rain, knucklehead), oil blades and moving parts (even a few drops of oil on a saw blade makes it cut more easily), and keep the blades sharp. Treat your pruning tools like old friends and they'll be there when you need them.

Your basic rose-tending toolbox should include:

- ✔ **Heavy gloves:** We shouldn't have to tell you this. You do know that roses have thorns, right? Choose gloves that are flexible but not easily punctured. We like gloves coated in nitrile (a strong plastic-like stuff). Your nursery can recommend some other types designed especially for roses.

- ✔ **Hand pruners:** Pruners do most of the work. We prefer by-pass pruners — the type with a curved blade and cutting arm, as shown in Figure 19-1. This tool provides the cleanest cut and is less likely to crush the cane below the cut, which often happens with anvil-type shears.

- ✔ **Loppers:** These are similar to hand pruners but have long handles to give you better leverage when cutting thicker canes. (See Figure 19-2.)

- ✔ **Pruning saw:** This saw is necessary for cutting really old, woody canes or dead wood. We like the folding type with a slightly curved blade, shown in Figure 19-3. This type fits neatly, if slightly uncomfortably, in your back pocket (folding the saw covers the blade, so you don't have to worry about injuring yourself).

- ✔ **Sharpener:** You need a sharpening stone or small file (we like those diamond-coated fingernail files) to keep your pruners sharp. Sharp blades do less damage to the plant. Move the stone or file down the beveled edge of the blade, starting from the base and ending at the tip (see Figure 19-4). Wear gloves when sharpening your pruners and apply gentle pressure. Some gardeners take the pruning shears apart before sharpening, but it's not necessary. Sharpening every time before you prune is a good idea. If you're pruning a lot of roses, like 10 to 20 bushes, you may want to carry your sharpener with you. When you notice that your cuts are getting harder and harder to make, or that the canes are getting crushed or torn with each cut, it's time to sharpen.

Figure 19-1:
By-pass pruners work better than anvil-type shears.

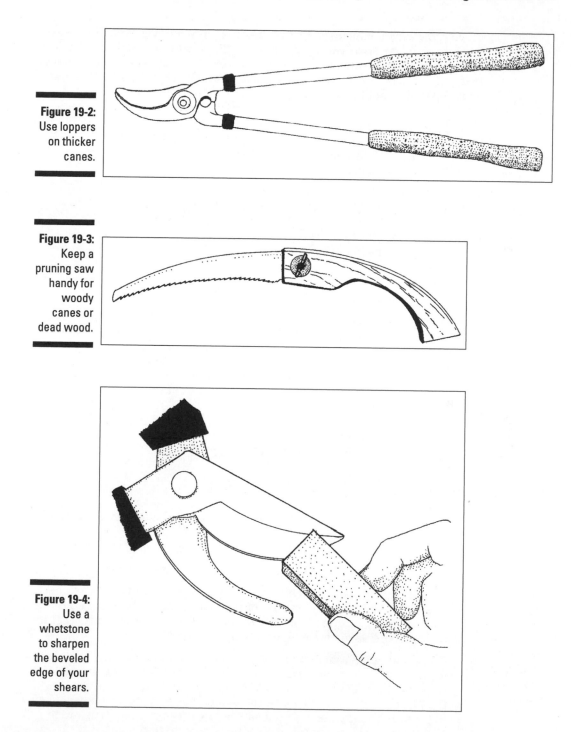

Figure 19-2:
Use loppers
on thicker
canes.

Figure 19-3:
Keep a
pruning saw
handy for
woody
canes or
dead wood.

Figure 19-4:
Use a
whetstone
to sharpen
the beveled
edge of your
shears.

If you grow a lot of landscape roses as hedges, groundcover, or in flower borders, you may also need a pair of hedge clippers or hedge shears. These long-bladed, scissor-like pruners (see Figure 19-5) let you whack back plants in quick and easy fashion, making short work of trimming thick hedges and shearing their tops.

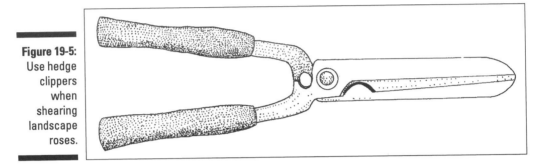

Figure 19-5:
Use hedge clippers when shearing landscape roses.

One thing you don't need is any kind of pruning paint or black goop to seal your pruning cuts. But if cane borers (see Chapter 21 for more information) are causing serious problems in your garden, you may want to treat the surface of your cuts with a dab of standard white glue to prevent pests from entering the canes. If you don't like the white color of the glue, smear a little green florist clay (ask your florist for some) on the cut end.

A Pruning Primer: Deep Cuts and the Same Old Response

We like to simplify rose pruning into three types of pruning cuts. Each one generates a very predictable response from the plant. As your pruning prowess grows, you'll find yourself using a combination of all three types of cuts:

- **Thinning** removes a branch at its origin — that is, it cuts a branch back to another branch or to the base of the plant. Usually, thinning does not result in vigorous growth below the cut. The result of thinning is that the plant is more open and less densely branched.

- **Cutting back** a dormant bud stimulates that bud to grow. If you're pruning during the dormant season — when the rose is resting and leafless in winter — the bud won't grow until spring, but this type of cut focuses the plant's energy into that one bud and maybe one or two buds below it. Pruning back to a bud is the best way to direct plant growth and to channel energy into specific canes that you want to bloom.

✔ **Shearing** is a more aggressive type of pruning but is sometimes effective. You simply use hedge clippers (refer to Figure 19-5) to whack off a portion of the plant. The result of shearing is vigorous growth below the cuts and a denser, fuller plant. Shearing is particularly effective with landscape roses, like shrubs and floribundas, especially if you plant them as hedges.

Getting after those hybrid teas and grandifloras for bigger flowers

Because hybrid teas and grandiflora roses are usually grown for large, long-stemmed flowers, you prune them more severely than other types of roses. Taking of more of the plant channels the plant's energy into fewer canes, which produce bigger and better flowers. (See Figure 19-6.)

You can see a color photo of hybrid tea canes before and after pruning in the color section, under "Spotting Garden Problems."

Here are the basic steps for pruning hybrid tea and grandiflora roses. Figure 19-7 shows the before and after picture.

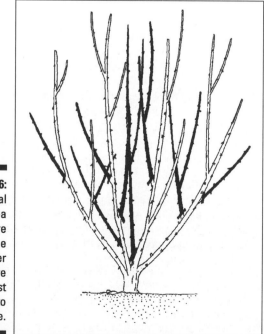

Figure 19-6: A typical hybrid tea bush before pruning. The darker canes are the best ones to remove.

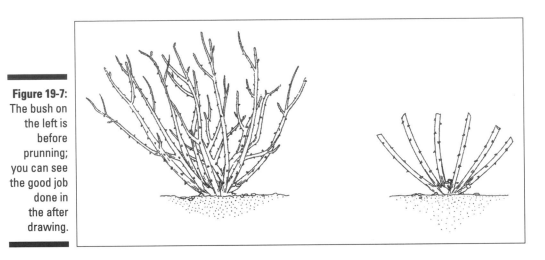

Figure 19-7:
The bush on the left is before prunning; you can see the good job done in the after drawing.

1. **Remove dead or damaged canes.**

   Cold temperatures, insects, and disease are likely to have done their fair share of damage to your plants since the last time you pruned them. So first, look over the plant. Notice that some of the canes are brownish or shriveled instead of bright green. Don't confuse these with older canes that are just thicker with rough bark. You can tell for sure by cutting off a piece. A dead cane is brown inside; a healthy one is whitish.

   Anyway, remove the dead canes using thinning cuts, cutting back at least far enough so that the insides of the canes are white again. You may have to use loppers or a saw to cut thick canes. After a really cold winter, you may have to prune all the way to the ground. If the plant looks dead, don't despair; wait a few weeks, and the plant may still put out new shoots. If it doesn't, you may have to practice another type of pruning — shovel pruning — removing the dead wimp and replacing it with it with something hardier.

2. **Remove suckers.**

   If you're pruning budded plants, and you probably are, remove any *suckers* — vigorous canes that arise from the rootstock below the bud union. You may to dig around at the base of the plant to fully expose the bottom of a sucker. Cut it flush to the rootstock. But be careful: Don't mistake desirable new canes for suckers. If you suspect that a new cane is a sucker, let it grow awhile. If its leaves are distinctly different from other leaves on the plant, go ahead and cut it away. (If you're growing own-root roses, or roses that have not been grafted but have their original roots, don't worry about suckers.) For more about rootstocks, bud unions, own-root roses, and the like, see Chapter 15.

3. **Select flowering canes.**

   Now you want to stop thinking about what you want to remove and decide what you want to save. The goal is to save the healthiest canes — these are the flowering canes that bloom in spring — and remove everything else. The healthiest canes are thicker and usually bright green; older canes are brown or gray and sometimes shriveled looking. Remove any twiggy (small and scraggly) branches. You want the flowering canes to be as evenly spaced around the plant as possible, and you should try to leave the center of the plant open, without any canes. After you finish, the plant should be sort of cup-shaped with flowering canes around the outside.

   The number of flowering canes you select depends on the vigor and age of the plant. With recently planted roses, leave about three to five flowering canes. Older plants can support more.

4. **Cut the flowering canes back by a third to a half.**

   Cut back to an outward-facing bud (this is a heading cut), about ¼ inch from the bud, as shown in Figure 19-8.

   In cold-winter climates, you may have to prune back a little farther to remove all the damaged wood — possibly leaving just 3 to 4 inches of cane.

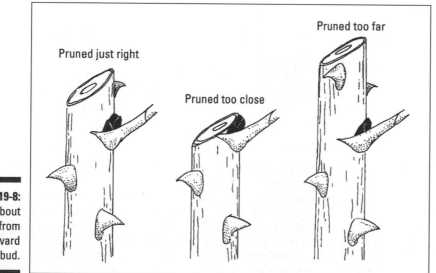

Pruned too far

Pruned just right

Pruned too close

Figure 19-8:
Prune about
¼ inch from
an outward
facing bud.

TIP

After your plants are in the ground for a few years, some of your flowering canes may get pretty thick and woody and lose some of their vigor and flower-power. These canes should be removed with a saw or loppers (now we're thinning). Allow a nearby *basal break* (a healthy new shoot from above the bud union at the base of the plant) to grow and replace it.

Pruning floribundas and polyanthas for shear pleasure

You can prune floribunda and polyantha roses much like hybrid tea roses, but because floribundas and polyanthas have a more twiggy growth habit (more, but smaller, stems and canes), you need to leave more flowering canes. Because most produce clusters of small flowers instead of those long-stemmed single beauties of the hybrid teas, and because floribundas and polyanthas are more often used en masse as landscape plants, you can prune in a much easier way — simply whack 'em back with hedge clippers.

Remove all canes that were damaged by winter. Then remove about one-third to one-half of the growth, shaping the plant into a nice, rounded dome, as shown in Figure 19-9. Then do a quick pass with a hand pruner, removing dead or very crowded branches and opening the center of the plant a bit. The result is a denser plant covered with blooms.

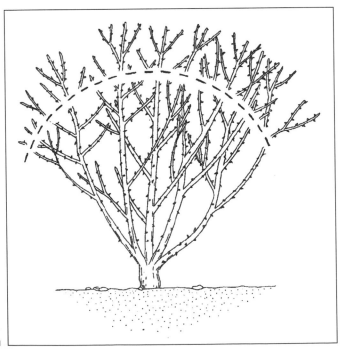

Figure 19-9:
Remove one-third to one-half the growth and shape the plant into a rounded dome.

Pruning a mixed bag of shrubs

Shrub roses represent a real mishmash of different kinds of plants, from low-growing, spreading ground covers to neat, compact shrubs to vigorous, upright monsters. Consequently, there are no hard-and-fast rules about how to prune them. Still, the basic techniques we present in this chapter work — remove dead and diseased branches, open the centers a bit, and whack back whatever gets out of bounds.

We prefer use hedge clippers to lightly shear back ground covers, such as the Meidiland roses and compact shrubs like 'Carefree Beauty'. David Austin English roses often have to be seriously cut back to be kept where they belong, and you need loppers to do the job.

With most of these plants, the amount of pruning you have to do depends on your climate. Where summers are long and winters are mild, plants grow more and need more pruning. In short-summer/cold-winter climates, the opposite is true; you have to cut off less.

On the other hand, many rose growers take a less-is-more approach to pruning shrubs and often just leave the plants alone. In the long run, not pruning usually results in fewer blooms and wild-looking plants. But in a fast-paced world, that low-maintenance approach is hard to argue with.

Using tiny pruners for tiny plants?

You can shear miniature roses the same way that you prune floribundas and polyanthas, which is especially timesaving if you have several plants on landscape duty.

But because miniatures are so diminutive and often admired up close, many gardeners prefer to handle them more carefully. If you are one of those gardeners, treat minis like hybrid teas, opening the center, removing dead or twiggy branches, and selecting healthy flowering canes. To keep the plants compact, shorten the flowering canes a little more than usual — by as much as three-quarters of their height.

Pruning antiquity

Old garden roses, like shrubs, are a greatly varied group of plants. We believe in a less-is-more approach to pruning. Take out the damaged and dead branches, shear back a bit — but not by over a third, or you may reduce bloom — and remove anything that's out of bounds.

Old roses that bloom only once in spring should be pruned after they flower. Pruning them during their dormant season reduces next season's blooms. But the rules still apply — go lightly.

Hybrid perpetuals are one exception to the go lightly rule. They like to be pruned hard, just like their close cousins, the hybrid teas.

Taking pruning to new heights

Pruning climbing roses is a bit different from pruning other roses.

The first thing you need to know is that climbing roses don't climb like true vines. They don't twist around or attach to whatever they come in contact with like ivy or grapes. Instead, they put out long, longer, and longer yet, vigorous, arching canes. If you just leave them alone, they form a huge, sprawling shrub. Consequently, to get them to climb, you have to tie them (we like to use the green plastic tape sold in any nursery) to some kind of a support, such as a fence, arbor, or trellis. Different types of supports for climbing roses are discussed in Chapter 5, "Landscaping with Roses."

The most common types of climbers are the climbing offshoots, or sports, of hybrid teas and large-flowered climbers, which bloom repeatedly throughout the growing season. (Climbing roses are further described in Chapter 12.) After planting, you should pretty much leave these climbers alone for two to three years so that they can develop long, sturdy canes. Just keep them within bounds and remove any dead or damaged growth. Tie them to the support if you need to keep them out of the way.

The fun begins after the second or third year of waiting. Think of your climbing rose as having two parts: the flowering shoots and the main structural canes on which they grow. Your goal in pruning is to select the sturdiest canes and tie them to the support in some evenly spaced manner, ideally in an angled or nearly horizontal fashion. The pattern doesn't have to be fancy. The number of canes you choose depends on the size of your support and the age of the plant. As the rose gets older, you can select more canes to fill up, say, a large fence. These main canes form the basic structure of the plant. Other canes should be removed.

After you bend these structural canes and tie them to the support, new growth sprouts along their length. These are the flowering shoots (sometimes called *laterals*) that — surprise! — flower. During dormancy, you should cut back these shoots to about two to three buds above the structural canes. After pruning, your climbing rose should look something like Figure 19-10.

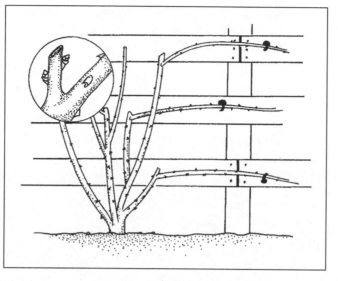

Figure 19-10:
A pruned climbing rose. The inset shows how to shorten flowering canes of climbing sports of hybrid teas and large-flowered climbers.

Occasionally, one of your structural canes may become too old and woody and not bloom as well as it used to. So get rid of it. New canes that you can train as replacements arise every year from the base of the plant. When you need these new canes, simply let them grow rather than pruning them as you've been doing since you selected your structural canes after the first two or three growing years. The rules change a bit with climbing roses that bloom only once in spring. Wait until after they bloom to prune; then remove more of the older structural canes and replace them with the new ones. These new canes produce most of the next season's bloom.

Deadheading for Grateful Roses

You do most of the pruning described up to this point during the dormant season, when plants are leafless. But you also need to prune a bit during the growing season. Most important, you have to deadhead. *Deadheading* is removing spent flowers — those that have withered and died — so that the plant can channel its energy into producing more flowers instead of seeds.

As with other types of pruning, you can deadhead the hard way or the easy way:

> ✔ **Take the hard way for hybrid teas:** Prune hybrid teas and grandifloras the hard way — cut back each spent flower shoot down to at least the first leaf with five leaflets, as shown in Figure 19-11. When you deadhead this way, the plants maintain a neater appearance, rebloom sooner, and produce sturdier stems that are less likely to result in droopy flowers.

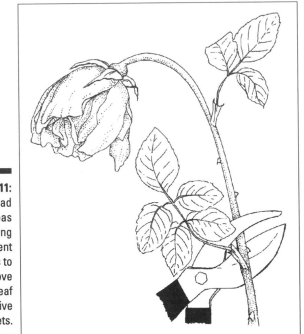

Figure 19-11:
Deadhead
hybrid teas
by cutting
back spent
flowers to
just above
the first leaf
with five
leaflets.

Remember, buds arising from thicker parts of a cane grow into sturdier canes themselves. Therefore, in order to get the largest possible new cane to grow from a bud eye, you have to cut down to where the main cane is fairly substantial. However, never remove more than a third of the plant at one time during the growing season. Doing so may weaken the plant.

✔ **Try the fast-track for multiple-flowered plants:** With more floriferous landscape roses like floribundas, shrubs, and miniatures, deadheading in the preceding manner can take forever. So if you don't have time, get out your trusty old shears or hedge clippers and whack off the faded flower clusters. The disadvantage of the whack method is that the plants take a little longer to rebloom. But the plants are much better off than if you don't whack at all.

There is one time and place you may not want to deadhead. Some rose growers believe that letting the hips develop in fall increases rose hardiness. So if you live in a cold winter climate, see Chapter 20 for more on hardiness.

Other than deadheading, prune during the summer as you see fit. If a branch gets in the way or is out of bounds, give it the ax.

Cleaning Up after Pruning

 After pruning, cleaning up and discarding or destroying the plant debris is important. Many insects and diseases live on dormant leaves and branches. So even though you remove dormant leaves and branches from the plant, pests can find their way back to the bush if you leave the prunings hanging around.

Start by removing any leaves left on the rose plant during dormancy. Then rake up all the plant debris and either discard or burn it. You can run the stuff through a shredder and add the debris to a compost pile, but you still risk harboring some pest organisms. To avoid future problems, keep the compost pile far away from your roses.

Right after dormant pruning is the ideal time to apply a dormant spray to your plants that smothers insect eggs and kills disease organisms; you can apply the spray as long as the plants are still dormant and leafless and have not started to grow. See Chapter 21 for instructions.

Chapter 20

Protecting Roses Where Winters Are Cold

. . . .

In This Chapter

▶ Determining rose hardiness

▶ Preparing roses for cold winters

▶ Protecting roses from cold weather

. . . .

*L*ove those hybrid teas but live in a freezing-cold winter climate? Have no fear. With a little extra effort (which is entirely worth it), you can keep those babies alive no matter how wild the winter gets. That's what this chapter is about: protecting roses — any kind of roses — where winters are cold. Mounding soil over the base of your plants is the secret, but you can make your mounding more effective in some easy and inexpensive ways, which we describe in this chapter.

Determining Hardiness — How Low Can They Go?

Most plants' *hardiness* is judged by the minimum low temperatures they can withstand in winter without being killed or damaged. Unfortunately, rose-hardiness is not a cut-and-dried matter because conditions other than cold temperatures can devastate a rose plant. And these conditions vary from winter to winter.

For example, if you get a foot of insulating snow in late November, and a thick snow cover stays around all winter long, your roses will be safe and cozy, even if you haven't spent a lot of time protecting them. But the following winter, you might get very little snow, devastatingly cold temperatures, and a strong, dry wind that sucks the moisture from everything. In this case, the same rose, if you haven't protected it properly, will most certainly be severely damaged or dead at winter's end.

Also, if your yard is protected from winter winds, or if you plant your roses close to your house, your roses are safer than if your yard is very open.

Even within rose classifications, different varieties can be hardier than others. For example, the new, fragile-looking, striped floribunda called 'Scentimental' is so surprisingly hardy that it doesn't need much winter protection, even where winters regularly dip to –20°F (–29°C). But the lovely white floribunda 'French Lace' is so tender that it often has to be replanted every year. Unfortunately, you have no sure-fire way to tell which varieties will be hardy in your yard, other than having experience with them in your yard.

But generally, if you live where winter temperatures predictably reach 10°F (–12°C), many of the most popular roses — such as hybrid teas, floribundas, grandifloras, and climbers — need some kind of protection to survive the winter. Miniature roses and shrubs are generally somewhat hardier, with many shrub and species roses being hardier still. You can find more information about rose hardiness, as well as a list of the hardiest varieties, in Chapter 4.

Without protection in areas where winters get colder than a variety's hardiness can tolerate, parts or all of the top of the plant will be killed or damaged. If a tender variety is budded onto a hardy rootstock, the rootstock may survive, but the flowering top of the plant can be killed or damaged. Who knows what will grow from the rootstock next spring? That's the main advantage of own-root roses — they sprout true from the base. (For more information about roses and rootstocks, see Chapter 15.)

Luckily, protecting roses is not a difficult task. You can do it by covering the base of the plant with soil.

Preparing for a Cold Winter: Bundle Up

Even though different types of roses have general hardiness ratings, how you care for specific plants prior to the onset of cold weather has an effect on their hardiness. A good analogy is the difference between a car with a radiator full of fresh antifreeze for the winter versus one that has only water.

A rose properly prepared for cold weather is said to be *hardened off*.

Most roses harden off by themselves during the gradual onset of fall and winter. During this time, the plant's cell walls thicken as they prepare for dormancy. In many rose varieties, this process manifests itself by the canes taking on a purplish cast. Unfortunately, purple canes indicate the onset of dormancy only and don't give much of an indication as to whether the variety is hardier than varieties that harden off without turning purple.

The fact remains, however, that the better care your roses receive throughout the growing season, the better chance they stand to get through the winter unscathed, or at least without too much damage. If the plant suffers from lack of water or nutrients or was devastated by disease during the summer and fall, it will be in a weakened state when winter arrives.

The key to hardening off a rose is to make sure that the plant stops growing and becomes fully dormant before the onset of the coldest weather. You can encourage full dormancy in two ways:

- **Stop fertilizing six weeks before the first frost.** Late applications of nitrogen fertilizers can keep a rose growing longer into fall or winter than is safe. If you don't know the average date of your first frost, ask an employee at your nursery or call your local cooperative extension office. It may also help to cut back on watering, but don't ever let your roses go into winter completely dry.

- **Let hips develop.** Instead of cutting off (deadheading) the spent flowers from late fall bloom, let the spent flowers go to seed. That is, let the hips — or the seed pods — develop fully. Not everyone believes that this increases dormancy, because many old roses develop hips in midsummer but then keep on growing quite nicely into fall. And we haven't seen any hard, fast research proving that letting the hips develop promotes dormancy. However, most plants slow down their vegetative growth while their seeds mature. Roses are no different. If the roses slow down, the slowing should combine with other factors (such as less fertilizer and no pruning) to increase dormancy. So there.

Keeping Roses Cold

Now why would you want to keep your roses cold? You're supposed to be trying to protect them from cold, not keeping them cold, aren't you?

Well, the two are kind of the same thing. You see, whether or not a rose plant is damaged by cold is not purely a matter of how low the temperatures get. Strong winter winds can dry out canes, and because the ground is frozen, the plant has no way to resupply the canes with water. And fluctuating temperatures, which can cause plants to freeze and thaw, refreeze, and thaw again (it hurts just to think about it!), can kill a cane in a snap or rip a miniature rose right out of the ground.

So what you really want to do when you winter-protect a rose is to insulate the plant not only from the coldest temperatures but also from unusually warm weather that may cause the plant to thaw prematurely. And you also want to protect the rose from drying winds.

Follow these steps for the easiest way to winter-protect roses:

1. **Make sure that your plants are well watered.**

   Fall rains usually do the job, but if the weather has been dry, water deeply (to a depth of at least 18 inches) after the first frost but before the ground freezes.

2. **In early to mid fall, when the nights are getting regularly frosty, mound several spadefuls of soil over the base of the plant, extending the soil up at least a foot above the bud union.**

   To make things easier, cut the canes back to 3 or 4 feet high and tie them together with string. Don't worry about the part of the canes above the mound; you're going to prune them off in the spring, anyway. Get the soil from somewhere other than your rose bed; you don't want to have to dig around your roses' tender roots.

3. **When the ground is thoroughly frozen, cover the mound with a thick layer — at least a foot — of mulch, such as straw, leaves, or compost.**

   Doing so ensures that the ground stays frozen and all of the plant is protected. If any leaves are left on the plant, pull them off. Besides harboring disease, leaves can increase drying. To keep the protective material in place in windy areas, enclose the rose with a cylinder of wire mesh and fill it with mulch or soil, as shown in Figure 20-1. Some gardeners prefer to simply wrap the top of the rose with a thick layer of newspapers, fill the inside with leaves or straw, and tie the whole thing together with string. You can also buy various types of Styrofoam or plastic cones that fit neatly over the top of the plant and which you can then fill with whatever insulating material you like.

4. **When the ground begins to thaw in the spring, gently start removing the soil from the base of the plant.**

Figure 20-1:
A mulched and wrapped rose ready for winter.

But don't get started too early; a sudden cold snap can be brutal. Watch for the yellow blooms of the forsythia. Once they are in bloom, it's usually okay to remove the mound of soil. Remove the soil carefully, because you may find that growth is beginning — look for buds that are swollen and beginning to stretch. Those new buds are very easy to break off, which is why working carefully around the plant is important. Applying a gentle stream of water to wash away the soil is often better than using your hands.

A good layer of snow provides insulation, too, but snow tends to be on the unreliable side — melting as it does.

Protecting Climbers and Tree Roses

Because climbing roses and tree roses are more upright and thus more exposed to cold and wind, they need special protection. If the rose is tied to a trellis or fence and the canes are not very flexible, untie the canes and wrap them with insulating material (like you'd wrap pipes to keep them from freezing). Then retie them to the trellis. If you need to cut the canes back a bit to make the job easier, go ahead. Also, cover the base of the plant with at least a foot of soil like we described for shrubbier roses previously. You may also be able to detach the canes from the trellis, lay the whole plant down (staking the canes in place if necessary), and cover it with soil and/or mulch (see Figure 20-2). When the weather warms in spring, gently remove the covering and retie the rose to the trellis.

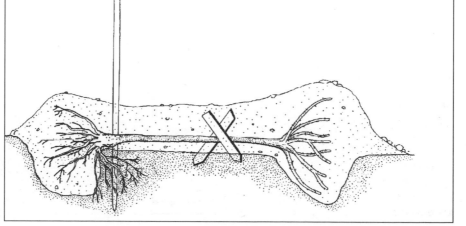

Figure 20-2:
Protect a tree rose through the winter by uprooting one side of the plant so that you can lean it over and bury it.

Dig up tree roses and store them for winter in a cool garage or basement. Or dig only one side of the tree roses' roots so that it can lie on its side. Then secure it in place with stakes and cover the whole thing with soil and mulch. Figure 20-3 shows you one of the best ways to protect a climbing rose.

Figure 20-3:
Protect climbing roses by untying them from their supports, staking the canes to the ground, and covering them with soil and other insulating material.

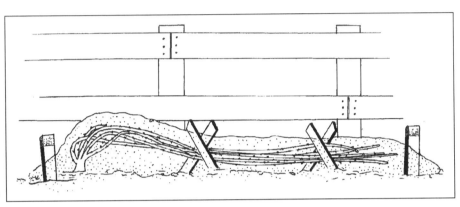

Chapter 21

Outsmarting Rose Pests and Diseases

. . . .

In This Chapter

▶ Commonsense pest prevention

▶ Preventing problems before they start

▶ Common rose pests . . . and how to control them

▶ Pitting beneficial bugs against troublemakers

▶ Managing pest levels

▶ Choosing safe and sane pest control products

▶ Heeding pesticide cautions

. . . .

Certain insects and plant diseases probably like your roses as much as you do — but not more than they like many other kinds of plants. Yeah, right. Then how come every nursery, garden center, even grocery store, has all these rose care products — sprays, dusts, combination fungicides and insecticides, and preventive three-way cure-alls — piled up to the roof?

Big surprise. Roses are, after all, among the most popular garden plants, and gardening is big business. Millions of dollars are made each year from products that catch the eye of rose growers, whether growers actually need those products or not.

The truth is that more than one approach to controlling rose pests exists. Some gardeners are determined to have their plants produce perfect flowers; these growers are looking for the perfect flower to display at a rose show, and they spray their plants every seven to ten days to prevent any insect or disease from touching their roses. On the other hand, many gardeners never spray with strong chemicals and still have beautiful roses.

We recommend a flexible, commonsense approach to controlling rose pests: Take a little and give a little. We can live with a few bugs — they make for a more diverse garden — and we can even get over some disease-splotched leaves. But if the pests try to wipe out our plants, we do something to stop them. Even then, we use only products that have the least impact on the environment. This commonsense approach to pest control is what this chapter is all about.

Preventing Problems

You can do several things to prevent insects and diseases from becoming problems for your roses:

- **Grow healthy plants.** A good, strong rose plant is less likely to be seriously bothered by pests or diseases than one that is weakened by under- or overwatering or that is planted where it doesn't get enough sunlight. Proper pruning to keep the plant open and free to good air circulation helps prevent disease. Even too much of a normally good thing — like nitrogen fertilizer — can result in excessive, lush growth that attracts insects like aphids. The tender leaves are just too luscious to pass up. So read Chapters 16 through 20 on caring for roses; they're the first step in preventing insects and disease.

- **Plant problem-free varieties**. Many rose varieties, especially the newer ones, have natural disease resistance bred into them. On the other hand, some of the loveliest roses are also the most disease-prone. It's like anything else — for the best you have to pay a price — in this case, more pests. Roses of all types vary in their susceptibility to disease and some insects, and where you live plays a part, too; some problems common in one region are rare in others. Regional disease problems are discussed in Chapter 4.

  If a rose has good disease resistance, we say so in the descriptions beginning with Chapter 8. Rose mail-order catalogs (see Appendix C) are also a good source of information about pest and disease resistance.

- **Encourage and use beneficial insects.** Beneficial insects are the good bugs in a garden — the insects that feed on the bugs that bother your roses. You probably have a bunch of different kinds of helpful insects in your garden already, but you can also purchase them and release them into your garden. The more beneficials, the fewer pests. File that in your memory for now; we give you specifics later in this chapter.

- **Keep your garden clean.** Many insects and diseases spend the winter, or go through various stages of their life cycle, in garden debris, like fallen leaves or prunings left on the ground. If you remove these hiding places, you also likely reduce the number of future pests. So, rake around the base of your plants occasionally to clean up fallen leaves, and always discard or burn your prunings. And apply a mulch to prevent water from splashing disease spores from the soil onto the foliage.

✔ **Know the enemy.** The more you know about specific pests and diseases common to your area — when they occur and how they spread — the more easily you can avoid them. For example, the fungal disease, black spot, runs rampant on wet foliage. By simply adjusting your watering so that you don't wet the leaves of your plants, or by watering early in the day so that your plants dry out quickly, you can reduce black spot's occurrence.

✔ **Apply a dormant spray.** Usually a combination of fairly benign horticultural oil and a fungicide like lime sulfur or fixed copper, a dormant spray smothers insect eggs and kills some disease organisms before they become a problem. This is the most important preventive spraying you can do, and the only spray we recommend that you apply every single year, especially if you live in an area where black spot is a problem. Apply the spray right after you prune in late fall or winter, and summer will be much easier.

Encouraging garden good guys

Okay, open your mental file on beneficial insects — the garden good guys — and fill it with some specifics. Following are some things you can do to encourage beneficial insects to populate your garden and reduce the number of rose pests:

✔ Avoid indiscriminate use of broad-spectrum pesticides, which kill everything — the good guys and the bad. If you do spray, use a spray that specifically targets the pest you want to eliminate.

✔ Have a diverse garden with many different kinds and sizes of plants. Doing so gives the beneficials places to hide and reproduce. Variety can also provide an alternate food source, because many beneficials like to eat pollen or flower nectar, too. Plants that attract beneficials include Queen Anne's lace, parsley (especially if you let the flowers develop), dill, clover, fennel, and yarrow. You can find many of these plants described in _Gardening For Dummies,_ 2nd Edition, by Michael MacCaskey, Bill Marken, and The National Gardening Association (IDG Books Worldwide, Inc.).

If beneficial insects are not as numerous in your garden as you would like, you can buy them from mail-order garden suppliers (we list several in Appendix C). If you know that a particularly difficult pest is likely to appear, order in advance. That way, you can release the beneficials in time to prevent problems.

Following are some of the good insects that you can buy to help control rose pests:

- **Lady beetles:** These are your basic ladybugs. Both the adult and the gila monster-like larvae are especially good at feeding on small insects like aphids and thrips. Releasing adults is sometimes not very effective because mother nature has preprogrammed them to migrate on down the road, so they leave your garden quickly. Try preconditioned lady beetles, which have been programmed (you don't want to know how) to be more likely to stick around, and release them just before sundown. That way, they'll at least spend the night. Release a few thousand of them in your garden in spring as soon as you notice aphids.

- **Green lacewings:** Their voracious larvae feed on aphids, thrips, mites, and various insect eggs. These insects occur naturally in most gardens are one of the most effective beneficials at controlling garden pests. Increase their numbers by scattering purchased eggs around your garden in late spring after the danger of frost has passed.

- **Parasitic nematodes:** These microscopic worms parasitize many types of soil-dwelling and burrowing insects, including the grubs of Japanese beetles, June beetles, and rose chafers. Because grubs usually inhabit lawns, you have to apply these worms there, too, as well as around the base of your plants. Apply parasitic nematodes to the soil around the base of your plants once a year in the spring.

- **Predatory mites:** This type of mite feeds on spider mites and thrips. Add them to your garden in spring as soon as frost danger has passed.

- **Trichogramma wasps:** Tiny wasps (harmless to people) that attack moth and butterfly eggs (in other words, they reduce the number of eventual, caterpillars). Release these garden good guys when the temperature is above 72°F (22°C).

Offering aphid hors d'oeuvres

Good bugs are no dummies; they hang out in gardens that offer the most diverse and reliable menu. That's why eliminating every last insect pest from your garden makes no sense.

As we said earlier, our approach to pest control is to have maximum diversity in the garden. That's why having some "bad" bugs around all the time is important. Aphids are like an hors d'oeuvre for so many helpful insects, so you always hope to have a few in your garden. Otherwise, what will the good bugs eat? But accepting the bugs also means that you have to accept a little pest damage once in a while. So you're really just trying to manage the pests, not nuke them off the face of the earth. You want to keep them at acceptable levels, without letting them get out of control.

Spend time in your garden. Poke around, turn leaves upside down. Investigate. Knowing what's out there is important.

Preparing your first line of defense

To manage insects and diseases successfully, you have to be a good observer, checking your roses frequently, if not daily, for developing problems. If an insect or disease does get out of hand, you want to treat it effectively without disrupting all the life in the garden. To do that, start with what we consider the first line of defense against pest outbreaks: pesticides that can be very effective against a certain pest, are pretty safe to use, and have a mild impact on the rest of the garden's life forms.

In general, these products are short-lived after you use them in the garden — that's what makes them so good. However, in order to get effective control, you have to use them more frequently than you do stronger chemicals.

Here are our favorites:

- **Biological controls:** This method involves pitting one living thing against another. Releasing beneficial insects is one example of biological control, but you can also use bacteria that, while harmless to humans, make rose pests very sick and eventually very dead. The most common and useful to rose growers are forms of *Bacillus thuringiensis,* or *Bt,* which kills the larvae of moths and butterflies — that is, caterpillars. However, some strains of Bt control other types of pests. For example, one type (sold as milky spore) kills the larvae of Japanese beetles.

- **Botanical insecticides:** These insecticides are derived from plants. The following two are especially useful against rose pests.

  - **Neem** comes from the tropical neem tree, *Azadirachta indica.* It kills young feeding insects and deters adult insects but is harmless to people and most beneficials. Neem works slowly and is most effective against aphids, and thrips, but it also repels Japanese beetles.

    We prefer neem oil over neem extract (check the product label) because the oil is also effective against all three common rose diseases: black spot, powdery mildew, and rust. Neem oil gets thick at cooler temperatures, so you need to warm it up a bit before trying to mix it with water. Just let the whole container sit in warm water a while before mixing.

    Use either kind of neem before you have a major pest problem. Neem is most effective when applied in early morning or late evening when humidity is highest. It can harm beneficials like lady beetles, so spray when they are not active. Reapply once a week or after rain.

- **Pyrethrins** are derived from the painted daisy, *Chrysanthemum cinerariifolium*. It is a broad-spectrum insecticide, which means that it kills a wide range of insects, both good (spray late in the evening to avoid killing bees) and bad. That it kills beneficials as well as pests is the downside. The upside is that this insecticide kills pests like thrips and beetles quickly, breaks down rapidly in sunlight, and has low toxicity to mammals, which means that it's essentially harmless to people, pets, and the environment.

  The terminology can be confusing, however. Pyrethrum is the ground-up flower of the daisy. Pyrethrins are the insecticide components of the flower. *Pyrethroids,* such as permethrin and resmethrin, are synthetic compounds that resemble pyrethrins but are more toxic and persistent. Consequently, we prefer to avoid pyrethroids for home garden use.

✔ **Horticultural oils:** When sprayed on a plant, these highly refined oils smother pest insects and their eggs. The words *highly refined* mean that sulfur and other components of the oil that damage plants are removed. They are relatively nontoxic and short-lived. Two types exist:

  - **Dormant oils** are sprayed on roses when they are leafless in winter. They are often combined with a fungicide like lime sulfur or fixed copper to help kill wintering disease spores.

  - **Summer oils** usually are more highly refined (or further diluted, or thinner) than dormant oils. They can be used on roses during the growing season, as long as the plants have been well watered and temperatures are not above 85°F (29°C).

    Avoid using oil sprays when temperatures are likely to reach above 85°F (29°C). When it's that hot, the oil can damage plant leaves.

✔ **Insecticidal soaps:** Derived from the salts of fatty acids, insecticidal soaps kill mostly soft-bodied pests like aphids, spider mites, and whiteflies. They can also be effective against Japanese beetles. They work fast, break down quickly, and are nontoxic to humans. Insecticidal soaps are most effective when mixed with soft water. Soaps sometimes burn tender foliage.

✔ **Baking soda (sodium bicarbonate):** The same stuff you put in cake batter has been a popular powdery mildew remedy (partially effective against black spot) in the rose underground for the past few years. If you want to try it, do it like this: Mix 1 rounded tablespoon of baking soda with 1 tablespoon of summer oil in a gallon of water. Apply weekly to well-watered plants, and don't spray if the temperature is above 85°F (29°C). The combination of the spray with the heat damages leaves. Ongoing research shows that potassium bicarbonate may work a little better and be less prone to damaging leaves. A new fungicide called Remedy contains potassium bicarbonate and can be purchased from Primary Products (see Appendix C for their address).

> Baking soda can burn leaves. Apply it in the early morning and not at all during very hot weather.

> ✔ **Antitranspirants:** When sprayed on plant foliage, antitranspirants form a thin, waxy layer that can prevent fungal disease like powdery mildew from invading the leaves. Antitranspirants don't kill disease, but they may prevent a disease from getting worse.

Rose Problems and How to Control Them

Before you wrestle with any insect or disease problem, make sure you know what the problem is. For a start, consult our list of common insects and diseases that follows, and also take a look at the information we give about the best products and materials to use. If you need further help, contact a local nursery — the folks there should be familiar with the common problems in your area. Often, a local nursery has a variety of reference books to consult and is familiar with local problems. Nearby botanical gardens and your local cooperative extension office also may be able to help.

Or better yet, contact the American Rose Society (see Appendix A) and ask about their Consulting Rosarian Program. Consulting Rosarians are recognized rose experts, and the ARS can put you in touch with the one nearest you. You can usually find several in any good-sized city, and nothing is better than asking a local expert for help. And the advice is free. (Appendix A also lists contact information for similar organizations around the world.)

If you like to look things up for yourself, ask at your local nursery or library for the *Ortho Problem Solver* (published by Ortho Books). It's a 1,000-page encyclopedia of garden pest problems, with a color picture of each one.

Insects that prey on roses

Following is a list of the most common insect pests you're likely to find infesting your roses, and the best ways to control them:

> ✔ **Aphids** are tiny, pear-shaped pests that come in many colors, including black, green, and red. (See Figure 21-1.) They congregate on new growth and flower buds, sucking plant sap with their needle-like noses. They leave behind a sticky, sugary substance called honey dew, that may turn black and ugly if infected with sooty mold. Honey dew also attracts ants.

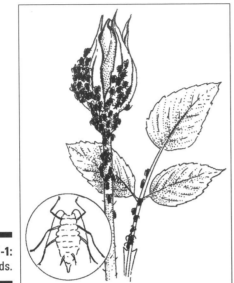

Figure 21-1:
Aphids.

Aphids are easy to control. You can knock them off a plant with a strong jet of water from a hose, or you can spray them with an insecticidal soap. The soap helps wash off sooty mold, too. But usually, if you just wait a week or two, the aphid population boom is followed by a buildup in beneficial insects, especially lady beetles, and these beneficials take matters into their own hands (er, mouths) before serious damage occurs. Malathion, and acephate are traditional chemical controls for aphids. A new product packaged under the name Merit (imidacloprid), is very effective against aphids, and is fairly environmentally friendly. However, it can be hard to find.

✔ **Cucumber beetles** are easy to recognize — they're about ¼-inch long and yellowish green, with black stripes or dots on their backs. Two different types exist. They feed mostly on cucumbers and vegetable plants, but they also love rose blossoms and take big bites out of them just as they open.

   Control is difficult. Try spraying spray with pyrethrum, neem, or insecticidal soap. Parasitic nematodes prey on the soil-borne larvae. Carbaryl is a traditional chemical control.

✔ **Japanese beetles** can really be a serious problem east of the Mississippi River. The ½-inch long beetles have coppery bodies and metallic green heads. (See Figure 21-2.) They feed on both flowers and foliage, often skeletonizing the leaves.

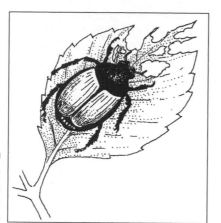

Figure 21-2:
A Japanese
beetle.

Control can be tough. Treating your lawn and garden soil with parasitic nematodes or milky spore may reduce the white, C-shaped larvae, but more adults will probably fly in from your neighbors' yards. Milky spore takes years to spread throughout your lawn. Turning the soil in the open areas of the rest of your yard to expose the grubs to birds may also help. Floral-scented traps that attract adult beetles are available, but the traps may bring in more beetles than you had before. If you try traps, keep them at least 100 feet away from your roses.

Neem, insecticidal soap, and pyrethrum are effective alternative sprays for controlling adult beetles. Traditional chemicals that may help include carbaryl and acephate. You can also just pick them off your roses (late evening is the best time) and or drop them into a can of soapy water.

✔ **June beetles** are about an inch long and reddish brown to black. They usually feed at night and prefer the foliage of various trees, but they also feed on roses. Control is the same as for Japanese beetles, but milky spore is not effective against June beetle grubs.

✔ **Caterpillars** are the larvae of moths or butterflies. They occasionally feed on the foliage or flowers of roses. You can control them with Bt or by releasing trichogramma wasps (they prey on caterpillar eggs). Acephate and carbaryl are traditional chemical controls that may be effective.

✔ **Rose midges** are small, almost invisible pests that rasp new growth, especially flower buds, causing it to shrivel and turn black. If your rose plants look healthy but do not produce flowers, suspect rose midge. Insecticidal soaps sometimes work. For better control, attack the soil-borne larvae with Diazinon or chloropyrifos.

✔ **Rose chafers** are tan-colored beetles with long legs, as shown in Figure 21-3. Again, control is the same as for Japanese beetles and June beetles, but milky spore is not effective against the grubs.

Figure 21-3:
A rose
chafer.

✔ **Rose stem borers** (shown in Figure 21-4) are tiny, worm-like larvae that bore into recently cut or new canes, and feed inside them, sometimes causing the cane to die. Several different insects can do this kind of damage, and they all are hard to control.

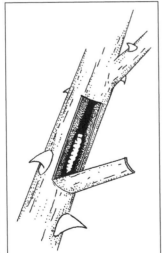

Figure 21-4:
A rose stem
borer.

Cut off the wilted stem well back into healthy tissue. (You may be able to see a small hole where the borer entered the stem. Cut back below that.) Look to see whether tissue inside the cane is damaged. If so, cut lower still until the inside of the cane is normal. If the borer has reached the base of the cane and bored into the bud union, you may lose the plant. Few sprays of any kind are effective, although you may get some of the larvae as they drop to the ground after feeding by using parasitic nematodes near the base of the plant.

If borers are really giving you fits, put a drop of white glue (Elmer's style) on the top of the cane after you cut a flower or prune. This keeps out the type of borer that enters through pruning cuts, but not the type that bores directly into new canes and causes them to wilt.

✔ **Spider mites** are tiny arachnids that you can barely see without a magnifying glass. If the population gets big enough, you can see their fine webbing beneath the leaves. As the mites suck plant juices, the leaves become yellowish with a silvery stippling or sheen. If things really get bad, the plant may start dropping leaves. Mites are most common in hot, dry summer climates and on dusty plants.

A daily bath with a strong spray from a hose should keep infestations down. Just make sure you work hardest on the undersides of the leaves. You can control spider mites with insecticidal soaps, which also help to clean off a plant's leaves. Summer oil is also effective, as is releasing predatory mites. If the pests get completely out of control, you may have to use a miticide, such as Avid (see Table 21-1 later in this chapter for a listing of effective pesticides).

✔ **Thrips** are another almost-invisible troublemaker. They feed on flower petals, causing them to become discolored and the buds to be deformed as they open. Thrips like all roses but are particularly fond of light-colored varieties.

Many beneficial insects feed on thrips, especially lacewings. Insecticidal soaps are also effective, as are several other insecticides, including acephate. Imidaclorid, mentioned previously under aphids, is also effective against thrips.

Troublesome rose diseases

The following sections talk about five of the most common rose diseases (some are pictured in the color section) and suggest some techniques for controlling them. It's important to realize that most fungicides work only as preventives. Once the disease is established, most are not effective. They work best when applied on a regular basis before a disease becomes a problem.

Black spot

Like its name says, this fungus causes small black spots on rose leaves and stems, as shown in Figure 21-5. The edges of the spots are fringed, and the tissue around the spots often turns yellow. In bad infections, the plant may drop all its leaves. This disease is most common in warm, humid climates with frequent summer rain (black spot is a water-borne disease).

Figure 21-5:
Black spot
disease.

The best advice we have to prevent black spot (besides planting disease-resistant varieties) is to clean up your winter prunings — the most common source of reinfection — and use a dormant spray that includes lime sulfur. Also, avoid overhead watering, or water early in the morning so that the leaves can dry out quickly. The baking soda-summer oil spray mentioned later in this chapter provides some control, as does neem oil. Effective traditional fungicides include triforine and chlorothalonil.

Downy mildew

Often confused with powdery mildew and black spot, but much more serious, downy mildew has the capability to defoliate a plant in 24 hours. Round, purple blotches with yellow edges form on the tops of leaves, usually around the leaf veins. They may also occur on the stems. Grayish white fuzz sometimes forms on the bottoms of the leaves, which often turn brittle and drop off. Fortunately, downy mildew is less common than other rose diseases. It usually shows up after long periods of cool, wet weather and then clears itself up when the weather warms.

The disease needs moist conditions to spread, so avoid overhead watering and water early in the morning — that way, everything has time to dry out.

Good cultural methods are the best control — prune to increase air circulation, and clean up plant debris. A dormant spray may help.

Powdery mildew

This grayish white, powdery fungus infects new leaves and flower buds, causing them to become distorted and crinkled-looking. (See Figure 21-6.) Unlike most other fungal diseases, powdery mildew spreads on dry foliage.

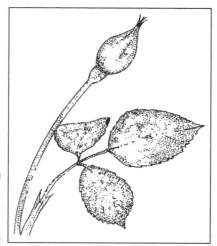

Figure 21-6:
Powdery
mildew.

Many rose growers prevent the spread of powdery mildew by watering overhead or with a sprinkling down each day late in the afternoon, thus washing the spores off the leaves before they can establish themselves. Other preventive measures include planting resistant varieties, planting in full sun, and pruning to encourage air circulation. Effective preventive sprays include antitranspirants, the baking soda-summer oil mentioned later in this chapter, and neem oil. Triforine is one of several traditional chemical fungicides used to control powdery mildew.

Rust

On a plant that has rust, small, orange pustules form on the undersides of the leaves. Yellow spots appear on the tops. (See Figure 21-7.) If the rust is severe enough, the plant can lose all its leaves. This disease is most troublesome when days are warm but nights are cool; prolonged hot, dry weather usually stops its development.

Prevention is similar to black spot — winter cleanup and dormant spray. Make sure that you also strip off infected leaves. Neem oil provides some control, as do traditional fungicides like triforine.

Figure 21-7:
Rust
disease.

Rose mosaic viruses

Rose mosaic viruses cause yellow mottling on the leaves and deformed new growth. Some plants affected by one of the viruses grow poorly. There's not much you can do about it. Most of the time, it shows up on a few leaves and doesn't do much harm to anything. It can't spread from plant to plant, but you should definitely avoid taking cuttings from or hybridizing with infected plants because the virus is passed on to offspring.

All reputable rose nurseries will replace a plant that has a virus. Large commercial nurseries that grow roses now supply plants that are 95 percent virus free, but some older plants may be infected. Severely infected garden plants should be destroyed.

Pesticide Double-Speak

People call pesticides such as carbaryl, Diazinon, and malathion the "traditional" pesticides. Such a label would make George Orwell proud. These pesticides are not traditional at all, unless by traditional you mean only what was developed after World War II. Most of the petroleum-derived pesticides that line the shelves in garden centers weren't available to home gardeners until the 1950s.

Many chemical pesticides are labeled for controlling rose pests. Most insecticides are generally effective but usually kill beneficial insects as well as insect pests. And in some cases, pests have developed resistance to a particular spray, so the spray no longer provides adequate control. When we mentioned a traditional pesticide in the earlier section on controlling pests, we used the generic name listed on the product label under "active ingredients." Most of these chemicals also have trade names, but they often vary by manufacturer. Table 21-1 lists some spray pesticides by trade name (and by chemical name in parentheses) and tells which pests they target.

Table 21-1	Spray Products for Perfect, Pest- and Disease-Free Roses
Product	*Pests and Diseases It Controls*
Avid (abamectin)	Spider mites only
Banner Max (propiconazole)	Black spot, powdery mildew, rust
Diazinon	Most insects
Fungi-Gard or Daconill (chlorothalonil)	Black spot, rust, powdery mildew
Funginex (triforine)	Many fungus diseases
Malathion	Aphids and many other insects
Merit (imidacloprid)	Thrips, aphids, and other insects
Orthene (acephate)	Thrips, whiteflies, aphids, and many other insects
Orthenex (several chemicals)	Insects, mites, and diseases
Protect T/O	Severe black spot
Rubigan (fenarimol)	Severe powdery mildew
Sevin (carbaryl)	Japanese beetles, rose chafers, and cucumber beetles

Most of the pesticides in Table 21-1 are widely available. A few — such as Avid, Rubigan, Banner Max, and Protect T/O — are hard to find. Check with your local rose society or a mail-order supplier such as Primary Products, 175-R New Boston Street, Woburn, Massachusetts 08101; phone 800-841-6630.

In the pest descriptions earlier in this chapter, we included both traditional chemical controls and less toxic alternatives, such as botanical insecticides and beneficial insects. We prefer to use alternatives first and turn to toxic materials only if the survival of a plant is threatened. We do not believe in using combination products (fertilizer, insecticide, and fungicide). They are a shot-gun approach to pest control that, although convenient, often results in excess use of unneeded, often harsh chemicals, which can harm the environment.

A Rosarian's Approach to Pest Prevention

Serious rose growers — less charitable folks might say obsessive — follow a preventive spray program to keep their roses in perfect shape and virtually pest free. They often use chemicals that are not widely available in nurseries and garden centers but which can be purchased through the mail (see Appendix C).

We've already stated our approach to controlling pests, but if you want "perfect" roses, you may decide that you want to go in a different direction. That's your choice. Here's one very knowledgeable rosarian's recommendations for preventing pests:

Spray every ten days with a good fungicide, but only when environmental conditions are optimal for disease development. When insect pests are present use a combination product like Orthenex, which has three different chemicals in one bottle, or use individual products listed in the table earlier in this chapter. A ten-day spray program plus good cultural practices keeps your roses looking great from spring to fall.

Pesticide Safety

No matter which pesticides you decide to use, you must use them safely. Even pesticides that have a relatively low impact on your garden environment can be dangerous to use and toxic to humans. This is true of several commonly used botanical insecticides. Here are some good guidelines to follow:

- Always follow instructions on the product label exactly. Both the pest you're trying to control and the plant you're spraying must be listed on the label. (Sometimes plants are listed in groups, such as *ornamental shrubs* or *flowering vines*.)
- Wear plastic gloves when mixing and spraying pesticides.
- Spray when winds are calm.
- Wear eye protection, a long-sleeved shirt, and long pants (wash everything after spraying).
- Store chemicals in the original manufacturer's, labeled containers well out of the reach of children (a locked cabinet is best).
- Dispose of empty pesticide containers as described on the label, or contact your local waste disposal company for appropriate disposal sites.

Again, always follow instructions on the product label exactly. Doing otherwise is against the law, as well as a violation of common sense. You're using these things to kill stuff!

Chapter 22

Making More Roses

So you bought a couple of rosebushes, and now they're growing great. You love the flowers; you love the fragrance. You're hooked. It's time for more roses!

What's the best way to increase your collection? The easiest and most obvious is to go to a garden center and buy more plants. Or, if you spend hours poring over the newest rose catalogs, why not order from them? Make no mistake: Buying new, healthy, vigorous, young rose plants is the very best way to increase your collection.

But noooo. You have to be the ultimate rosarian and make your own plants. Okay, we can help. But know right now that there's nothing simple about it, no matter which method you use. The concept is simple enough, but a rose isn't a geranium or an impatiens. Roses are as easy to grow as other flowers, but they're not as easy to propagate. Roses certainly are fun to propagate (a heavy term for increasing their numbers), though, if you really enjoy the hobby.

You can propagate a rose plant in two ways:

✔ **Asexual propagation:** Like cloning, asexual propagation creates new plants identical to the original plant. You can use several methods to create new plants of the same variety: transplant new shoots from own-root plants, root cuttings from the original plant, and bud the original variety onto rootstock. Also, if you have an expensive tissue culture lab, you can clone a new plant from just a single cell. But, as you can imagine, cloning a plant is complicated, so we won't get into it here.

One warning, however. As we mention in Chapter 1, many new roses are patented (you see that weird little symbol on the rose label); therefore, asexually propagating patented roses is illegal. Although we doubt that the rose police will come to your yard to check for illegal propagation, out of respect for hybridizers who work so hard to bring new roses into the world, most rosarians gladly comply with the law. Don't worry; plenty of great rose varieties are off-patent and are prime candidates for propagating.

✔ **Sexual propagation (also known as hybridizing):** Pollen taken from one rose fertilizes the eggs of another rose. Roses self-pollinate because they have both male and female parts. But the result is rarely as good as the original plant. So hybridizers take pollen from one plant, called the *pollen parent,* or dad, and brush it onto the female parts of another rose, called the *seed parent,* or mom. After seeds develop, they are planted to grow new varieties of roses. Sexually propagating patented roses, even the very newest varieties, is not illegal.

Raiding a Rose Garden

Own-root roses, usually of the old garden type of rose and some modern shrubs, are not budded onto a rootstock (see Chapter 15 for more information about this rootstock business). Therefore, new canes grow from the *crown* (the base of the plant, right at ground level) of the plant. Often, the plant throws up a new shoot several inches from the main plant. You can dig up this cane, plant it elsewhere, and leave it to grow into a whole new plant.

Friends who grow roses, particularly the old garden roses, which are more inclined to produce this type of growth, are often willing to share their bounty and give you new shoots to plant in your own garden. New shoots from own-root plants are always identical to the original plant.

To plant a new shoot, do the following:

1. **In early spring, dig up the new shoot with a spade, taking along a big clump of the soil in order to keep the roots relatively undamaged.**

2. **Plant the whole thing in a beautifully prepared hole, just like one you'd prepare for any other rosebush (see Chapter 16 for pointers).**

3. **Water thoroughly and mound the plant with soil, leaving the soil in place until new growth begins to appear, which indicates that the roots are working on their own to nourish the plant.**

In a month or two, you should have a healthy new rose plant.

Growing New Plants from Cuttings

Growing roses on their own roots has some advantages, such as increased winter hardiness. Although many rosarians and commercial growers believe that a plant must be budded to reach its full potential, that's not true for all varieties. Why not try rooting a few cuttings (pieces of rose stem) and compare for yourself?

Rooting new plants from softwood cuttings sounds easy, but unless you know what a cutting needs and faithfully provide those things, you will not have a successful experience. Here's how to do the job right:

1. **Take a cutting from a fairly young cane coming from a bud eye along a main cane.**

   The best time to take cuttings is in late spring or early summer, just after a new cane flowers. The diameter of the cane should be about the same size as a drinking straw.

2. **Cut off the bottom of the severed cane at a very sharp angle so that the cut is as close as possible to a bud eye.**

   Make this angled cut with a very sharp pruner.

3. **With a razor blade or X-ACTO knife, lightly score the bark vertically from the bottom, and up about an inch, on the side of the stick opposite a bud eye.**

   Doing so encourages roots to form along the score.

4. **From the bottom of the cutting, measure up about 6 inches, leaving two to three sets of leaflets. Cut the top off the stick, about ¼ inch above a bud eye.**

5. **Dip the bottom, angled end of the cutting into a liquid rooting hormone (such as Dip 'n Grow), mixed according to package directions.**

   Dip the cutting to a depth of about 1 inch so that the score you made on the cane is immersed.

6. **Insert the coated cutting into a small peat pot filled with wet, sterile potting soil.**

   With your fingers, squeeze down the soil so that the cutting stands up and is fairly stable in the pot.

7. **Place your cutting into a misting tent.**

   Making an effective misting tent is easy: Simply mist the cutting with water, place a clear plastic bag over the container, and secure the bag around the top of the pot with a piece of string, as shown in Figure 22-1. The tent prevents the cutting from drying up and dying by keeping it moist.

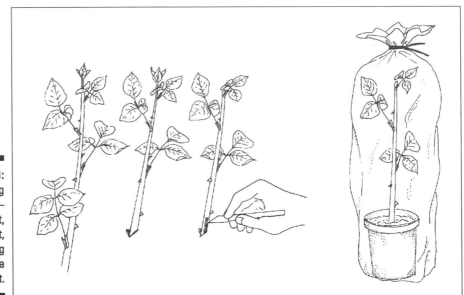

Figure 22-1:
Rooting
a rose —
cutting it,
scoring it,
and putting
it in a
misting tent.

8. **Place the cutting, enclosed in its misting tent, outdoors in a spot that gets morning and afternoon sun but is in shade at midday, such as the north side of your house.**

   You must mist the leaves several times each day, more often if it's sunny. Misting keeps moisture in the cutting, which it needs because it has no roots to get its own moisture. Don't forget to mist, or your cutting will die.

   If the leaves turn yellow and fall off before the first week ends, you may as well give up and start again. If the leaves fall off after three weeks, it's not a great sign, but you still have hope. Mix 1 tablespoon of a high-nitrogen liquid fertilizer in 1 gallon of water and lightly mist your plant with the solution. Doing so may stimulate new leaf growth from the bud eye.

   If all goes well, your cutting should root in less than a month. When strong white roots grow from the bottom of the cutting and fill the small pot, it's time to transplant into a larger pot.

9. **Place the cutting, peat pot and all, into a 6-inch pot filled with regular potting mix, harden it off, then put it in full sun to grow.**

   To *harden off* a plant, move it into full, outdoor sun slowly, keeping it outdoors in the sun a little longer each day for a ten-day to two-week period, never letting the soil dry out.

10. **When the plant starts putting out strong, healthy growth, transplant it into the garden and treat it as you do your other rose plants.**

    See Chapter 16 for planting instructions.

Sexual Propagation

You've heard about this kind of thing before, haven't you? Well, the process is pretty much the same for roses as it is for people, give or take a few steps. This section tells you how to go about it the rose way.

If you want to try your hand at creating a new variety of rose without a lot of effort, try growing the seeds in the hips that form on your roses in the fall. The hips are already pollinated — by bees or by themselves. So the sex part is already over.

Follow these steps:

1. **After the hips (seed pods) change color from green to orange or red, pick them off the plant.**

2. **Carefully cut open the hip with a knife, trying not to injure the seeds inside. Gently remove the seeds.**

3. **Wrap the seeds in a damp paper towel and place them in a plastic bag.**

4. **Keep the bag in the vegetable crisper section of your refrigerator for 60 days.**

5. **Remove the seeds from their cool packaging and plant them ¼ inch deep in a shallow container, or flat, filled with sterile potting soil.**

6. **Place the container under lights or on a really sunny windowsill and wait for the seeds to sprout.**

   Not all the seeds will sprout, but that's normal.

7. **Leave the seedlings to grow in the container, keeping them moist — but not soggy — at all times.**

   They should bloom in about six weeks. The plant and the bloom will be small, and although you won't get a very accurate idea of what the flower will look like on a mature plant, you can tell whether it has potential.

8. **Destroy plants with really ugly flowers or those that become diseased when the others in the flat stay healthy.**

9. **After the first flower blooms, carefully transplant the seedling into a larger pot.**

   To keep from damaging the fragile roots, take plenty of the surrounding soil along with the roots when you transplant.

10. **After the plant grows several new canes, harden it off (see Step 9 in "Growing New Plants from Cuttings" earlier in this chapter) and then plant it in the garden to mature.**

Roses are heavy feeders, so give your new seedling plenty of nutrients to enable it to achieve maximum growth in its first season. (Chapter 18 explains fertilizing roses.) With proper care, many seedlings can reach a large size in the first season.

Hybridizing Roses

Hybridizing is best done in a greenhouse, rather than outdoors where bees can interfere with cross-breeding and where your plants are subject to the whims of the weather. Of course, you can hybridize outside if you want to. Here goes:

1. **Choose two rose varieties of roses whose characteristics you'd like to see passed on to a new variety.**

2. **Decide which rose will be the *seed parent,* or female plant. When a flower on that plant opens its first couple rows of petals, but the center is still tightly furled, gently remove all the petals from the flower.**

   Without the petals, the yellow stamens are exposed. The *anthers,* or male parts that produce pollen, are at the top of the stamens. If you have any questions about what part of the flower is what, see Chapter 2.

3. **Gently bending the rose stem, cut off or remove the anthers from the stamens with manicure scissors or a pair of tweezers.**

   Removing the anthers ensures that the rose does not self-pollinate, ruining your cross-breeding plan.

   Never allow the anthers to fall into the center of the flower. (That would botch the whole thing up.)

   Now your seed parent is emasculated.

4. **Cover the seed parent with a bag so that no new pollen drifts in.**

   Leave the flower alone for 24 hours so that the female parts can ready themselves to accept pollen.

5. **In the meantime, collect some pollen from the *pollen parent,* or male.**

   Pollen requires a couple of days to ripen after being harvested, so collect the anthers from the second rose (removing them just like you did when you emasculated the seed parent) well in advance. Let the tiny anthers sit in an uncovered shallow container in a warm place until you can easily shake off the yellow pollen.

6. **When both the pollen and the seed parent are ready, use a small paintbrush to dab pollen onto the center of the seed parent.**

   To simplify this step, just cut the pollen source from the rosebush and dab the pollen on the seed parent when its center looks slightly sticky.

(See Figure 22-2.) The results are less reliable, but this method is much easier. Whichever method you use, place a bag back over the seed parent for a week.

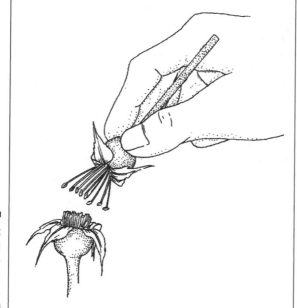

Figure 22-2:
Dabbing pollen onto the seed parent.

If the cross-pollination is successful, the hip begins to swell, as shown in Figure 22-3. The hip is ripe, and when the hip turns red or orange after six to eight weeks, you can harvest the seeds. Like the self-pollinated seeds we discuss earlier in this chapter, you must chill the seeds for 60 days before planting them.

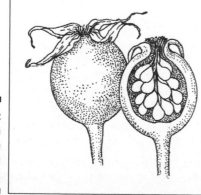

Figure 22-3:
A swollen rose hip filled with seeds.

7. **Plant the seeds ¼- to ½-inch deep in a pot or tray filled with sterile potting soil.**

   Put the tray in a warm, brightly lit area indoors (a heated greenhouse is ideal) and keep the soil moist. The seeds should germinate in about six to eight weeks.

8. **When the seedlings have two true leaves, transplant them into individual small pots.**

   Keep the seedlings in a bright windowsill until the weather is nice enough to plant them outdoors. But make sure to harden off the seedlings first, conditioning them to outdoor sun and temperatures gradually.

Keeping track of the cross you made is always a good idea. You can do so by attaching a label to the stem of the hip as you leave it to ripen. Write the seed parent's name first, then an *x,* meaning "crossed with," and then the pollen parent's name. For example:

‘Pristine’ x ‘Folklore’

Some rose varieties make better seed parents, and some make better pollen parents. Hybridizers who have worked with roses for years have learned which is which, and you can share their experience by reading any of the books they've published or by subscribing to the Rose Hybridizers' Association Newsletter, published by the Rose Hybridizers' Association.

If you want to get rich hybridizing roses, try to come up with a large, red, fragrant hybrid tea with excellent form. It has to grow on long, sturdy stems and produce flowers generously. It must be disease-resistant and do well in a greenhouse. If it does well outside, too, that's a great bonus. The color must stay true for a long time, not bluing or blackening on the edges, and the flower should have a long vase life. Good luck!

For more information about hybridizing your own roses, contact the Rose Hybridizers' Association, 21 South Wheaton Road, Horseheads, NY 14845; phone: 607-562-8592. An annual membership fee of $10 brings its quarterly bulletin to your door.

One More Thing, Sport!

One other way to come up with a new variety of rose is to find a sport on an existing plant. A *sport* is an anomaly in a plant's cells that causes an entirely different cane and flower to grow from a bud eye on the original plant. Often these sports are really wonderful roses, sometimes even better than the original plant. For example, 'Chicago Peace', a sport of 'Peace', was discovered by a gardener in Chicago. And 'Gourmet Popcorn', a sport of the white miniature 'Popcorn', was discovered by a rosarian in Los Angeles. Many of the roses you can buy today are sports.

As with many types of plants, sporting is a fairly common occurrence, but finding a sport is always fun — especially if it's a good one.

If you observe a sport on one of your plants, make a cutting and grow the new variety. The plant may be wonderful beyond your wildest dreams. If so, invite one of the large commercial growers to take a look. If they like your rose, test it, and introduce it to the public, you're entitled to a royalty!

Chapter 23

Drying Roses and Making Potpourri

. . . .

In This Chapter
▶ Drying whole roses in silica gel
▶ Making potpourri
▶ Pressing roses

. . . .

*E*ver walk into one of those wonderful-smelling shops where they sell cookbooks, kitchen utensils, things to hang on the wall, soaps and towels — you know, just about anything homey — including perfect bouquets of dried roses and intensely fragrant potpourris filled with dried rose petals? Where does that stuff come from? A herd of hard-working grandmas must be out there somewhere growing and drying a heck of a lot of roses.

Actually, those grandmas may not be working as hard as you think. Drying roses and making potpourri is not that difficult. In fact, it's pretty easy, as we show you in this chapter. And in the process, you not only find out how to preserve and spread the beauty of roses around your house 12 months a year, but you also can make great gifts to share with friends.

Drying Roses in Silicon Valley

In Silicon Valley, computer nerds use silica gel to dry roses, of course. What did you expect? (Okay, so it's not funny and doesn't make sense. But every *For Dummies* book has to have a reference to computer nerds, and that was ours.) Silica gel is actually a sugar-like substance that sucks the moisture right out of a rose, leaving a perfectly dried flower. You can get the stuff from a florist or at a craft shop.

Because they dry so quickly, miniature roses are favorites for preserving in silica gel. But with some practice, you can also dry larger roses successfully.

Which colors are best? Many of the deepest red roses dry black. However, some bright orange roses dry bright red. Deep pink roses usually dry nicely. White, light pink, and yellow roses tend to fade to dishwater white. Blended roses dry beautifully, but again they tend to fade after a while.

We asked some members of the American Rose Society (see Appendix A for more information), who have been drying roses for years, which varieties they get the best results with. They made the following suggestions:

- **Reds:** Use hybrid teas 'Old Smoothie' and 'Olympiad'; and miniatures 'Acey Deucy', 'Debut', 'Old Glory', and 'Starina'.

- **Pinks:** Try 'Century Two', 'Color Magic', 'Dainty Bess', 'Electron', 'Miss All-American Beauty', 'Perfume Delight', 'Pink Peace', 'Prima Donna', 'Sheer Elegance', and 'Touch of Class' among the hybrid teas; and 'High Jinks' and 'Winsome' (actually a mauve rose) from the miniatures.

- **Oranges:** Good choices (which, oddly, dry to red) include 'Bing Crosby', 'Cary Grant', 'Command Performance', 'Dolly Parton', 'Fragrant Cloud', and 'Tropicana' of the hybrid teas; grandifloras 'Olé' and 'Prominent'; and floribundas 'Impatient' and 'Marina'.

- **Multis:** Good choices include 'Milestone' and 'Mon Cheri' of the hybrid teas; and 'Child's Play', 'Holy Toledo', and 'Kristin' of the miniatures.

To get the best results when drying roses with silica gel, cut your roses in the morning after the dew dries. Pick the best roses, open just the way you want them and free of insects and disease. Leave very little, if any, stem on the flower. Then do the following:

1. **Spread about an inch of silica gel in the bottom of a flat, wide container that has a snug-fitting top.**

   A plastic Tupperware tray works well.

2. **Set the roses upright in the gel, making sure that they don't touch each other.**

3. **Gently add more gel until the flowers are completely covered.**

4. **Seal the container.**

   The roses take anywhere from a day or two to two weeks to dry, depending on their size and how humid the air is where you live. The roses are dry when they feel like crisp paper.

5. **Carefully remove the blossoms from the gel and blow on them gently to remove the excess gel.**

   If some gel sticks, use an artist's brush to remove it.

6. **Don't leave the roses in the gel too long, or the color will fade quickly after you take them out.**

You can also dry rose leaves for making more realistic dried bouquets, but you should do them in a separate container from the flowers. They become too brittle if left on the stem, and they may take longer to dry than the flowers do.

Your local florist or craft shop can recommend one of several products you can use on dried roses to help preserve their color. Rose growers we talked to like a product called Craft Flex, made by the Craft Flex Company, 36046 Riverside Drive SW, Albany, OR 97321; phone 800-800-1981. A pint costs about $25.

You can display dried roses in bowls or dishes with other dried flowers, or you can use them to make arrangements. However, to make arrangements like you do with fresh flowers, you need to attach the blooms to flower sticks, floral wire, or something stiff to support the dry flower. Again, a florist or craft shop is the best place to look for materials and ideas.

Making Really "Rotten Pot"

Who'd want to make "rotten pot"? Well, maybe the idea sounds better when you translate "rotten pot" into French, making it "potpourri." *Potpourri* is an aromatic and colorful mixture of dried rose petals, herbs, spices, and aromatic oils. (You can make moist potpourri, but this chapter describes the dry kind, which is a lot easier to make, anyway.) The word *potpourri* is derived from a French process of aging rose petals in some type of container — the rotting pot.

Any rose, as long as it's fragrant, makes a good potpourri. Collect the petals in the morning after they have dried. Flowers that are about three-fourths to fully open are best. Anything older loses its fragrance. To dry the petals, spread them out on an elevated screen placed in a well-ventilated, warm, dry area away from direct sun. The petals are dry enough when they break when bent — the process takes anywhere from a day or two to a week.

You usually can find everything you need for making potpourri in craft shops. You can also find aromatic oils in drugstores and health food stores.

The basic procedure for mixing potpourri is as follows:

1. **Mix the dry petals with your favorite aromatic herbs and spices — cloves, allspice, mint, and cinnamon work well.**

   Use an ounce of dry herbs for every quart of dried petals. You can also throw in dried citrus peel and other dried flowers.

2. **Add some aromatic oils, like lavender, clove, or cinnamon, and a preservative.**

Powdered or chopped orris root (available at craft shops) is a favorite preservative. You can either put a few drops of oil on the small pieces of orris root or drop the oil over the whole potpourri mixture, which includes the powdered orris root you added.

3. **Mix everything gently and place the potpourri in a sealed container.**

   Store the potpourri in a cool, dark place. Gently shake or toss the mixture every so often. The whole mess should be ready in a few weeks, although the scent is pretty strong at first.

You can put your potpourri out in any attractive container, but a glass bowl looks especially nice. To prolong the aroma, keep the potpourri covered and then open and gently stir it when you want to release the essence (like when guests come over). You may want to add more dried flowers occasionally to intensify the color. When covered, potpourri can last for years.

Pressing Flowers

You can dry roses one other way — by pressing them. The process is simple but works best with single roses or flowers with fewer than 10 or 12 petals. You can find flower presses in nurseries or craft stores, but you can just as effectively press flowers between the pages of a heavy book. Here's how:

1. **Place two pieces of blotter paper (even paper towels work) between the pages of a heavy book.**

2. **Pick some roses in the morning after they dry and place the roses between the pieces of blotter paper, arranging the petals just the way you want the flower to dry.**

3. **Close the book carefully and pile some other heavy books on top.**

4. **Check the flowers every few days.**

   If the blotter paper looks wet, replace at least one piece of it, carefully moving the flowers with tweezers, if necessary. The flowers dry in about two weeks.

Store the flowers in an airtight container, between pieces of paper, or even in the book itself. You can mount pressed roses in picture frames or use them to make greeting cards or decorate festive tables.

Part V

The Part of Tens

The 5th Wave — By Rich Tennant

"Well, that's a lovely hybrid rose, Muriel. But why do you call it 'Whack-on-the-head'?"

In this part . . .

This is a fun part of the book, filled mostly with ways to fine-tune your enjoyment of roses. Here, you can get answers to those burning questions about roses that you always wanted to ask, discover which roses you should avoid (unless you're an expert), find out about the interesting history of roses, and see how to cut those beautiful roses you're growing so that they last for days in vases all over your house.

Chapter 24

The Ten Most Frequently Asked Questions about Roses

- -

In This Chapter

▶ All the things you wanted to know about roses but were afraid to ask

- -

The following sections answer ten of the most frequently asked questions about roses, as received by the National Gardening Association.

How soon can I prune?

Never prune for the sake of pruning. Cut off dead parts of the canes in late winter or early spring after removing winter protection. Prune off dead or dying flowers (which is called deadheading). Prune out spindly growth from the bottom of the plant as soon as you see it. And cut as many flowers as make you happy. (See Chapter 19 for more information about pruning.)

Where can I shop for roses?

Have you seen a rose that you simply must have, but you can't find it anywhere? Check the Combined Rose List. It tells you where you can buy nearly any rose that's for sale. You can order the list for $20 at P. O. Box 677, Mantua, OH 44255. Or call your ARS Consulting Rosarian. He or she should have a copy. You can also find roses on the Internet at www.findmyroses.com, which lists thousands of varieties of roses and tells you where to get them.

What's wrong with my roses?

If your plants don't seem to have any of the pests or diseases that we describe in Chapter 21, get a soil test. Your county cooperative extension service or a private laboratory can tell you the pH of your soil and whatever else may be the cause of sickly roses. You can find out more about soil tests in Chapter 16. You can also contact a Consulting Rosarian from the ARS; see the appendix for details.

Why won't my climbing roses bloom?

Some older varieties of climbing roses bloom on old wood — that is, stems that are two years old or older. If you chop those climbers to the ground every spring, you'll never see a flower. In cold climates, your best bet is to protect your climbers really well. Tie up all the canes together and wrap the whole thing with burlap or those plastic mesh bags that horse feed comes in. (Don't use plain old plastic — it provides a great place for disease to proliferate.) If all else fails, dig the thing up and plant an ever-blooming climber.

Why do my rose leaves turn yellow and fall off?

First, check for spider mites by looking on the undersides of the leaves. You may need a magnifying glass. If you see little spiders, they're sucking the very life from your rose plant. Try a spray with summer oil, which smothers the little suckers. If you don't see tiny spiders, check Chapter 21 about rose pests and diseases and see whether your plant has black spot or any other fungal disease. If you're still stumped, call your nearest ARS Consulting Rosarian to come and take a look.

What are the easiest roses to grow?

It really depends on the kind of gardener you are. But if you have absolutely no confidence in your ability to grow roses, give it a rest! You're as good a grower as anyone else. To start with, try 'The Fairy', 'Betty Prior', 'Sunsprite', 'Mister Lincoln', 'Iceberg', 'Baby Love', or one of the tough shrubs like 'Carefree Delight', 'Knockout', or 'Flower Carpet'. In addition, we've marked the most universally recognized easy-growers with a Can't Miss icon throughout the book.

What's the difference between bareroot and potted roses?

One has its roots growing in a pot of soil, and the other has all the soil removed from the roots. We'll let you figure out which is which. For more information about how roses are sold, see Chapter 15.

Why are my rose leaves covered with a silvery white powder and shriveled?

Your roses have powdery mildew. Control it by removing severly infected leaves, then try the summer oil and baking soda routine described in Chapter 21.

Why aren't my roses fragrant?

You may be growing varieties that have little or no fragrance. Or perhaps you're smelling them at the wrong time of day. Choose fragrant varieties if fragrance is important to you. See the list of fragrant roses in Chapter 3. We also identify fragrant roses in the color section.

When should I prepare my roses for winter?

Wait until you think that your plants are pretty dormant. Some people wait until the ground is frozen, but chances are you'll have to do your winter preparing in the snow if you wait that long. Where average annual minimum temperatures are 5°F (–15°C) and below, late November (Thanksgiving week-end in the United States) is a good time.

Chapter 25

Ten Roses to Avoid If You're Not an Expert (Or a Masochist)

• •

In This Chapter

▶ Roses that are more trouble than most people find them worth

• •

*T*hese roses aren't bad plants (because, of course, there are no bad roses!), but you can find better ones, especially if you just want to add a couple of rose plants to spice up your garden.

Austrian Copper Rose (Rosa foetida): Yellow with Black Spot

The original source of yellow color in roses, this old garden rose is also the original source of black spot disease. The plant is never without it. When you plant it by itself, it loses all its leaves. And when you plant it with other roses, it infects them all.

'Brandy': Just Too Tender

A tender, fragile rose that's guaranteed to die in cold-winter climates. But the color is so unique and the form is so wonderful, that it's worth growing as an annual. In warm winter areas, it abhors even the lightest pruning (branches die). In fact, it shudders at the sight of pruning shears.

'Climbing Orchid Masterpiece': Prone to Disease

A 1960 large-flowered climber, 'Climbing Orchid Masterpiece' is pretty, but every disease that attacks roses will find it and spread to other plants in your garden. Best to avoid this one, even if you spray enough chemicals to keep birds from flying over.

'French Lace': Lovely but Fragile

One of the loveliest floribundas, but sooooo tender in northern gardens. If you live where temperatures don't fall below 10°F (–12°C), you can protect, protect, and protect against winter, but that's no guarantee. 'French Lace' is so pretty that you may want to grow it as an annual and buy a new one every year. On the other hand, it's a favorite perennial of a friend of mine who lives in Los Angeles. But he says, like 'Brandy', it doesn't like heavy pruning.

Lady Banks' Rose (Rosa banksiae): Space Hog

This old garden rose takes over everything in its path, occasionally, of course, in a completely charming manner. It is thornless and has pretty little yellow flowers (a white form also exists), but if you grow roses for pleasure, don't mess with this one — unless you know Edward Scissorhands.

'Mermaid': Takeover Artist

Another rampant grower, this plant with its yellow and white single flowers will kill a tree if it's allowed to climb into it. Best to avoid this variety because even when you dig it up, it sprouts somewhere else in the yard. If you're a northern gardener and think 'Mermaid' would be great to go over the top of that pergola you're planning, forget it. It's too tender.

'Mint Julep': No Beauty in This Beast

Avoid this rose because it's just so ugly. 'Mint Julep' is a hybrid tea that was introduced in 1983, probably because its color is unique — a washed-out gray-green with a blush of pink on the edges of the petals. In fact, it's so ugly that you probably can't buy it anywhere, anyway.

'Newport Fairy': It Keeps Growing

With *Rosa wichuriana* as its seed parent (which tells you that it's a strong grower), this pink and white single rose grows prettily in small clusters. And then the plant keeps growing and growing and growing. It eats your yard, then it eats small children and dogs, and then it eats your house. It's not worth the effort of trying to keep it from devouring your life.

'Snowfire': A Thorn among Roses

This rose is oh so incredibly thorny. Lots of people love the flowers, which are red with a silvery white on the reverse of the petals. You wonder how the plant can even be bothered to produce flowers because it's so busy putting out loads of big, nasty thorns. Most roses have thorns, but these are beyond all reason. If you like the color combination, try 'Love' instead.

'Sterling Silver': Faded and Fading

Unique and wonderful when it was introduced in 1957, 'Sterling Silver' was one of the first mauve hybrid teas and was popular as a greenhouse rose for many years. But compared to the new mauves, it looks washed out and unattractive. In the garden, it's not very vigorous and is a disease hound. Most of the newer mauves are so much better. Try 'Blue Girl', 'Paradise', 'Lady X', 'Fragrant Plum', or 'Stainless Steel'.

Chapter 26

Ten Tips for Cutting Roses

· ·

In This Chapter

▶ Getting the most from a cut rose

▶ The best roses for cutting

· ·

A nyone who grows roses and doesn't cut some to bring their beauty and fragrance indoors is missing the boat. No matter what your home looks like, from campy to castle, bringing some roses inside can make it look regal. And having roses around the house makes you feel great, too. Try it if you don't believe us.

Really, almost any rose makes a great cut flower. It's true that some varieties last longer than others, and we tell you about those varieties in this chapter. But if you like a rose — any rose — then cut it, bring it inside, and put it in a vase. Who cares whether it lasts two days or ten; this isn't a contest! If the thing wilts, you can always cut another one.

Anyway, that's our approach to cutting roses. But we may be in the minority. To many people, cutting roses is an art. And artists can be a little nutty. You know the type:

"My cut roses last longer than anyone's. The secret is to cut them while standing on your head and singing John Denver songs. Then chew off all the thorns while gargling with beer and put them in water measuring exactly 47 degrees Celsius."

Yeah, right.

To be honest, cutting roses is a little bit craziness and a little bit science. And that's what this chapter is about. If you want your cut roses to last as long as possible, follow as many of our ten suggestions as possible. If you don't care whether they last five days or six, do whatever you want.

Following a Flipped-Out Florist

These ten tips help you get the longest-lasting cut roses:

- Cut flowers late in the afternoon, when stem and flower are loaded with food reserves.

- Make sure that the plant you're cutting from is not dry, especially in hot weather. If it is, water it several hours prior to cutting flowers.

- Choose flowers at the right stage — roses that are one-third to one-half open, or still closed in the bud but whose sepals are separated and turned downward. The bud shouldn't be rock hard. Instead, it should be slightly soft when you squeeze it.

- Carry a bucket of water with you. Cut the stem at a 45-degree angle and place it immediately in the bucket of water. You can cut as far down the stem as you want, but try to leave at least two or three leaves on the stem below the cut. Those leaves feed the remaining stem.

- When you get inside, cut the ends of the stems again, but this time cut them under water. That's right, under water. Doing so supposedly keeps the stem's vessels open so that it can take up water. Just use a pruner or a pair of scissors that you don't mind getting wet and cut the stems at an angle right in your bucket. Can't handle this? Us either. The point is to keep the roses out of water for the shortest possible time.

- Let the flowers stand in the bucket in a cool, dark place for at least a few hours before arranging them. This conditions the roses so that they'll have a longer vase life.

- Doctor the water in the vase. Roses last longer in clean water that is a little on the acidic side. You can buy little packs of flower preservative at florists' shops that add all the right stuff, or you can make your own. Our favorite mix adds one part lemon-based soda pop, like Sprite or 7-Up, to three parts water. Or just add two good squeezes from a fresh lemon, a tablespoon of sugar, and a few drops of household bleach to a quart of water.

- Before putting the flowers in a vase, remove the leaves that will be beneath the water. If left on the stem, they rot quickly and mess up the water. Leave the thorns. Breaking them off merely provides more places for bacteria to enter. Also, use a clean vase.

- Change the vase water often. The cleaner you keep the water, the longer the flowers will last.

- Last but not least, say something nice to the roses. It can't hurt. Besides, if you do all the other stuff, you probably talk to your flowers already.

If, even after all this, your roses still wilt (or maybe the phone rang and you forgot all about the flowers in the yard), recut the ends, submerge the entire bunch in very warm water (if you can put your hand in it, it's not too hot), and let them sit for an hour.

The Best Roses for Cutting

In general, the bigger and thicker a rose's petals are, the longer it lasts as a cut flower. Most double modern roses, especially hybrid teas, are ideal as cut flowers because they usually have those great long, sturdy stems. Old rose roses tend to have a shorter life than modern varieties, but the great character and fragrance of most old roses really make them wonderful in bouquets. The same is true for heavily petaled newer roses like the David Austin English roses.

Over the years, many people and groups have tested different rose varieties for longevity as cut flowers. We compiled a bunch of the tests, threw in some of our own experience, and came up with the following list of roses that are long-lasting cut flowers, which means that they usually last over five days when handled properly:

- **'America':** Pink climber (shown in color section)
- **'Cherish':** Pink floribunda
- **'Duet':** Pink hybrid tea
- **'French Lace':** White floribunda
- **'Gingersnap':** Orange floribunda
- **'Gold Medal':** Yellow grandiflora (shown in color section)
- **'Honor':** White hybrid tea
- **'Intrigue':** Purple floribunda
- **'Iceberg':** White floribunda (shown in color section)
- **'Marina':** Orange floribunda
- **'Mister Lincoln':** Red hybrid tea (shown in "Fragrant Favorites")
- **'New Day':** Yellow hybrid tea

- ❀ **'Olé':** Orange-red grandiflora
- ❀ **'Olympiad':** Red hybrid tea (shown in color section)
- ❀ **'Paradise':** Mauve-blend hybrid tea (shown in color section)
- ❀ **'Pascali':** White hybrid tea (shown in color section)
- ❀ **'Prominent':** Orange-red grandiflora
- ❀ **'Sonia':** Pink grandiflora
- ❀ **'St. Patrick':** Yellow hybrid tea
- ❀ **'Touch of Class':** Pink hybrid tea (shown in color section)
- ❀ **'Viva':** Red floribunda
- ❀ **'Voodoo':** Salmon-pink hybrid tea

Chapter 27

Ten Roses and Rose Gardens That Made History

• •

In This Chapter

▶ Facts and fancy on roses throughout history

• •

oses have a royal history that few plants can match. You can trace roses back over 5,000 years, when they were grown by many an ancient civilization, including the Egyptians, Chinese, Greeks, and Romans. Even Confucius wrote about roses around 500 B.C. Since then, roses have been cherished by kings and queens, described by poets and philosophers, and just plain loved by us commoners.

Even if you're not a history buff, you can't ignore the historical significance of roses and some rose gardens. This chapter talks about roses and gardens that made history, giving you just enough to whet your appetite for what may be the start of a new career: Rosarian Historian. Or is it Historian Rosarian?

The Rose the Romans Loved

Rosa damascena sempervirens, known as the autumn damask rose, caused quite a stir in ancient Rome around 50 B.C. Until then, the Romans knew only roses that bloomed once a year. When they saw this new rose from North Africa that bloomed twice a year, they went bonkers. Imagine what would have happened if someone had walked into Rome with the floribunda 'Iceberg' — which never stops blooming. A Caesar might still rule the world!

Cleopatra's Secret Weapon

The cabbage rose, *Rosa centifolia* (at least we think the plant was a cabbage rose — we weren't actually there), was another rose that those decadent Romans loved. They learned how to grow them in heated greenhouses so that they flowered almost year-round. Picture this: Emperor Nero, sipping wine while lounging on cushions filled with rose petals. Fountains flowing with rose-scented water, with guests strolling through halls strewn with rose petals. And — how come we didn't see this in the movie? — Cleopatra supposedly had rose petals piled knee-deep in the room where she first entertained Mark Antony.

Fighting over Roses in England . . .

Roses were even involved in the fight over who would be king of England. The five-petaled White Rose of York, *Rosa alba,* is infamously linked to the House of York, which used it as its emblem in the 15th-century Wars of the Roses. Their enemies, the House of Lancaster, chose the red apothecary's rose, *Rosa gallica officinalis,* as its symbol. One fable says that the two parties stopped fighting when they found a rosebush bearing both red and white individual flowers, and flowers that were both red and white, in the English countryside. The pink and white damask rose 'York and Lancaster' is often credited with being that rose, but it actually wasn't introduced to England until later.

. . . and the Rose to Commemorate the War's End

The 'Peace' hybrid tea has long been one of the world's favorite roses. In the 1994 American Rose Annual published by the American Rose Society, Dr. Tommy Cairns traced the history of 'Peace'. We borrowed liberally from his story.

'Peace' can be traced back to Antibes, France, where, in 1935, the 23-year-old hybridizer Francis Meilland made the cross that would first be known as #3-35-40. The rose caught everyone's eye; Meilland himself described it, saying that it "produced flowers quite marvelous in shape and size with a greenish tinge, warming to yellow, and progressively impregnated with carmine around the edges of the petals."

Buds from #3-35-40 were passed to several nurseries around the world. In the confusion surrounding the start of World War II, the rose was given three different names: 'Gloria Dei' by a German company, 'Gioia' by an Italian nursery, and 'Mme. A. Meilland' in memory of the hybridizer's mother.

Even during the war, #3-35-40 gained notoriety. The Duke of Windsor himself said, "I have never seen another rose like it. It is most certainly the most beautiful rose in the world."

Meanwhile, the Conard Pyle Company introduced #3-35-40 as 'Peace' to commemorate the end of World War II. Under the auspices of the American Rose Society, 'Peace' was formally introduced on April 29, 1945, a date that also marked the fall of Berlin. Shortly after this event, at a meeting of 49 delegations of the United Nations in San Francisco, the head of each delegation received in his or her hotel room a small vase with a single 'Peace' rose accompanied by a card carrying the following message:

> *This is the 'Peace' rose, which was christened by the Pacific Rose Society exhibition in Pasadena on the day Berlin fell. We hope the 'Peace' rose will influence men's thoughts for everlasting world Peace.*

Besides being inseparably linked to world peace, the 'Peace' rose is also one of the most widely used roses for creating new varieties. No fewer than 285 progeny of 'Peace' exist, including 236 hybrid teas, 32 floribundas, 11 grandifloras, and 6 shrubs.

What a rose!

The World's Biggest Rose Plant

"The Tombstone rose," a single Lady Banks rose growing in Tombstone, Arizona, was originally planted in 1885. It now covers over 8,000 square feet and has a trunk that is 95 inches in diameter. It is listed in the *Guinness Book of World Records* as the world's largest rose plant.

Build It and They Will Come

Empress Josephine, wife of France's Napoleon I, put together probably the world's most famous, if not most important, rose garden at her imperial chateau, Malmaison. In 1798, she started collecting every species and natural hybrid of rose she could find. Plants came from all over the world until she had a collection of about 250 rosebushes.

Visitors who saw the great garden were stunned. At once, the great diversity in the rose family was plainly visible, and people saw the possibilities of new varieties and types. Soon there were new hybrids galore, heralding the era of modern roses to come.

The Hangover Rose?

Roses have a long history as medicinal and perfume plants. Rose oils were used to treat everything from eye problems to wrinkled skin to hangovers. As far back as the 13th century, the apothecary's rose, *Rosa gallica officinalis,* was widely used to make perfume and medicine in the French town Provins. Eventually, the apothecary's rose became a symbol for modern pharmacology.

Political Roses

Four roses are official U.S. state flowers. The Cherokee rose, *Rosa laevigata,* is the state flower of Georgia. The wild rose is the state flower of Iowa. The prairie rose, *Rosa setigera,* belongs to North Dakota. And last, but not least, the rose, any rose, is the state flower of New York. Oh, and the rose is the national floral emblem of the United States.

Roses on the Gridiron

Pasadena, California's annual Rose Parade and Rose Bowl football game is an all-American tradition on New Year's Day. The parade got its start in 1890 as a celebration of California's mild winter climate, where roses still bloom in January. The founders of the Tournament of Roses, as the day's events are called, created a floral festival patterned after the Battle of the Flowers held in Nice, France. Initially, the Tournament was a modest procession of flower-covered carriages. The afternoon "games" included foot races, tug-of-war contests, and sack races.

Today, the Rose Parade features animated floral floats, high-stepping equestrian units, and precision marching bands and is viewed by an estimated 425 million people worldwide. In the afternoon, the champion collegiate football teams of the Pac-10 and the Big Ten conferences meet for a gridiron showdown in the Granddaddy of Them All (a trademarked name, no less), the Rose Bowl.

'Tournament of Roses', the pink grandiflora rose, was named to celebrate the 100th anniversary of the Tournament of Roses.

Part VI
Appendixes

The 5th Wave   By Rich Tennant

"Well that's just amazing! Look at the size of those Grandifloras, and with the heat we've had!"

In this part . . .

Because you're having so much fun growing roses, you're going to need more of them. So in this part, we show you how to increase your supply without having to visit a nursery — by buying roses through the mail! Now that's fun. Here's also where you can find out how to contact the American Rose Society and other rose societies around the world, as well as find out the location of a public rose garden near you.

Appendix A

Rose Societies

● ●

*W*ith such widespread love for the rose as a flower and a plant, it's no surprise that people get together to share their experiences. Joining a rose society is a great way to meet people with similar interests and a fantastic way to get information about growing roses, particularly on a local level.

The American Rose Society

The American Rose Society was founded in 1899 and now has more than 20,000 members in local affiliates throughout the U.S. As a member, you receive the monthly magazine, *The American Rose* and the yearly, *American Rose Annual*. These publications include the latest information about growing techniques, new varieties, and annual get-togethers like conventions, symposiums, and guided tours of well-known rose gardens. The *American Rose Annual* also includes the very valuable "Roses in Review," which compiles regional evaluations of rose varieties. You also receive a copy of the "Handbook for Selecting Roses," which rates all roses on a scale of 1 to 10, based on members' experience throughout the country. The American Rose Society also publishes *Modern Roses,* a comprehensive, descriptive list of all known roses.

Through the Consulting Rosarian Program, you can get advice on varieties and growing techniques from local experts. Local chapters also put on rose shows, where you can enter your best rose and have it judged against others grown in your area.

For information about the American Rose Society, write to American Rose Society, P. O. Box 30,000, Shreveport, LA 71130-0030, or call 318-938-5402 or fax 318-938-5405.

The Heritage Rose Group

The Heritage Rose Group shares information and experience with old garden roses. Its $5 membership includes the quarterly newsletter, "The Rose Letter." For information, send a self-addressed, stamped envelope to 100 Bear Oaks Drive, Martinez, CA 94553.

More Rose Societies

Argentina
Rose Society of Argentina
Libertador 408 16B
1001 Buenos Aires
Phone: 54-1-327-1435

Australia
National Rose Society of Australia
271b Balmore Road
North Malwyn, Victoria 3104
Phone: 61-3-9857-9656

Austria
Osterreichische Rosenfreünde
Gartenbau-Gesellschaft
A-1010 Vienna
Parkring 12
Phone: 43-1-512-84-16

Belgium
Societe Royale Nationale
Les Amis de la Rose
Korte Aststraat 12
B-9750 Huise-Zingem
Phone: 32-9-384-83-39

Canada
The Canadian Rose Society
20 Portico Drive
Scarborough, Ontario M1G 3R3

Germany
Verein Deutscher Rosenfreünde
Waldseestrasse 14
D-76530 Baden-Baden
Phone: 49-7221-31302

Great Britain
The Royal National Rose Society
Chiswell Green
St. Albans, Hertfordshire AL2 3NR
Phone: 44-1727-850461
E-mail: mail@rnrs.org.uk

India
Indian Rose Federation
852 Napier Town
Jabalpur 482 001 (MP)
Phone: 91-761-315744

Israel
Israel Rose Society
Wohl Rose Park of Jerusalem
P. O. Box 10185
91101 Jerusalem
Phone: 972-2-637233

Northern Ireland
Rose Society of Northern Ireland
10 Eastleigh Drive
Belfast BT4 3DX
Phone: 44-232-651-989

Norway
Norwegian Rose Society
Smiuvn 8
N-0982 Oslo
Phone: 47-22-108-417

Pakistan
Pakistan National Rose Society
395-396 Sector 1-9
Industrial Area
Islamabad
Phone: 92-51-41-17-52

Poland
Polish Society of Rose Fanciers
ul. Broniewskiego 19/7
01-780 Warszawa
Phone: 48-22-6211964

Romania
Asociatia Amicii Rozelor din Romania
Univ. Stiinte Agricole
Calea Manastur 3
RO-3400 Cluj-Napoca
Phone: 40-64-195-825

Zimbabwe
Rose Society of Zimbabwe
P. O. Box 366
Highlands
Harare

Appendix B

Where to See Roses

● ●

*M*any beautiful rose gardens can be found in the United States. If you're at all interested in planting and growing roses, visiting a public rose garden is one of the best ways to learn. Most importantly, you can actually see many different kinds of roses at once, making comparisons easy. Of course, simply enjoying the roses is good enough, but in these rose gardens, all the roses are labeled, meaning you can compare specific varieties with one another.

When you visit a public rose garden, take along a pencil and note paper. Your notes will prove invaluable the next time you shop for roses at either the local nursery or in mail-order catalogs.

This listing may not include every single public rose garden in the United States, but it does include all those that are sanctioned by the All-America Rose Selections. Here's the listing, organized by state:

ALABAMA

Dunn Rose Garden
Birmingham Botanical Gardens
2612 Lane Park Rd.
Birmingham, AL 35223
205-879-1227
2,700 plants, 185 varieties

Fairhope City Rose Garden
1 Fairhope Ave.
Fairhope, AL 36532
334-928-8003
800 plants, 41 varieties

David A. Hemphill Park of Roses
(Mobile Public Rose Garden)
Springdale Plaza, Airport Blvd.
Mobile, AL 36606
334-479-3775
800+ plants, 300 varieties

Battleship Memorial Park
2703 Battleship Parkway
Mobile, AL 36601
334-433-2703
700 plants, 22 varieties

Bellingrath Gardens
12401 Bellingrath Gardens Rd.
Theodore, AL 36582
334-973-2217
3,500 plants, 130 varieties

ARIZONA

Mesa-East Valley Rose Society/
Mesa Community College Rose Garden
1833 W. Southern Avenue
Mesa, AZ 85202

Valley Garden Center Rose Garden
1809 North 15th Ave.
Phoenix, AZ 85007
602-461-7000
1,270 plants, 117 varieties

Gene C. Reid Rose Garden
900 South Randolph Way
Tucson, AZ 85716
520-791-4874 ext. 215
1,000 plants, 150 varieties

ARKANSAS

State Capitol Rose Garden
Arkansas State Capitol
Little Rock, AR 72201
501-324-1010
1,200 plants, 75 varieties

CALIFORNIA

Fountain Square Rose Garden
7115 Greenback Lane
Citrus Heights, CA 95621
916-969-6666
402 plants, 162 varieties

Roger's Garden Rose Garden
2301 San Joaquin Hills Rd.
Corona del Mar, CA 92625
714-721-2100 ext. 328
52 plants, 52 varieties

Descanso Gardens International Rose
Garden
1418 Descanso Dr.
La Canada, CA 91011
818-952-4396
5,000 plants, 1,900 varieties

Exposition Park Rose Garden
701 State Dr.
Los Angeles, CA 90037
213-748-4772
16,000 plants, 165 varieties

Watts Senior Citizen Center Rose Garden
1657 East Century Blvd.
Los Angeles, CA 90002
213-564-9440
480 plants, 12 varieties

Mary Balen Zaninovich Memorial Rose
Garden
31381 Pond Rd.
McFarland, CA 93250

Morcom Amphitheater of Roses
700 Jean St.
Oakland, CA 94610
510-597-5039
1,500 plants, 200 varieties

South Coast Botanic Garden
James J. White Rose Garden
26300 Crenshaw Blvd.
Palos Verdes Peninsula, CA 90274
310-544-1948
2,000 plants, 100 varieties

Tournament of Roses Wrigley Garden
391 South Orange Grove Blvd.
Pasadena, CA 91184
818-794-4414
1,350 plants, 100 varieties

McKinley Park Rose Garden
601 Alhambra Blvd.
Sacramento, CA 95816
916-264-7316
1,240 plants, 170 varieties

Capitol Park Rose Garden
1300 L St.
Sacramento, CA 95814
916-445-3658
1,000 plants, 150 varieties

Inez Parker Rose Garden
Park Blvd. at Plaza de Balboa
San Diego, CA 92101
619-235-1114
2,213 plants, 178 varieties

Golden Gate Park Rose Garden
Golden Gate Park, Section 7
San Francisco, CA 94117
415-666-7003
2,000 plants, 142 varieties

San Jose Heritage Rose Garden
Spring and Taylor Streets
San Jose, CA
408- 298-7657
A world-class collection of almost 5,000
plants of more than 3,400 varieties of heritage, modern, and miniature roses

San Jose Municipal Rose Garden
Naglee & Dana Avenues
San Jose, CA 95121
408-277-5422
4,500 plants, 187 varieties

The Huntington Library, Art Collections, and
Botanical Gardens
1151 Oxford Road
San Marino, CA 91108
626-405-2100
1,500 cultivars

A. C. Postel Memorial Rose Garden
555 Plaza Rubio
Santa Barbara, CA 93101
805-564-5437
1,400 plants, 200 varieties

Westminster Civic Center Rose Garden
8200 Westminster Blvd.
Westminster, CA 92683
714-895-2876
1,542 plants, 178 varieties

Pageant of Roses Garden
3888 South Workman Mill Rd.
Whittier, CA 90601
310-692-1212 ext. 300
6,000 plants, 600 varieties

COLORADO

Jefferson County Sheriff's Complex Rose
Garden
200 Jefferson County Parkway
Golden, CO 80401
303-422-5905
1,440 plants, 221 varieties

War Memorial Rose Garden
5804 South Bemis St.
Littleton, CO 80121
303-721-8478
800 plants, 100 varieties

Longmont Memorial Rose Garden
Roosevelt Park
700 block of Bross St.
Longmont, CO 80501
303-651-8446
1,350 plants, 110 varieties

CONNECTICUT

Pardee Rose Garden
180 Park Rd. East Rock Park
Hamden, CT 06517
More than 36,000 rose bushes in formal and
informal plantings

Norwich Memorial Rose Garden
Mohegan Park
400 Rockwell St.
Norwich, CT 06360
203-823-3759
1,500 plants, 150 varieties

Boothe Park Wedding Rose Garden
Boothe Memorial Park & Museum
Stratford, CT 06497
203-377-3116
950 plants, 40 varieties

Elizabeth Park Rose Garden
Prospect & Asylum Avenues
West Hartford, CT 06119
860-722-4321
15,000 plants, 800 varieties

FLORIDA

Walt Disney World Company
AARS Display Garden
P. O. Box 10,000
Lake Buena Vista, FL 32830
407-824-6256
225 plants, 40 varieties

Sturgeon Memorial Rose Garden
13401 Indian Rocks Rd.
Largo, FL 33774
813-595-2914
850 plants, 125 varieties

GEORGIA

Elizabeth Bradley Turner Memorial Rose
Garden
State Botanical Garden
2450 South Milledge Ave.
Athens, GA 30605
706-369-5884
330 plants, 70 varieties

Atlanta Botanical Rose Garden
Piedmont Park at the Prado
Atlanta, GA 30309
404-876-5859
475 plants, 72 varieties

HAWAII

University of Hawaii
Maui County Research, CTAHR
209 Mauna Place
Kula Maui, HI 96790
808-878-1213
504 plants, 28 varieties

IDAHO

Julia Davis Rose Garden
Julia Davis Dr.
Boise, ID 83706
208-384-4327
2,000 plants, 200 varieties

ILLINOIS

Nan Elliott Memorial Rose Garden
Gordon F. Moore Community Park
4550 College Ave.
Alton, IL 62002
618-463-3580
1,800 plants, 155 varieties

Merrick Park Rose Garden
Southwest corner of Oak Ave. &
Lake St.
Evanston, IL 60201
847-866-2911
2,000 plants, 110 varieties

Bruce Krasberg Rose Garden
Chicago Botanic Garden
Lake Cook Rd., ½ mile east of Edens Exp.
Glencoe, IL 60022
847-835-8325
5,000, plants, 150+ varieties

Lynn J. Arthur Rose Garden
Cook Memorial Park
211 West Rockland Rd.
Libertyville, IL 60048
847-918-8671
833 plants, 76 varieties

George L. Luthy Memorial Botanical Garden
2218 North Prospect Rd.
Peoria, IL 60613
309-686-3362
1,000 plants, 120 varieties

Rockford Park District Sinnissippi Rose
Garden
1300 North Second St.
Rockford, IL 61107
815-987-1661
3,500 plants, 40 varieties

Washington Park Rose Garden
Washington Park
Springfield, IL 62704
217-753-6228
3,000 plants, 304 varieties

INDIANA

Lakeside Rose Garden
Lakeside Park
1401 Lake Ave.
Fort Wayne, IN 46805
219-427-6402
1,500 plants, 180 varieties

Richmond Rose Garden
Glenn Miller Park
2500 National Rd. East
Richmond, IN 47374
317-966-3425
2,000 plants, 100 varieties

IOWA

Iowa State University
Horticultural Garden
1407 Elwood Dr.
Ames, IA 50011
515-294-2117
1,100 plants, 115 varieties

Vander Veer Park Municipal Rose Garden
215 West Central Park Ave.
Davenport, IA 52803
319-326-7894
2,000 plants, 55 varieties

Greenwood Park Rose Garden
Greenwood Park
4700 Grand Ave.
Des Moines, IA 50310
515-271-8727
2,200 plants, 70 varieties

Dubuque Arboretum & Botanical Gardens
3100 Arboretum Dr.
Dubuque, IA 52001
319-582-8621
872 plants, 200 varieties

Weed Park Memorial Rose Garden
Park Dr.
Muscatine, IA 52761
319-263-0241 or 5465
1,000 plants, 150 varieties

State Center Public Rose Garden
300 3rd St. Southeast
State Center, IA 50247
515-483-2081
1,400 plants, 74 varieties

KANSAS

E. F. A. Reinisch Rose Garden
Gage Park
4320 West Tenth St.
Topeka, KS 66604
913-272-6150
6,500 plants, 400 varieties

KENTUCKY

Kentucky Memorial Rose Garden
Kentucky Fair & Exposition Center
Louisville, KY 40232-7130
502-267-6308
1,580 plants, 102 varieties

LOUISIANA

LSU/Burden Research Plantation
AARS Rose Garden
4560 Essen Lane
Baton Rouge, LA 70809
504-763-3990
1,450 plants, 134 varieties

Hodges Gardens
P. O. Box 900
Hwy. 171 South
Many, LA 71449
318-586-3523
2,700 plants, 200 varieties

American Rose Center
8877 Jefferson-Paige Rd.
Shreveport, LA 71119
318-938-5402
More than 20,000 rose bushes comprising
nearly 400 varieties of modern and old roses

MAINE

City of Portland Rose Circle
Deering Oaks Park, High St. Ext.
Portland, ME 04101
207-756-8388
600 plants, 28 varieties

MASSACHUSETTS

James P. Kelleher Rose Garden
Park Dr.
Boston MA 02118
617-635-7381
2,000 plants, 103 varieties

The Stanley Park of Westfield, Inc.
400 Western Ave.
Westfield, MA 01086
413-568-9312
2,000 plants, 50 varieties

MICHIGAN

Michigan State University
Horticultural Demonstration Gardens
Plant & Science Bldg.
East Lansing, MI 48823
517-353-4800
1,000 plants, 150 varieties

MINNESOTA

Palma Wilson/Marylin Nafsted/Nelson Shrub
Rose Garden
Minnesota Landscape Arboretum
3675 Arboretum Dr.
Chanhassen, MN 55317
612-443-2460
1,050 plants, 520 varieties

Leif Ericson Rose Garden
1301 London Rd.
Duluth, MN 55805
218-723-3581
2,800 plants, 93 varieties

Lyndale Park Rose Garden
4125 East Lake Harriet Parkway
Minneapolis, MN 55409
612-661-4875
3,000 plants, 150+ varieties

MISSISSIPPI

Hattiesburg Area Rose Society Garden
University of Southern Mississippi
Hattiesburg, MS
601-268-9990
1,200 plants, 40 varieties

Mississippi Agriculture Museum
1150 Lakeland Dr.
Jackson, MS 39216
601-354-6113
950 plants, 186 varieties

MISSOURI

Laura Conyers Smith Municipal Rose Garden
Jacob L. Loose Memorial Park
52nd & Pennsylvania Ave.
Kansas City, MO 64112
816-333-6706
4,000 plants, 125 varieties

Gladney & Lehmann Rose Gardens
Missouri Botanical Garden
4344 Shaw Blvd.
St. Louis, MO 63110
314-577-5189
3,500 plants, 312 varieties

Unity Rose Garden
1901 Northwest Blue Parkway
Unity Village, MO 64065
816-524-3550
720 plants, 35 varieties

MONTANA

Missoula Memorial Rose Garden
700-800 Brooks St.
Missoula, MT 59806
406-549-8905
1,000 plants, 40 varieties

NEBRASKA

Boys Town AARS Constitution Rose Garden
Father Flanagan's Boys Home
Boys Town, NE 68010
402-498-1104
2,000 plants, 55 varieties

Lincoln Municipal Rose Garden
Antelope Park, 27th & C Sts.
Lincoln, NE 68502
402-441-8267
3,000 plants, 120 varieties

Memorial Park Rose Garden
58th & Underwood Ave.
Omaha, NE 68132
402-444-5497
1,700 plants, 80 varieties

NEVADA

Reno Municipal Rose Garden
2055 Idlewild Dr.
Reno, NV 89509
702-334-2270
2,500 plants, 500 varieties

NEW HAMPSHIRE

Fuller Gardens Rose Gardens
10 Willow Ave.
North Hampton, NH 03862
603-964-5414
2,000 plants, 150 varieties

NEW JERSEY

Rudolf W. van der Goot Rose Garden
Colonial Park
Mettler's Rd.
Franklin Township, NJ 08873
908-873-2459
3,000 plants, 250 varieties

Lambertus C. Bobbink Memorial Rose
Garden
Thompson Park
Newman Springs Rd.
Lincroft, NJ 07738
908-842-4000 ext. 260
770 plants, 63 varieties

Jack D. Lissemore Rose Garden
Davis Johnson Park & Gardens
137 Engle St.
Tenafly, NJ 07670
201-569-7275
900+ plants, 87 varieties

NEW MEXICO

Albuquerque Rose Garden
Wyoming Regional Library
8205 Apache Ave., NE
Albuquerque, NM 87110
505-821-8053
1,052 plants, 405 varieties

NEW YORK

The Peggy Rockefeller Rose Garden
New York Botanical Garden
Bronx, NY 10467
718-817-8700
2,700 plants, 241 varieties

Cranford Rose Garden
Brooklyn Botanical Garden
1000 Washington Ave.
Brooklyn, NY 11225
718-622-4433
5,000+ plants, 1,500+ varieties

Joan Fuzak Memorial Rose Garden
Erie Basin Marina
Buffalo, NY 14202
716-851-4268
700 plants, 40 varieties

Delaware Park
Delaware Park Casino
Buffalo, NY 14222
716-882-5920
1,000 plants, 100 varieties

Sonnenberg Gardens Rose Garden
151 Charlotte St.
Canandaigua, NY 14424
716-394-1727
2,600 plants, 50 varieties

United Nations Rose Garden
United Nations
New York, NY 10017
212-963-1739
1,445 plants, 42 varieties

Old Westbury Gardens
71 Old Westbury Rd.
Old Westbury, Long Island, NY 11568
516-333-0048
2,500 plants, 75 varieties

Maplewood Rose Garden
100 Maplewood Ave.
Rochester, NY 14615
716-647-2379
4,000 plants, 327 varieties

Central Park Rose Garden
Central Park
Schenectady, NY 12305
518-370-8250
2,600 plants, 130 varieties

E. M. Mills Memorial Rose Garden
Thornden Park
Ostrom Ave. & University Pl.
Syracuse, NY 13207
315-473-2631
3,200 plants, 300 varieties

NORTH CAROLINA

The Biltmore Estate
1 Lodge St.
Asheville, NC 28803
704-274-6246
3,000 plants, 250 varieties

McGill Rose Garden
940 North Davidson St.
Charlotte, NC 28206
More than 1,000 rose bushes

Tanglewood Park Rose Garden
Tanglewood Park
Hwy. 158 West
Clemmons, NC 27102
919-788-6268
750 plants, 75 varieties

The Gardens at Witherspoon
3312 Watkins Rd.
Durham, NC 27707

Raleigh Municipal Rose Garden
301 Pogue St.
Raleigh, NC 27607
919-821-4579
1,200 plants, 60 varieties

Reynolda Rose Garden of Wake Forest
University
100 Reynolda Village
Winston-Salem, NC 27106
910-759-5593
1,050 plants, 102 varieties

OHIO

Stan Hywet Hall & Gardens
714 North Portage Path
Akron, OH 44303
330-836-0576
800 plants, 130 varieties

Cahoon Memorial Rose Garden
Cahoon Memorial Park
Cahoon Rd.
Bay Village, OH 44140
216-835-3617
1,000 plants, 250 varieties

Columbus Park of Roses
3923 North High St.
Columbus, OH 43214
614-645-6648
11,113 plants, 382 varieties

Charles E. Nail Memorial Rose Garden
Kingwood Center
900 Park Ave. West
Mansfield, OH 44906
419-522-0211
900 plants, 250 varieties

Fellows Riverside Gardens
123 McKinley Ave.
Youngstown, OH 44509
330-740-7116
1,744 plants, 1,255 varieties

OKLAHOMA

J. E. Conrad Municipal Rose Garden
Honor Heights Park
641 Park Dr.
Muskogee, OK 74403
918-684-6302
2,000 plants, 150 varieties

Charles E. Sparks Rose Garden
Will Rogers Park & Arboretum
Oklahoma City, OK 73112
405-951-0108
600 plants, 150 varieties

Tulsa Municipal Rose Garden
Woodward Park
21st & Peoria
Tulsa, OK 74114
918-746-5155
9,000 plants, 250 varieties

OREGON

Shore Acres Botanical Garden/State Park
10965 Cape Arago Hwy.
Coos Bay, OR 97420
541-888-3732
900 plants, 78 varieties

Corvallis Rose Garden
Avery Park
Corvallis, OR 97333
541-752-2123
750 plants, 140 varieties

George E. Owen Memorial Rose Garden
300 North Jefferson
Eugene, OR 97401
541-687-5347
6,000 plants, 500 varieties

International Rose Test Garden
400 Southwest Kingston Ave.
Portland, OR 97201
503-823-3636
10,000 plants, 450 varieties

PENNSYLVANIA

Malcolm W. Gross Memorial Rose Garden
2700 Parkway Blvd.
Allentown, PA 18104
610-437-7628
2,640 plants, 62 varieties

Hershey Gardens
P. O. Box 416, Hotel Rd.
Hershey, PA 17033
717-534-3493
8,000 plants, 450 varieties

Garden Club of McKeesport
Renziehausen Park
McKeesport, PA 15131
412-672-1050
1,500 plants, 250 varieties

Morris Arboretum Rose Garden
University of Pennsylvania
9414 Meadowbrook Ave.
Philadelphia, PA 19118
215-247-5777 ext. 114
2,500 plants, 250 varieties

Robert Pyle Memorial Rose Garden
Rts. I & 796
Jennersville, PA 19390
800-458-6559
2,100 plants, 100+ varieties

SOUTH CAROLINA

Edisto Memorial Gardens
200 Riverside Drive
Orangeburg, SC 29115
803-533-5870
5,000 plants, 95 varieties

SOUTH DAKOTA

Rapid City Memorial Rose Garden
444 Mt. Rushmore Rd.
Rapid City, SD 57702
605-394-4175
1,000 plants, 94 varieties

TENNESSEE

Chattanooga Choo Choo
1400 Market St.
Chattanooga, TN 37402
423-266-5000
800 plants, 65 varieties

Warner Park Rose Garden
1254 East 3rd St.
Chattanooga, TN 37404
423-757-5056
1,000 plants, 40 varieties

Memphis Municipal Rose Garden
750 Cherry Road
Memphis, TN 38117
901-685-1566
1,600 plants, 51 varieties

TEXAS

Mabel Davis Rose Garden
Zilker Botanical Gardens
2220 Barton Springs Rd.
Austin, TX 78746
512-478-6875
850 plants, 80 varieties

El Paso Municipal Rose Garden
1702 North Copia (corner of Copia & Aurora Sts.)
El Paso, TX 79901
915-541-4331
1,157 plants, 236 varieties

Fort Worth Botanic Garden Rose Garden
3220 Botanic Garden Blvd.
Fort Worth, TX 76107
817-871-7671
2,400 plants, 200 varieties

Gleaves James Centennial Rose Garden
10th & Market Sts.
Galveston, TX 77555
409-772-5026
1,370 plants, 41 varieties

J. M. Stroud Rose Garden
Hermann Park
Houston, TX 77004
713-529-5371
2,799 plants, 102 varieties

Tyler Municipal Rose Garden
420 South Rose Park Dr.
Tyler, TX 75702
903-531-1200
30,000 plants, 400 varieties

Victoria Memorial Rose Garden
476 McCright
Victoria, TX 77901

UTAH

Nephi Federated Women's Club
Memorial Rose Garden
100 North & 100 East
Nephi, UT 84648
801-623-0747 or -1199
1,000 plants, 100 to 125 varieties

Sugar House Park Municipal Rose Garden
1602 East 2100 South
Salt Lake City, UT 84010
801-250-3741
1,200 plants, 150 varieties

Territorial Statehouse State Park Rose
Garden
50 West Capitol Ave.
Fillmore, UT 84631
801-743-5316
330 plants, 33 varieties

VIRGINIA

Bon Air Memorial Rose Garden
Bon Air Park
Wilson Blvd. & Lexington St.
Arlington, VA 22152
703-644-4954
2,800+ plants, 137 varieties

Norfolk Botanical Gardens Bicentennial Rose
Garden
Azalea Garden Rd.
Norfolk, VA 23518
804-441-5830
4,000 plants, 290 varieties

WASHINGTON

Fairhaven Park Rose Garden
Chuckanut Dr.
Bellingham, WA 98225
206-676-6801
1,000 plants, 100 varieties

City of Chehalis Municipal Rose Garden
80 Northeast Cascade Ave.
Chehalis, WA 98532
360-748-0271
300 plants, 100+ varieties

Woodland Park Rose Garden
5500 Phinney Ave. North
Seattle, WA 98103
206-684-4863
5,000 plants, 260 varieties

Rose Hill - Manito Park
4 West 21st Ave.
Spokane, WA 99203
509-625-6622
1,700+ plants, 200 varieties

Point Defiance Rose Garden
5400 North Pearl
Tacoma, WA 98407
206-591-5328
1,470 plants, 150 varieties

WEST VIRGINIA

Ritter Park Rose Garden
1500 McCoy Rd.
Huntington, WV 25701
304-696-5587
2,000 plants, 160 varieties

The Palace Rose Garden
(Formerly Prabhupadas Palace Rose
Garden)
Rd. 1, Box 319
Moundsville, WV 26041
304-845-4175
2,000 plants, 100 varieties

WISCONSIN

Boerner Botanical Gardens
5879 South 92nd St.
Hales Corners, WI 53130
414-425-1131
3,500 plants, 350+ varieties

Olbrich Botanical Gardens
3330 Atwood Ave.
Madison, WI 53704
608-246-4683
600 plants, 114 varieties

Where to Find Roses and Rose-Growing Equipment

*I*f you're lucky enough to live down the street from a Home Depot, a Lowe's, or some great garden center, you can find most everything you need to garden. Your fate is different if you live out in the boondocks, or if you're looking for a plant or product that isn't mainstream — and that includes most of the nifty stuff that makes gardens and gardening fun. It's when you're looking for something special that you'll love the following companies. These are our favorite mail-order suppliers of plants, gardening tools, and equipment. Through them, you can find the latest and the weirdest, as well as the run-of-the-mill.

If you want even a bigger list of rose sources, or are having trouble finding a certain variety, look on the Internet at www.helpmefind.com/roses or www.findmyroses.com.

We note in these lists which suppliers charge a fee for sending their catalog. If no fee is listed, the catalog is free.

Many Kinds of Roses

Arena Rose Company
P.O. Box 3096
Paso Robles, CA 93447-3096
Catalog $5. Antique, Generosa, exhibition,
and landscape roses.
805-227-4094

Butner's Old Mill Nursery
806 South Belt Highway
St. Joseph, MO 64507
800-344-8107

Carlton Rose
P.O. Box 366
Carlton, OR 97111
Phone: 503-852-7135
www.carltonrose.com/
Specialists in roses the florists grow.

Carroll Gardens
444 East Main St.
P. O. Box 310
Westminster, MD 21157

Edmunds' Roses
6235 Southwest Kahle Rd.
Wilsonville, OR 97070
503-682-1476, fax 503-682-1275
www.edmundsroses.com
Specialist in exhibition and European varieties of modern roses.

Garden Valley Ranch Nursery
498 Pepper Rd.
Petaluma, CA 94952
707-795-0919
www.gardenvalley.com

Hortico Inc.
723 Robson Rd., RR#1
Waterdown, ON, Canada, LOR 2H1
905-689-6984
www.hortico.com
Catalog $3. Importers offering huge selection of old and new roses.

Jackson & Perkins
P.O. Box 1028
Medford, OR 97501-0400
800-292-4769
www.jacksonandperkins.com
The world's largest producer of roses.

J.W. Jung Seed Company
333 South High St.
Randolph, WI 53957
800-297-3123

Lowe's Own Root Roses
6 Sheffield Rd.
Nashua, NH 03062-0328
603-888-2214, fax 603-888-6112
Many kinds of roses, including climbers and rare varieties.
Catalog $3.

Petaluma Rose Company
P. O. Box 750953
Petaluma, CA 94975
707-769-8862
www.sonic.net/~petrose

Pickering Nurseries, Inc.
670 Kingston Rd.
Pickering, Ontario
Canada L1V 1A6
905-839-2111
www.pickeringnurseries.com/
Catalog: $4

Regan Nursery
4268 Decoto Rd.
Fremont, CA 94555
510-797-3222
www.regannursery.com

The Roseraie at Bayfields
P. O. Box R
Waldoboro, ME 04572-0919
207-832-6330,
www.roseraie.com
Free consultations by phone. Practical roses for hard places.

Roses Unlimited
Route 1, Box 587
North Deer Wood Drive
Laurens, South Carolina 29360
http://members.aol.com/rosesunlmt/index.html
Carries over 900 varieties of container-grown own-root roses.

Russian Roses for the North
5680 Hughes Rd
Grand Forks, British Columbia VOH 1H4
250-442-1266
Explorer and Parkland roses, old garden roses, Austin roses, and miniatures, all on their own roots.

Sam Kedem Greenhouse & Nursery
12414 – 191st St. East
Hastings, MN 55033
612-437-7516
www.kedemroses.com
Great selection of hardy roses.

Spring Hill Select Roses
110 W. Elm St.
Tipp City, Ohio 45371
800-582-8527
www.gardensolutions.com

Stanek's Nurseries
2929 East 27th Ave.
Spokane, WA 99223
509-535-2939

Wisconsin Roses
7939 31st Avenue
Kenosha, WI 53142-4617
414-694-7696 (4pm-9:30pm CST)
www.darkwave.net/wiroses/
Specalizes in exhibition and fragrant roses.

Witherspoon Rose Culture
P. O. Box 52489
Durham, NC 27717-2489
800-643-0315
www.netmar.com/~wrc

Mostly Miniature Roses

Bridges Roses
2734 Toney Rd.
Lawndale, NC 28090-9497
704-538-9412
www.shelby.net/briroses/
Miniature roses and own-root hybrid teas.

Justice Miniature Roses
5947 S. W. Kahle Rd.
Wilsonville, OR 97070
503-682-2370

Michael's Premier Roses
9759 Elder Creek Road
Sacramento, CA 95829
916-369-ROSE
www.michaelsrose.com
More than 700 rose varieties.

The Mini Rose Garden
P. O. Box 203
Cross Hill, SC 29332
864-998-4331
www.minirose.ais-gwd.com.

Nor'East Miniature Roses, Inc.
58 Hammond St.
P. O. Box 307
Rowley, MA 01969
800-426-6485 or 978-948-7964
www.noreast-miniroses.com

Oregon Miniature Roses, Inc.
8285 Southwest 185th Ave.
Beaverton, OR 97007
503-649-4482
Miniature roses, climbers, and ground
covers.

Pixie Treasure
4121 Prospect Ave.
Yorba Linda, CA 92886
714-993-6780
Many varieties of miniature roses.
Catalog $1.

**Sequoia Nursery, Moore
Miniature Roses**
2519 East Noble Ave.
Visalia, CA 93292
559-732-0309
www.biggermall.com
Home base for Ralph Moore, renowned
hybridizer of miniature roses. Also sells
other types of roses. Catalog $1.

Taylor's Roses
P.O. Box 11272
Chicksaw, AL 36671-0272
205-456-7753
About 40 Miniatures bred by the Taylors.
Catalog: Free.

Tiny Petals Mini Rose Nursery
489 Minot Ave.
Chula Vista, CA 91910
619-422-0385
www.tinypetalsnursery.com
Specializes in miniature roses.

Mostly Old Garden Roses

Antique Rose Emporium
9300 Lueckemeyer Rd
Brenham, TX 77833
800-441-0002
www.heirloomroses.com
Specialist in easy-to-grow old garden roses.
Catalog $5.

David Austin Roses Limited
15393 Highway 64 West
Tyler, TX 75704
903-526-1800
www.davidaustinroses.com
Beautiful, free catalog of David Austin roses
and many heirloom varieties.

Heirloom Old Garden Roses
24062 Northeast Riverside Dr.
Saint Paul, OR 97137
503-538-1576
Glorious catalog and supplier of new and
old roses.
Catalog $5.

High Country Roses
PO Box 148
Jensen, UT 84035
800-552-2082.
www.highcountryroses.com
Specializes in hardy and old garden roses.

Liggett's Rose Nursery
1206 Curtiss Ave.
San Jose, California 95125-2319
408-295-6014
www.liggettroses.com/

Rose of Yesterday
803 Brown's Valley Road
Watsonville, CA 95076
831-728-1901
www.rosesofyesterday.com
Catalog $5. This old reliable is back in busi-
ness. Excellent selection of old and new varieties. Extensive garden open to the public.

Royall River Roses
P.O. Box 370
Yarmouth, ME 04096
800-820-5830
www.royallriverroses.com
250 varieties of bareroot, hardy roses.
Catalog $3.

Vintage Gardens Antique Roses
2833 Old Gravenstein Hwy. South
Sebastopol, CA 95472
707-829-2035 or 707-829-5342
www.vintagegardens.com
About 2,000 antique roses, many not offered
elsewhere.
Catalog: $5 for 160-page, well-written, com-
plete catalog describing nearly 2,000 varieties of roses and their growth habits. Rose
list available free.

Wayside Gardens
1 Garden Lane
Hodges, SC 29695-0001
800-845-1124
www.waysidegardens.com
Wide variety of modern, shrub, and antique
roses.

White Rabbit Roses
P.O. Box 191
Elk, CA 95432
707-877-1888
www.mcn.org/b/roses/
Between 300-400 varieties of classic roses
Catalog: Free upon request.

Rose Publications

American Rose Magazine
American Rose Society
P. O. Box 30,000
Shreveport, LA 71130
Magazine is free with $32 membership in
society.

Combined Rose List
P. O. Box 677
Mantua, OH 44255
Complete listing of all roses currently
available; $19.50.

Handbook for Selecting Roses
American Rose Society
P. O. Box 30,000
Shreveport, LA 71130
Lists most roses in commerce and their
ratings; $4 or free with membership.

Modern Roses 10
American Rose Society
P. O. Box 30,000
Shreveport, LA 71130
Lists all roses of the world, color class, clas-
sification, denomination, brief description;
$50. Modern Roses 11 available spring 2000,
$99.50 plus shipping, 1000 pages.

Rose Hybridizers' Association
21 South Wheaton Road
Horsehead, NY 14845
Quarterly newsletter with membership; $5.

Tools and Supplies

Garden Trellises, Inc.
P. O. Box 105N
LaFayette, NY 13084
315-498-9003
Galvanized steel trellising for vegetables
and perennials.

Gardener's Supply Company
128 Intervale Rd.
Burlington, VT 05401
800-863-1700, fax 800-551-6712
www.gardeners.com/gardeners
Hundreds of innovative tools and products
for gardeners.

Gardeners Eden
P. O. Box 7307
San Francisco, CA 94120-7307
800-822-9600
Stylish garden supplies and
accessories.

Gardens Alive
5100 Schenley Pl., Dept. 5672
Lawrenceburg, IN 47025
812-537-8650
www.gardens-alive.com
One of the largest organic pest control
suppliers.

E. C. Geiger, Inc.
Rt. 63, P. O. Box 285
Harleysville, PA 19438
800-443-4437, fax 215-256-6100
Wide selection of horticultural supplies.

Harlane Company
P.O. Box 39
Perrineville, NJ 08535
Pruning tools, gloves, and other
rose-growing equipment.

Harmony Farm Supply
P. O. Box 460
Graton, CA 95444
707-823-9125, fax 707-823-1734
Drip and sprinkler irrigation equipment,
organic fertilizers, beneficial insects, power
tools, and composting supplies.
Catalog $2.

Hoop House Greenhouse Kits
Department N
1358 Route 28
South Yarmouth, MA 02664
800-760-5192

IPM Labs
P. O. Box 300
Locke, NY 13092-0300
315-497-2063
Specialist in beneficial insects.

Kinsman Company
River Rd., FH
Pt. Pleasant, PA 18950
800-733-4146, fax 215-297-0450
Gardening supplies and quality tools.

Langenbach
P. O. Box 1420
Lawndale, CA 90260-6320
800-362-1991, fax 800-362-4490
Fine-quality tools and garden gifts.

A. M. Leonard, Inc.
241 Fox Dr.
Piqua, OH 45356
800-543-8955
www.amleo.com
Professional nursery and gardening supplies. Catalog $1.

Mellinger's, Inc.
2310 West South Range Rd.
North Lima, OH 44452
800-321-7444
www.mellingers.com
Broad selection of gardening tools, supplies, fertilizers, and pest controls, as well as plants.

Natural Gardening
217 San Anselmo Ave.
San Anselmo, CA 94960
415-456-5060
Organic gardening supplies; tomato seedlings.

Peaceful Valley Farm Supply
P. O. Box 2209 #NG
Grass Valley, CA 95945
916-272-4769
www.groworganic.com
Organic gardening supplies and quality tools.

Planet Natural
P. O. Box 3146
Bozeman, MT 59772
800-285-6656 or 406-587-5891, fax 406-587-0223
e-mail ecostore@mcn.net
www.planetnatural.com/
Environmentally friendly products for lawn, garden, and farm.

Plow & Hearth
P. O. Box 5000
Madison, VA 22727
800-627-1712
www.plowhearth.com
A wide variety of products for home and garden.

Primary Products
100E Tower Office Park
Woburn, MA 01801
617-932-8509
www.primaryproducts.com
Especially for rose growers: growth stimulants, fertilizers, and hard-to-find sprays.

Smith & Hawken
2 Arbor Ln.
P. O. Box 6900
Florence, KY 41022-6900
800-776-3336, fax 606-727-1166
www.smithhawken.com
Wide selection of high-end tools, furniture, plants, and outdoor clothing.

The Urban Farmer Store
2833 Vicente St.
San Francisco, CA 94116
800-753-3747 or 415-661-2204
Drip irrigation supplies.
Catalog $1.

Walt Nicke Company
P. O. Box 433
Topsfield, MA 01983
800-822-4114, fax 508-887-9853
Good selection of gardening tools.

Index

Notes

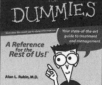

FOR DUMMIES®

Plain-English solutions for everyday challenges

COMPUTER BASICS

0-7645-0838-5

0-7645-1663-9

0-7645-1548-9

Also available:

PCs All-in-One Desk Reference For Dummies (0-7645-0791-5)

Pocket PC For Dummies (0-7645-1640-X)

Treo and Visor For Dummies (0-7645-1673-6)

Troubleshooting Your PC For Dummies (0-7645-1669-8)

Upgrading & Fixing PCs For Dummies (0-7645-1665-5)

Windows XP For Dummies (0-7645-0893-8)

Windows XP For Dummies Quick Reference (0-7645-0897-0)

BUSINESS SOFTWARE

0-7645-0822-9

0-7645-0839-3

0-7645-0819-9

Also available:

Excel Data Analysis For Dummies (0-7645-1661-2)

Excel 2002 All-in-One Desk Reference For Dummies (0-7645-1794-5)

Excel 2002 For Dummies Quick Reference (0-7645-0829-6)

GoldMine "X" For Dummies (0-7645-0845-8)

Microsoft CRM For Dummies (0-7645-1698-1)

Microsoft Project 2002 For Dummies (0-7645-1628-0)

Office XP For Dummies (0-7645-0830-X)

Outlook 2002 For Dummies (0-7645-0828-8)

Get smart! Visit www.dummies.com

- **Find listings of even more *For Dummies* titles**

- **Browse online articles**

- **Sign up for Dummies eTips™**

- **Check out *For Dummies* fitness videos and other products**

Available wherever books are sold. Go to www.dummies.com or call 1-877-762-2974 to order direct.